Penguin Books
The Lake District

The editor, Norman Nicholson, is probably
the best-known Cumbrian-born poet of our
time, and is the author of several highly
praised books in prose, including *Portrait of
the Lakes* and *The Lakers*.

THE LAKE DISTRICT

AN ANTHOLOGY
Compiled by Norman Nicholson

PENGUIN BOOKS

Penguin Books Ltd, Harmondsworth,
Middlesex, England
Penguin Books, 625 Madison Avenue,
New York, New York 10022, U.S.A.
Penguin Books Australia Ltd, Ringwood,
Victoria, Australia
Penguin Books Canada Ltd, 2801 John Street,
Markham, Ontario, Canada L3R 1B4
Penguin Books (N.Z.) Ltd, 182–190 Wairau Road,
Auckland 10, New Zealand

First published by Robert Hale 1977
Published in Penguin Books 1978

Made and printed in Great Britain by
Cox & Wyman Ltd, London, Reading and Fakenham
Set in Monotype Bembo

Contents

Contents

DALES

LAKES AND WATERFALLS

THE LAKE COAST

NATURE'S PLAN

Contents

WIND AND WEATHER

THE PICTURESQUE

LEGEND AND HISTORY

THE LAKE POETS

Contents

CUSTOMS AND SOCIAL CONDITIONS

WORK

PLAY

Contents

CANNY CUMMERLAN' OR OOR MAK O' SANG

Introduction

Lake District literature started rather late in our history, for, in Cumberland, the early Celtic or British language lingered on for centuries longer than in any other part of England except the South-west. Cumberland, in fact, means the land of the Cymru or Welsh, but, while South-western Scotland gave to literature the work of some of the greatest of the early Welsh poets, nothing remains of the Welsh-speaking days of Cumberland except for folk-memories of King Arthur and the evidence of place-names.

Then, when the Welsh-speaking tribes died out, they were followed in the Lake District by the Norsemen who reached Cumberland from Ireland and the Isle of Man during the two or three hundred years that preceded the Norman Conquest. For centuries after this, the dialect of the Cumberland and Westmorland dales remained so Scandinavian as to be almost unintelligible to anyone from south of Morecambe Bay, while, to this day, the Norse vocabulary is inscribed across the landscape as if it had been carved into the very rock: fell, dale, tarn, scree, scar, gill, force, spout, thwaite and keld. Again, the Lake District proper, right up to the seventeenth century, was a poor country, with few great houses and few men of education. A lively ballad literature did arise in the northern part of Cumberland, but this dealt almost entirely with the lore of the Scottish Border or the outlaws of Inglewood, the medieval forest that stretched, south of Carlisle, from the Pennines to the sea. The ballads touched the Lakes scarcely at all.

Apart, then, from a few attempts by local landowners and antiquaries to make some topographical or historical survey of the area, the Lake District does not come into English literature until it was discovered by visitors from the outside world. The first of these, journalists and diarists like Daniel Defoe and Celia Fiennes, hardly knew what to say. Indeed, the charm of Miss Fiennes's writing lies in

13

that very fact. She was never at a loss for words, but they had to be her own words – she had no ready-made conventional vocabulary with which to describe what she saw.

William Gilpin was the man who supplied the convention. He was Cumberland-born of a family long-established in the county, but he spent most of his life as a schoolmaster and parson in the south of England, and, on his retirement, set out to teach the people of his time how to look at and appreciate the world around them. It was Gilpin who popularized the term 'picturesque', which meant, quite literally, a way of looking at a landscape *as if it were a picture*. Gilpin was a man with an acute visual sense, but, as more and more people read him and more and more tourists came to the Lakes, the 'picturesque' hardened into a habit. Everyone now knew exactly what to say, and the same adjectives began to echo from book to book like the sound of the horns on Ullswater: grand, sublime, horrid, stupendous, irregular, precipitous and the like. To us, Gilpin and the travellers who succeeded him sound artificial, exaggerated, yet they record, sometimes very vividly, what the Lake District looked like to the men of the late eighteenth century. For, though the fells and dales may not have changed a great deal, the way we look at them has changed enormously.

The main reason for that change, of course, is the poetry of William Wordsworth. Wordsworth broke down the picture-frame and saw the Lakes, not through Gilpin's, but through his own eyes. At the same time, he expressed what he saw, what he felt, what he experienced, so passionately, so intensely, that, once we have read him, the Lake District can never look quite the same again. With Wordsworth, the mountains of Cumberland passed into World Literature, became, like the music of Beethoven and the paintings of Turner, symbols of the power, the vitality, the force of nature and super-nature which haunted and compelled the imagination of the nineteenth century.

And because of Wordsworth, directly or indirectly, an oddly varied but influential group of poets and prose-writers settled in Keswick, Ambleside, Windermere and Coniston – S. T. Coleridge, Southey, De Quincey, Harriet Martineau, 'Christopher North', with many lesser figures, and, a generation later, John Ruskin. For a time the Lakes became one of the power-houses of the Romantic Movement, and helped to change, not just the course of English literature, but the way people live in Cumberland and Westmorland. The Lake Poets, in fact, became part of our social history.

It would be possible to compile an anthology of the Lake District entirely from the work of Wordsworth. Even at his second-best, his powers of description are usually more accurate, more perceptive and far more felicitous in expression than those of almost anyone who has succeeded him. I have tried, then, to make sure that he is represented in this book at all levels of his accomplishment, from the prophetic incantation of *The Prelude* to comparatively pedestrian – but, topographically, extremely interesting – pieces such as the lines 'Written with a Slate Pencil on a Stone on the Side of the Mountain of Black Combe'.

The influence of Wordsworth's topographical prose was rather different from that of his poetry. His *Guide to the Lakes*, as can be seen from the successive editions published both during and after his lifetime, foreshadowed a new tendency – that of taking a less 'picturesque' and more factual look at the landscape. Men like Jonathon Otley, John Gough and William Green began to study the geology, botany, meteorology of the Lakes, but, though their work was important at the time, it is mostly too dull, as prose, to allow me to quote more than one or two examples. There was another reaction, however, which gave rise to a livelier style of writing. This was a kind of local backlash, from men who felt that Wordsworth had idealized the inhabitants of the Lakes, had over-romanticized his shepherds and 'statesmen', and, above all, had made them speak in a language no dalesman would ever use. Dr Alexander Gibson of Coniston and John Briggs of Furness were typical anti-Wordsworthians, who looked around them with realistic and often ironic eyes. Gibson and Briggs probably exaggerated in their own way, every bit as much as the Romantics did in theirs, but they were born and brought up in the district, they mixed with men of all classes and could talk to the dalesman in his own language. So that, along with other writers all born or long-resident in the Lakes, they give perhaps the truest picture we have of Cumbrian people in the years between Waterloo and the First World War.

A word about dialect. There was, in the late eighteenth and early nineteenth centuries, a very lively school of Cumberland dialect poets most of whom lived in the north of the county and were greatly influenced by the vernacular poets of Lowland Scotland. Susanna

Blamire, of Carlisle, perhaps the best-known of them all, wrote much of her best work actually in Scots. Moreover, some of these North Cumberland poets – such as John Stagg, the blind fiddler – wrote in a dialect so 'thick' that it would need pages of glossary to make it intelligible today even to the average Cumbrian. Wigton at that time became known as 'a nest of singing birds', but since few of their songs were Lake District songs they do not really belong in this collection.

Of the dialect poets who lived in true Lake country, Josiah Relph – though his home, at Sebergham, lay just outside the boundary of the present National Park – was one of the earliest and most important. He was a clergyman with a classical education, and his Pastorals, based on the idylls and eclogues of Ancient Greece and Rome, were, so far as I know, the first attempts to write serious and scholarly verse in any local English vernacular dialect. John Richardson, who comes next, perhaps, in importance after Relph, was a man of quite a different type – a schoolmaster, admittedly, but self-taught and essentially a man of the common people. On the whole, however, the dialect writers of the Lake District, as distinct from many of those of the Solway area, were men of education, men of the middle or lower-middle class, who, though they understood the dialect very well, approached it with a certain detachment, even, in the case of Dr Gibson, a certain condescension. Gibson's songs are adroit, sympathetic, often charming, but in his prose stories – as also in Thomas Farrall's popular *Betty Wilson's Teals* – the rural characters are too often turned into hobbledehoys, figures of quiet though affectionate fun to amuse the more sophisticated readers of the tourist towns and the then booming industrial coast.

This fashion, fortunately, died out before the revival of dialect writing, led by Ernest Denwood of Cockermouth in the years following the First World War. His work and that of others – including the talented and amiable William Sanderson of Wigton – is quite free from the giggles of *Betty Wilson*, but it is free, also, from any apparent awareness of what was happening in contemporary poetry outside Cumberland. There is nothing in the twentieth-century vernacular verse of the county to be compared with the magnificent use of Lallans by Hugh MacDiarmid, who, after all, was born and brought up only a few miles north of the Cumbrian Border.

Many of the dialect writers show little consistency in spelling. Canon Rawnsley, for instance, gives three different renderings of the dialect pronunciation of the name of 'Wordsworth' in the course of one paragraph! Writers of this century show rather more consistency, but, or so it seems to me, they make too much use of quasi-phonetic spelling. I cannot see the point, for instance, of spelling 'of' as 'ov'. However, I have not felt it my business to alter whatever spelling the poet chose, though, as a contrast, I include one poem by Margaret Cropper which catches the true vernacular tone without any use of eccentric spelling at all. Throughout the book, indeed, except in the case of titles, I have retained the period spelling, which, especially in the place-names, can vary considerably. Right up to the 1920s, for instance, writers and printers were still undecided between 'Westmorland' and 'Westmoreland'. I have, however, allowed myself to make a few, very slight, alterations in the punctuation wherever it seemed that the original might give rise to confusion or ambiguity.

In this anthology I have tried to give at least a sample of some of the splendid work that has come out of the Lake District, to show how the landscape looked to men of different types and different generations, and to evoke something of the life, customs, speech and attitudes of the ordinary men and women of the dales throughout the last two or three centuries. Novels I have largely ignored, since most of them seem to me to be melodramatic and over-blown and to give a false idea of Cumbrian people. Three fictional extracts, however, I have felt that I could not do without: a short paragraph from Jane Austen, and two solidly factual descriptions – the one of iron-smelting and the other of a fell hunt – from two notable Cumberland-born novelists of this century, Graham Sutton and Melvyn Bragg. It is interesting to remember that Bragg is yet another voice from Wigton's 'nest of singing birds'.

Acknowledgements

My thanks are due to the staff of the Cumbria County Library and the public libraries at Barrow-in-Furness, Carlisle, Kendal, Millom and Whitehaven. I should like to make particular mention of Mrs J. Savage, who gave me special facilities for working in the Millom Library; and of Miss Christine Stockdale, of the Local Collection at Kendal Library, and Mr R. Smith, of the similar collection at Barrow, both of whom went to much trouble to track down material not easily available. For special information, I am grateful to Mr Daniel Hay and Mr George Bott; for advice and help on various matters, to Mr David Wright and Mr Irvine Hunt; for the loan of rare books, pamphlets and manuscripts in the Cumberland dialect, to Mr T. Foster and Mr J. Park of Millom and Mr G. Barnes of Barrow.

Lastly, as always, thanks go to my wife for help in typing and the correction of proofs, for much research in encyclopedias and catalogues, and for the encouragement that cannot be catalogued.

Acknowledgements
for the use of copyright material are due to the following:

To J. M. Dent & Sons Ltd for the extract from the Everyman's Library edition of Bede's *Ecclesiastical History of the English Nation*;

to the author and Martin Secker & Warburg Ltd for the extract from *The Hired Man* by Melvyn Bragg;

to the author for 'Dorothy Wordsworth Wakes' and 'The Four-Year-Old Boy' from *Collected Poems* by Margaret Cropper;

to the author and Robert Hale Ltd for the extract from *The Roof of England* by A. H. Griffin;

to Irvine Hunt for 'The Charcoal Burners' and 'Tyson';

to J. D. Marshall for 'Slater's Bridge';

to Faber & Faber Ltd for 'To the River Duddon' from *Five Rivers* and 'On Duddon Marsh' from *The Pot Geranium*, to the Ceolfrith Press for 'Wall' from *Stitch and Stone*, and to Robert Hale Ltd for the extract from *The Lakers*, all by Norman Nicholson;

to David Watkin Price for 'On Meeting Sheep';

to the author and Hamish Hamilton Ltd for 'At the Waterfall' from *Collected Poems* by Kathleen Raine;

to John Short for 'Carol';

to Collins Publishers for the extract from *Shepherd's Warning* by the late Graham Sutton;

to the Oxford University Press, Oxford, for the extract from the 1805–6 version of *The Prelude*, from *The Poems of William Wordsworth* edited by E. de Selincourt;

to the author for 'Valley' and 'Cockermouth', and to the author and Hodder & Stoughton Ltd for 'Storm', from *Nerve Ends*, all by David Wright;

to the author and The Garnstone Press for the extract from *The Shining Levels* by John Wyatt;

and to the literary executors and Martin Secker & Warburg Ltd for 'The Thunderstorm' from *Complete Poems* by the late Andrew Young.

I have been unable to trace the relatives or descendants of one or two authors, mostly in the dialect, who have died within the last twenty or thirty years, and my apologies are due for any inadvertent infringement of copyright. From my personal knowledge of the authors, while they were alive, I am sure that they would all have been very ready to allow their work to appear in this anthology.

N.N.

A Broad View

Dear Native Regions

Dear native regions, I foretell,
From what I feel at this farewell,
That, wheresoe'er my steps may tend,
And whensoe'er my course shall end,
If in that hour a single tie
Survive of local sympathy,
My soul will cast the backward view,
The longing look alone on you.

Thus, while the Sun sinks down to rest
Far in the regions of the west,
Though to the vale no parting beam
Be given, not one memorial gleam,
A lingering light he fondly throws
On the dear hills where first he rose.

William Wordsworth (1770–1850)
(written at the age of sixteen, in anticipation of leaving school)

A Western Moorish Country

Daniel Fleming's Description of Westmoreland was compiled in 1671 and used by Nicolson and Burn in their history of Westmorland and Cumberland, though they do not seem to have known Fleming's companion survey of Cumberland. His picturesque derivation of the name of the county, however, is no longer acceptable, and 'Westmorland' is now understood to mean 'the district of the people living west of the moors' – i.e. west of the Pennines.

Beyond the farthest parts of Lancashire, more northward, lyeth another lesser country of the Brigantes, called by modern Latin writers Westmoria and Westmorlandia, in our tongue Westmoreland, bounded on the west and north with Cumberland and part of Lancashire, on the south with Lancashire, and on the east with Yorkshire and Bishoprick of Durham, which, because it lyeth among moors and high hills, and was antiently for the most part unmanured, came by this name in our language, for such barren places which cannot easily by the painful labour of the husbandman be brought to fruitfulness, the northern English men call *moores*, and Westmoreland is nothing else but a western moorish country . . .

The air in winter especially, is a little sharp and piercing, yet very healthful; the soil for a great part of it is but barren, being full of great moors and high mountains, called in the north Fells, yet there are many fruitful valleys in it, abounding with good arable, meadows, and pasture grounds, and commended for plenty of corn and cattle.

Sir Daniel Fleming of Rydal
Description of the County of Westmoreland, A.D. 1671

Barren and Frightful

Defoe's famous Tour *was published, in three volumes, between 1724 and 1727, and the evidence seems to suggest that he drew his material from memories of his own travels over a period of many years, together with research carried out in 1722.*

This part of the country seemed very strange to us, after coming out of so rich, populous and fruitful a place, as I have just now described [i.e. Preston]; for here we were, as it were, locked in between the hills on one side high as the clouds, and prodigiously higher, and the sea on the other, and the sea it self seemed desolate and wild, for it was a sea without ships, here being no sea port or place of trade, especially for merchants; so that, except colliers passing between Ireland and Whitehaven with coals, the people told us they should not see a ship under sail for many weeks together.

Here, among the mountains, our curiosity was frequently moved to enquire what high hill this was, or that. Indeed, they were, in my thoughts, monstrous high; but in a country all mountainous and full of innumerable high hills, it was not easy for a traveller to judge which was highest.

Nor were these hills high and formidable only, but they had a kind of unhospitable terror in them. Here were no rich pleasant valleys between them, as among the Alps; no lead mines and veins of rich ore, as in the Peak; no coal pits, as in the hills about Hallifax, much less gold, as in the Andes, but all barren and wild, of no use or advantage either to man or beast. Indeed here was formerly, as far back as Queen Elizabeth, some copper mines, and they wrought them to good advantage; they are all given over long since, and this part of the country yields little or nothing at all ...

Here we entered Westmoreland, a country eminent only for being the wildest, most barren and frightful of any that I have passed over in England, or even in Wales it self; the west side, which borders on Cumberland, is indeed bounded by a chain of almost unpassable mountains, which, in the language of the country, are called Fells, and these are called Fourness Fells, from the famous promontory bearing that name, and an abbey built also in ancient times, and called Fourness.

> Daniel Defoe (*c.* 1660–1731)
> *A Tour through the Whole Island of Great Britain*

Copeland

The medieval Forest of Copeland covered a large area of West Cumberland, and the name has now been given to the new County Borough that stretches from Whitehaven as far south as the River Duddon and the old Lancashire boundary. Drayton is mistaken in his derivation of the name 'Copeland' which is now understood to signify 'bought land'. His account of the pearls in the River Mite is copied from Camden.

But southward sallying hence, to those sea-bordring sands,
Where Dudden driving downe to the Lancastrian lands,
This Cumberland cuts out, and strongly doth confine,
This meeting there with that, both meerly maratine.
Where many a daintie rill out of her native dale,
To the Virgivian [i.e. the Irish Sea] makes, with many a pleasant gale:
As Eske her farth'st, so first, a coy bred Cumbrian lasse,
Who commeth to her road, renowned Ravenglasse,
By Devoke driven along, (which from a large-brim'd lake,
To hye her to the sea, with greater haste doth make)
Meets Nyte [Mite], a nimble brooke, their rendevous that keepe
In Ravenglasse, when soone into the blewish deepe
Comes Irt, of all the rest, though small, the richest girle,
Her costly bosome strew'd with precious orient pearle,
Bred in her shining shels, which to the deaw doth yawne,
Which deaw they sucking in, conceave that lusty spawne,
Of which when they grow great, and to their fulnesse swell,
They cast, which those at hand there gathering, dearly sell.
This cleare pearle-paved Irt, Bleng to her harbor brings,
From Copland comming downe, a forrest-nymph, which sings
Her owne praise, and those floods, their fountains that derive
From her, which to extoll, the forrest thus doth strive:

Yee northerne Dryades all adorn'd with mountaines steepe,
Upon whose hoary heads cold winter long doth keepe,
Where often rising hils, deepe dales and many make,
Where many a pleasant spring, and many a large-spread lake,
Their cleere beginnings keepe, and doe their names bestow
Upon those humble vales, through which they eas'ly flow.
Whereas the mountaine nymphs, and those that doe frequent
The fountaines, fields, and groves, with wondrous meriment,
By moone-shine many a night, doe give each other chase,
At hood-winke, barley-breake, at tick, or prison-base,
With tricks, and antique toyes, that one another mocke,
That skip from crag to crag, and leape from rocke to rocke.
Then Copland, of this tract a corner, I would know,
What place can there be found in Britan, that doth show

A surface more austere, more sterne from every way,
That who doth it behold, he cannot chuse but say,
Th'aspect of these grim hills, these darke and mistie dales,
From clouds scarce ever cleer'd, with the strongst northern gales,
Tell in their mighty roots, some minerall there doth lye,
The islands generall want, whose plenty might supply:
Wherefore as some suppose of copper mynes in me,
I Copper-land was cald . . .

> Michael Drayton (1563–1631)
> From *Poly-Olbion*, The Thirteenth Song

A Cabinet of Beauties

The five finest things in Scotland are – (1) Edinburgh; (2) The ante-chamber of the Fall of Foyers; (3) The view of Loch Lomond from Inch Tavannach, the highest of the islands; (4) The Trossachs; (5) The view of the Hebrides from a point, the name of which I forget. But the intervals between the fine things in Scotland are very dreary; – whereas in Cumberland and Westmorland there is a cabinet of beauties, – each thing being beautiful in itself, and the very passage of one lake, mountain or valley, to another, is itself a beautiful thing again. The Scotch lakes are so like one another, from their great size, that in a picture you are obliged to read their names; but the English lakes, especially Derwent Water, or rather the whole vale of Keswick, is so rememberable, that, after having been once seen, no one ever requires to be told what it is when drawn. This vale is about as large a basin as Loch Lomond; the latter is covered with water; but in the former instance, we have two lakes with a charming river to connect them, and lovely villages at the foot of the mountain, and other habitations, which give an air of life and cheerfulness to the whole place.

> S. T. Coleridge (1772–1834)
> *Table Talk*

The Image of a Wheel

To begin, then, with the main outlines of the country; – I know not
how to give the reader a distinct image of these more readily, than by
requesting him to place himself with me, in imagination, upon some
given point; let it be the top of either of the mountains, Great Gavel
[Gable] or Scawfell; or, rather, let us suppose our station to be a cloud
hanging midway between those two mountains, at not more than
half a mile's distance from the summit of each, and not many yards
above their highest elevation; we shall then see stretched at our feet a
number of valleys, not fewer than eight, diverging from the point,
on which we are supposed to stand, like spokes from the nave of a
wheel. First, we note, lying to the south-east, the vale of Langdale,
which will conduct the eye to the long lake of Winandermere,
stretched nearly to the sea; or rather to the sands of the vast bay of
Morcamb, serving here for the rim of this imaginary wheel; – let us
trace it in a direction from the south-east towards the south, and we
shall next fix our eyes upon the vale of Coniston, running up likewise
from the sea, but not (as all other valleys do) to the nave of the wheel,
and therefore it may be not inaptly represented as a broken spoke
sticking in the rim. Looking forth again, with an inclination towards
the west, we see immediately at our feet the vale of Duddon, in which
is no lake, but a copious stream winding among fields, rocks, and
mountains, and terminating its course in the sands of Duddon. The
fourth vale, next to be observed, viz. that of the Esk, is of the same
general character as the last, yet beautifully discriminated from it by
peculiar features. Its stream passes under the woody steep upon which
stands Muncaster Castle, the ancient seat of the Penningtons, and after
forming a short and narrow estuary enters the sea below the small
town of Ravenglass. Next, almost due west, look down into, and
along the deep valley of Wastdale, with its little chapel and half a
dozen neat dwellings scattered upon a plain of meadow and corn-
ground intersected with stone walls apparently innumerable, like a
large piece of lawless patchwork, or an array of mathematical figures,
such as in the ancient schools of geometry might have been sportively
and fantastically traced out upon sand. Beyond this little fertile plain
lies, within a bed of steep mountains, the long, narrow, stern, and

desolate lake of Wastdale; and, beyond this, a dusky tract of level ground conducts the eye to the Irish Sea. The stream that issues from Wast-water is named the Irt, and falls into the estuary of the river Esk. Next comes in view Ennerdale, with its lake of bold and somewhat savage shores. Its stream, the Ehen or Enna, flowing through a soft and fertile country, passes the town of Egremont, and the ruins of the castle – then, seeming, like the other rivers, to break through the barrier of sand thrown up by the winds on this tempestuous coast, enters the Irish Sea. The vale of Buttermere, with the lake and village of that name, and Crummock-water, beyond, next present themselves. We will follow the main stream, the Coker, through the fertile and beautiful vale of Lorton, till it is lost in the Derwent, below the noble ruins of Cockermouth Castle. Lastly, Borrowdale, of which the vale of Keswick is only a continuation, stretching due north, brings us to a point nearly opposite to the vale of Windermere with which we began. From this it will appear, that the image of a wheel, thus far exact, is little more than one half complete; but the deficiency on the eastern side may be supplied by the vales of Wytheburn, Ullswater, Haweswater, and the vale of Grasmere and Rydal; none of these, however, run up to the central point between Great Gavel and Scawfell. From this, hitherto our central point, take a flight of not more than four or five miles eastward to the ridge of Helvellyn, and you will look down upon Wytheburn and St John's Vale, which are a branch of the vale of Keswick; upon Ullswater, stretching due east: – and not far beyond to the south-east (though from this point not visible) lie the vale and lake of Haweswater; and lastly, the vale of Grasmere, Rydal, and Ambleside, brings you back to Winandermere, thus completing, though on the eastern side in a somewhat irregular manner, the representative figure of the wheel.

William Wordsworth
Guide to the Lakes

Rock Bottom

Within the central area of the Lakes the travellers find three main types of scenery. In the north there is the Skiddaw range, and the block of fells round Bassenthwaite, Buttermere, Crummock and Loweswater, together with the country as far west as the borders of the Egremont iron-ore district. These are all of Skiddaw slate, which appears also in several outlying patches, notably that of Black Combe, above Whicham Valley, in the extreme south of the county. Now these fells, which were the last to be seen by the eighteenth and nineteenth-century traveller who approached from the south, probably impressed him more immediately than the rest, for they are bolder, more obtrusive, more self-assertive. They tend to be rather isolated, standing apart as individuals, unlike the fells of the central dales, which lap and fold over and around one another like the sheaths of a houseleek. No doubt Skiddaw has its secrets, but, on first meeting, it is frank and open, hands on the table – not particularly friendly, but with nothing to conceal. Even Charles Lamb, who was far from being a mountain lover, could not ignore it. 'Oh, its fine black head,' he wrote in 1802, 'and the bleak air atop of it, with a prospect of mountains all about and about, making you giddy.' The average traveller rarely got himself into the right position to see the more tucked-away and secluded fells, such as Langdale Pikes, but he could not help but get a clear view of Skiddaw.

Now the rock of these northern mountains is a dark mud rock, which does not easily disintegrate into scree or splinter into crag. Its typical form is a solid smooth-sided block, rounded like Dent above Egremont, or pyramidal like Melbreak. From the bottom its slopes seem to slide so evenly upwards that they look neither steep nor high until some object catches your eyes – perhaps a stone wall which runs up and up till it is no more than a pencil mark on the flank of the fell. At Grasmoor, beside Crummock, the broom grows alongside the road, lemon tags and curlings of bloom with the stamens cocked like little fingers, and the eye follows them up a slope no steeper, apparently, and not much longer than the high street of a country town. Then, all at once, you realize that where the broom gives way to bracken, the yellow bunches seem the size of pollen grains, and immediately the fellside comes into perspective and you feel the whole height and weight and mass of it hulking above you like a boot above a beetle.

Because this rock is uniformly more durable than the rocks of the central dales, it has worn into simpler, more regular shapes, and has less variety of texture than, say, the fells of Eskdale or Langdale; instead of a continual contrast of crag and turf, we find an even surface of grass and bracken or sometimes heather. It is smooth, even sleek, yet it is tough and alive like the hide of an animal. In those places (as on Skiddaw Dodd) where the Forestry Commission have planted rectangles of fir trees crossed by geometrical rides, the effect is that of a green tartan pulled round its haunches.

The early traveller, looking north and west from Friar's Crag at the foot of Derwentwater, had a view of Skiddaw and the Newlands Fells that was so deliberate, so self-explanatory, that it might be called a demonstration. It was magnificent and, as he would say, 'awful', yet it seemed to be within his powers of understanding. But if he turned and gazed to the fells round the head of the lake, he was face to face with a different sort of country altogether, a country which seemed to him to have all the mystery and secretiveness which were what he asked from romantic scenery. It might not impress itself on his mind as clearly as Skiddaw and Saddleback, but nevertheless it blew across his imagination like the wind across the strings of an Aeolian harp.

This was the country of the dales, the hub of the lakes; the land of the passes, and tight, crooked valleys, where the fells queued up one behind the other, so packed, close and anonymous, that you scarcely realized that from many of them you could look down on Grasmoor and Saddleback, and even, from one or two, on Skiddaw. This central area is of the volcanic rocks which Professor Sedgwick called 'green slates and porphyries'. The rock here, being formed of different sorts of volcanic matter – lava, ashes, breccias and conglomerates – varies very greatly in hardness, and therefore weathers in many different ways even in the same fellside. At times it is as hard as steel, thrusting a great plated hulk into the rough seas of cloud, letting the waters run away down spouts and grooves of rock. Such is the rock face of Pavey Ark above Great Langdale, or the knob of Castle Head near Derwentwater which may perhaps have been the central neck of lava in one of the former lake volcanoes. In other places the rock wears no better than plaster, rotting and crumbling in the rain, slithering into scratchings and slaverings of scree. Such are the screes of Wastwater, where a whole fellside has disintegrated, turning back into its own element, and seeping down to the water which once shaped and raised it from mud to mountain.

Yet it is not these vast exhibitions of crag or scree which are typical of the dales, but rather the continual juxtaposition of each to each, so that even the lower hills are both bony and scurfy, are knobbed and scabbed, gnarled and scraped, whiskered and downy, almost at one and the same time. The turf climbs among the crags, carrying sedges and the mountain flowers, and larches heave in great heaped tidal waves up the narrowing channels of gills and clefts. Gorse swarms like bees, and rowans and thorn trees grow high up in hollows and clearings scythed out of the bracken by a beck. From lakeshore to the tops the land is populous with flower and seed and bird and living water.

Moreover, it is not just the substance of the rock which has given the dales their character, but the forces which have been at work on it, and, in particular, that of glaciation. In the Ice Ages, the Lake valleys manufactured each its own glacier which squirmed to the lowlands along the track taken now and before by the rivers. But this ice-flood left the shape of the dales greatly changed. It sliced away the sides giving a U-shape to a cross-section of the valleys instead of the former V-shape. Today, a flat matting of meadowland is laid along the beck-side right up to the dale-heads, while the fells, cut clean to the bone, look on with water dribbling down their chins. Where the streams were of any size they were often left 'hanging' in the air, so that now they may drop all at one go in a waterfall, or bob and bubble and bounce their way down a gill carved out of the rock like a slice cut from a cake. When the drop is steep, even a beck so small that it would not drown a hedgehog can dig a trough deep enough to hide a house.

It was the glaciers, too, which gave the dales their lakes, either by damming the exit with a moraine, or by scooping beneath the old river-bed and then leaving the water to flood the hole. For this reason the lakes of the dales are very like rivers. Bassenthwaite and lower Derwentwater spread out beneath a wide sky, with plenty of room for the sun to shine on them and for the traveller to view them whole. They seem detached, separate from the fells, pretending to be under no obligation, and the fells, for their part, seem aloof. Buttermere and Crummock are more hemmed in, lying as in the bottom of a cup, but they too are curiously independent, not accepting High Style or Robinson or Melbreak as being of their order or genus. But the lakes of the central dales are the brides and bed-mates of the rocks. Ullswater links arms with the crags, crooking elbow and ankle around them, turning back to see itself, bending at the knees and again at the hips, slapping the masculine thighs of the fells and wriggling like an adolescent. Elterwater, which drains both of the Langdales, never quite makes up its mind when to cease to be a lake and begin to be the Brathay. Just below the entrance of the stream from Colwith, the lake is narrowed by a long promontory, but it opens out again into another reach almost as large as the higher one. Then it contracts itself to a river, shallow enough for a dog to wade through, flows a hundred yards or so between widening meadows and woods, and, without any excuse, opens out into a pool nearly as deep as the lake. But from that moment there is no more shilly-shallying, for Skelwith Force has got its pull on the water which now flows straight and fast till it makes that full-bodied dive into the rock-pools above Skelwith Bridge.

It is futile to assess such country in terms of views. The view flattens the scene into a man-made dimension; it measures the landscape from the borders of an imaginary picture-frame; it reduces life to a post-card. It imposes a rigid and unnatural rule of proportion on our eyes, and makes us reject so much of what our other senses tell us. Even in our own memories, Coniston Old Man is not just a design in shape and colour seen from this or that angle – a double-propped marquee from the Duddon Estuary; a single-ridged peak, like a shoe-nut, from Torver; a great kangaroo-bellied amphibian, seen from the opposite side of Coniston Lake. It is also the man-made screes beside the quarries; the whitewash on old miners' cottages; a stone playing ducks and drakes on Levers Water, making the black tarn throw up waves like a magician's steel rings; a small dog nosing its way up the track from Low Water to the summit; a scrap of silver paper curled round a stone like lichen; dirty snow in a culvert of rock; rowan berries, the red-green of mouldy raspberry jam, making the end twigs bend under their weight; wheatears; the split and spit of thin ice; a pulled muscle in the thighs; a wind making a spread map roll and ripple like the sea; herdwicks; the smell of cut bracken; clouds; handkerchiefs. And yet all these impressions, and a thousand more, add up only to a one-sided, personal and entirely superficial memory, which ignores all that the mountain may mean to those who have lived for years beside it. It ignores still more what the mountain may mean to itself – not as a thing to be seen or climbed or thought about, but merely as a thing that is.

Looking east from Coniston Old Man, towards Kendal and the Yorkshire border, you see the third main division of the Lake scenery: the Windermere country. It includes no fells of any great height, no crags, no screes, no major waterfalls. Instead, it consists of easy-going hills, undulating as gently as an eiderdown, with wood, park-land, gardens, garages and country houses. Much of it is now turned into a mountain watering-place, an upper-outer-suburb, yet in its less publicized spots it is still as homely and wholesome as new-made bread. There are gulleys and gills in the hills behind Brantwood which are far less visited than the top of Scafell Pike.

Norman Nicholson (1914–   )
The Lakers

Fells

Of Mountains in General, with Their Natural Uses

For a short account of the author, the Rev. Thomas Robinson, see page 345.

Some of our late *Theorists*, who have undertaken to give us some new Schemes and Descriptions of this Terraqueous Globe, and to entertain us with Theories of it, seem to be of Opinion, that the *Antidiluvian* Earth was mathematically round, without Mountains, Hills, or Vallies, as if these exuberances of its Surface, like Warts and Wens, were the Deformities of it. But this *Hypothesis*, or rather Conceit, seems to be the effect of their Ignorance in Divinity, as well as Natural Philosophy. For if these new *Theorists* had considered that God hath made nothing in the whole Creation in vain, but to wise Ends, and the best of Purposes, tho' the narrowness of our dark Intellect is not able fully to comprehend them, they would have been convinced of their Mistake, and retracted their ill grounded *Hypothesis*. For as God was pleased to make, not only the Earth it self, but all the several Ranks and Species of Creatures which live upon it, and are subordinate to our Nature, for our Use, Pleasure, and Diversion; so these high and lofty Mountains do not only contribute to the Entertainment of our visive Faculty, with most curious and delightful Landskips, but present us with a Set of Vegetables peculiar to their cold and elevated Soil, and most proper and agreeable with the hot Natures of Sheep and other Creatures bred upon them, which are most refreshed with the coldness and frigidity of the Mountain-Air. But as the whole Frame and Fabrick of the World is supported and preserved in order by the Agreement, Conspiracy, and Subserviency of one Part to another, so one Part of the Earth is serviceable to another, and the *Mountains* to the Whole: For I cannot yet understand how this Earth could have been an habitable World without a distribution of Rain, Wind, Air, and Dews; for all which those *warm* and *spacious Plains* and *Vallies* are in a great measure indebted to the high and lofty Tops of Mountains, that seem with Pride and Contempt so much to overlook them.

Thomas Robinson
*An Essay towards a Natural History of
Westmorland and Cumberland* (1709)

Mountains as Picturesque Objects

*The Rev. William Gilpin did more than any other writer to make popular
the idea of 'Picturesque Beauty' in the second half of the eighteenth century.
His* Observations, *made on a tour of the Lakes in 1772, influenced many
who followed him in that region, and are quoted again and again in the early
guide-books. His determination to see the whole landscape in terms of a
picture is often carried to near-absurdity, but he taught a generation of
travellers to use their eyes as never before.*

With regard to *mountains*, it may be first premised, that, in a pic-
turesque view, we consider them only as *distant objects*; their enormous
size disqualifying them for objects at hand. In the removed part of a
picture therefore, the mountain properly appears; where its immen-
sity, reduced by distance, can be taken in by the eye; and its mon-
struous features, losing their deformity, assume a softness which
naturally belongs not to them.

I would not however be understood to mean, that a mountain is
proper only to close an *extended* view. It may take its station in a
second, or third distance with equal propriety. And even on a fore-
ground, a rugged corner of its base may be introduced; tho its upper
regions aspire far beyond the limits of any picture.

The beauty of a distant mountain in a great measure, depends on
the line it traces along the sky; which is generally of a lighter hue. The
pyramidal shape, and easy flow of an irregular line, will be found in
the mountain, as in other delineations, the truest source of beauty.

Mountains therefore rising in regular, mathematical lines, or in
whimsical, grotesque shapes, are displeasing. Thus . . . a mountain in
Cumberland, which from its peculiar appearance in some situations,
takes the name of *Saddle-back*, [forms] disagreeable lines . . . Such
forms also as suggest the idea of lumpish *heaviness* are disgusting –
round, swelling forms, without any break to disincumber them of
their weight.

Indeed a continuity of line without a break, whether it be *concave*,
straight, or *convex*, will always displease, because it wants variety;
unless indeed it be well contrasted with other forms. The effect also
of a broken line is bad, if the breaks are regular.

The sources of *deformity* in the mountain-line will easily suggest those of *beauty*. If the line swell easily to an apex, and yet by irregular breaks, which may be varied in a thousand modes, it must be pleasing.

The same principles, on which we seek for beauty in *single* mountains, will help us to find it in a *combination* of them. Mountains *in composition* are considered as *single* objects, and follow the same rules. If they break into mathematical, or fantastic forms – if they join heavily together in lumpish shapes – if they fall into each other at right-angles – or if their lines run parallel – in all these cases, the combination will be more or less disgusting: and a converse of these will of course be agreeable.

> William Gilpin (1724–1804)
> *Observations Relative Chiefly to Picturesque*
> *Beauty in the Mountains and Lakes*
> *of Cumberland and Westmorland*

Mountains: Their Forms and Colours

Their *forms* are endlessly diversified, sweeping easily or boldly in simple majesty, abrupt and precipitous, or soft and elegant. In magnitude and grandeur they are individually inferior to the most celebrated of those in some other parts of this island; but, in the combinations which they make, towering above each other, or lifting themselves in ridges like the waves of a tumultuous sea, and in the beauty and variety of their surfaces and colours, they are surpassed by none.

The general *surface* of the mountains is turf, rendered rich and green by the moisture of the climate. Sometimes the turf, as in the neighbourhood of Newlands, is little broken, the whole covering being soft and downy pasturage. In other places rocks predominate; the soil is laid bare by torrents and burstings of water from the sides of mountains in heavy rains; and not unfrequently their perpendicular sides are seamed by ravines (formed also by rains and torrents) which, meeting in angular points, entrench and scar the surface with numerous figures like the letters W and Y.

In the ridge that divides Eskdale from Wastdale, granite is found; but the MOUNTAINS are for the most part composed of the stone by mineralogists termed schist, which, as you approach the plain country, gives place to lime-stone and free-stone; but schist being the substance of the mountains, the predominant *colour* of their *rocky* parts is bluish, or hoary grey – the general tint of the lichens with which the bare stone is encrusted. With this blue or grey colour is frequently intermixed a red tinge, proceeding from the iron which interveins the stone, and impregnates the soil. The iron is the principle of decomposition in these rocks; and hence, when they become pulverized, the elementary particles crumbling down, overspread in many places the steep and almost precipitous sides of the mountains with an intermixture of colours, like the compound hues of a dove's neck. When in the heat of advancing summer, the fresh green tint of the herbage has somewhat faded, it is again revived by the appearance of the fern [i.e. bracken] profusely spread over the same ground: and, upon this plant, more than upon anything else, do the changes which the seasons make in the colouring of the mountains depend. About the first week in October, the rich green, which prevailed through the whole summer, is usually passed away. The brilliant and various colours of the fern are then in harmony with the autumnal woods; bright yellow or lemon colour, at the base of the mountains, melting gradually, through orange, to a dark russet brown towards the summits, where the plant, being more exposed to the weather, is in a more advanced state of decay. Neither heath nor furze are *generally* found upon the *sides* of these mountains, though in many places they are adorned by those plants, so beautiful when in flower. We may add, that the mountains are of height sufficient to have the surface towards the summit softened by distance, and to imbibe the finest aerial hues. In common also with other mountains, their apparent forms and colours are perpetually changed by the clouds and vapours which float round them: the effect indeed of mist or haze, in a country of this character, is like that of magic. I have seen six or seven ridges rising above each other, all created in a moment by the vapours upon the side of a mountain, which, in its ordinary appearance, showed not a projecting point to furnish even a hint for such an operation.

William Wordsworth
A Guide to the Lakes

Skiddaw

The mountain *Skiddaw* is about eleven hundred yards perpendicular from the Broadwater [i.e. Bassenthwaite Lake]. It rises with two heads, like unto Parnassus; and with a kind of emulation beholds Scruffel [Criffel] hill before it in Annandale in Scotland. By these two mountains, according as the misty clouds rise or fall, the people dwelling thereabouts make their prognostication of the change of the weather, and have a common expression,

> If Skiddaw hath a cap,
> Scruffel wots well of that.

Like as there goes also another saying concerning the height of this hill with two others in this kingdom,

> Skiddaw, Lanvellin [Helvellyn], and Casticand [Catstye Cam]
> Are the highest hills in all England.*

Joseph Nicolson and Richard Burn
*The History of the Antiquities of
Westmorland and Cumberland* (1777)

* This is incorrect, of course, none of these mountains being as high as Scafell or Scafell Pike.

A Letter from the Top of Scafell

*The following extract is taken from the Notebook kept by Coleridge on a
solitary tour of the Western Lakes, during the summer of 1802. He had taken
a previous tour, some years earlier, in the company of William and, part of
the way, John Wordsworth.*

Thursday Morning, Augt 5th [1802].

I ascended Sca' Fell by the side of a torrent, and climbed and rested,
rested and climbed, 'till I gained the very summit of Sca' Fell – be-
lieved by the Shepherds here to be higher than either Helvellyn or
Skiddaw. Even to Black Coomb, before me all the Mountains die
away running down westward to the Sea, apparently in eleven ridges
and three parallel Vales with their three Rivers, seen from their very
Sources to their falling into the Sea, where they form (excepting their
Screw-like flexures) the *Trident* of the Irish Channel at Ravenglass.
O my God! what enormous Mountains these are close by me, and
yet below the Hill I stand on, Great Gavel [Gable], Kirk Fell, Green
Crag, and behind, the Pillar, then the Steeple, then the Hay Cock, on
the other side and behind me, Great End, Esk Carse [Hause], Bow-
fell and close to my back two huge Pyramids, nearly as high as Sca'
Fell itself, and indeed parts and parts of Sca' Fell known far and near
by these names, the hither one of Broad Crag, and next to it (but
divided from it by a low Ridge) Doe Crag, which is indeed of itself
a great Mountain of stones from a pound to 20 Ton weight embedded
in woolly Moss. And here I am *lounded* [sheltered] – so fully lounded –
that tho' the wind is strong, and the Clouds are hasting hither from
the sea – and the whole air Seaward has a lurid Look – and we shall
certainly have Thunder – yet here (but that I am hunger'd and
provisionless) *here* I could lie warm, and wait methinks for tomorrow's
Sun, and on a nice Stone Table am I now at this moment writing to
you – between 2 and 3 o'clock as I guess – surely the first Letter ever
written from the Top of Sca' Fell! But O! what a look down just
under my feet! The frightfullest Cove that might ever be seen, huge
perpendicular Precipices, and one Sheep upon its only Ledge, that
surely must be crag! Tyson told me of this place, and called it Hollow
Stones. Just by it and joining together, rise two huge Pillars of bare

lead-coloured Stone. I am no measurer, but their height and depth is terrible. I know how unfair it is to judge of these Things by a comparison of past Impressions with present – but I have no shadow of hesitation in saying that the Coves and Precipices of Helvellyn are nothing to these! From this sweet lounding Place I see directly thro' Borrowdale, the Castle Crag, the whole of Derwent Water, and but for the haziness of the Air I could see my own House. I see clear enough where it stands –

Here I will fold up this Letter.

S. T. Coleridge
Tour in the Lake Country, 1802

Descent of Scafell

Eskdale, Friday, Augt 6th at an Estate House called Toes [Taw House]

A Ridge of Hill lay low down, and divided this Crag (called Doe-Crag) and Broad-crag – even as the hyphen divides the words broad and crag. I determined to go thither; the first place I came to, that was not direct Rock, I slipped down, and went on for a while with tolerable ease – but now I came (it was midway down) to a smooth perpendicular Rock about 7 feet high – this was nothing – I put my hands on the Ledge, and dropped down, In a few yards came just such another. I *dropped* that too. And yet another, seemed not higher – I would not stand for a trifle, so I dropped that too – but the stretching of the muscle of my hands and arms, and the jolt of the Fall on my Feet, put my whole Limbs in a *Tremble*, and I paused, and looking down, saw that I had little else to encounter but a succession of these little Precipices – it was in truth a Path that in a very hard Rain is, no doubt, the channel of a most splendid Waterfall. So I began to suspect that I ought not to go on; but then unfortunately tho I could with ease drop down a smooth Rock of 7 feet high, I could not *climb* it, so go on I must: and on I went. The next 3 drops were not half a Foot, at least not a foot, more than my own height, but every Drop increased the Palsy of my Limbs. I shook all over, Heaven knows without the least influence of Fear. And now I had only two more to drop down – to return was impossible – but of these two the first was tremendous, it was twice my own height, and the Ledge at the bottom was exceedingly narrow, that if I drop down upon it I must of necessity have fallen backwards and of course killed myself. My limbs were all in a tremble. I lay upon my Back to rest myself, and was beginning according to my custom to laugh at myself for a Madman, when the sight of the Crags above me on each side, and the impetuous Clouds just over them, posting so luridly and so rapidly to northward, overawed me. I lay in a state of almost prophetic Trance and Delight and blessed God aloud for the powers of Reason and the Will, which remaining no Danger can overpower us! O God, I exclaimed aloud, how calm, how blessed am I now. I know not how to proceed, how to return, but I am calm and fearless and confident. If this Reality were a Dream, if I were asleep, what agonies had I suffered! what screams! When the Reason and the Will are away, what remain to us but Darkness and Dimness and a bewildering Shame, and Pain that is utterly Lord over us, or fantastic Pleasure that draws the Soul along swimming through the air in many shapes, even as a Flight of Starlings in a Wind. I arose, and looking down saw at the bottom a heap of Stones which had fallen abroad and rendered the narrow Ledge on which they had been piled doubly dangerous. At the bottom of the third Rock that I dropt from, I met a dead Sheep quite rotten. This heap of stones, I guessed, and have since found that I guessed aright, had been piled up by the Shepherd to enable him to climb up and free the poor Creature whom he had observed to be crag-fast, but seeing nothing but rock over rock, he had desisted and gone for help and in the mean time the poor Creature had fallen down and killed itself. As I was looking at these I glanced my eye to my left, and observed that the Rock was rent from top to bottom. I measured the breadth of the Rent, and found that there was no danger of my being *wedged* in, so I put my knap-sack round to my side, and slipped down as between two walls, without any danger or difficulty. The next Drop brought me down on the Ridge called the How. I hunted out my Besom Stick, which I had flung before me when I first came to the Rocks, and wisely gave over all thought of ascending

Doe-Crag, for now the Clouds were again coming in most tumul-tuously. So I began to descend, when I felt an odd sensation across my whole Breast – not pain nor itching – and putting my hand on it I found it all bumpy – and on looking saw the whole of my Breast from my Neck – to my Navel, exactly all that my Kamell-hair Breast-shield covers, filled with great red heat-bumps, so thick that no hair could lie between them. They still remain but are evidently less and I have no doubt will wholly disappear in a few Days. It was however a startling proof to me of the violent exertions which I had made. I descended this low Hill which was all hollow beneath me – and was like the rough green Quilt of a Bed of Waters. At length two streams burst out and took their way down, one on one side a high Ground upon this Ridge, the other on the other. I took that to my right (having on my left this high ground, and the other Stream, and beyond that Doe-crag, on the other side of which is Esk Halse [Hause], where the head-spring of the Esk rises, and running down the Hill and in upon the Vale looks and actually deceived me, as a great Turnpike Road – in which, as in many other respects the Head of Eskdale much resembles Langdale) and soon the Channel sank all at once, at least 40 yards, and formed a magnificent Waterfall – and close under this a succession of Waterfalls 7 in number, the third of which is nearly as high as the first. When I had almost reached the bottom of the Hill, I stood so as to command the whole 8 Waterfalls, with the great triangle-crag looking in above them, and on the side of them the enormous and more than perpendicular Precipices and *Bull's-Brows*, of Sca' Fell!

S. T. Coleridge
Tour in the Lake Country, 1802

Black Combe

The usual spelling is 'combe', a word derived not from the British 'cumba', a valley, but from the Old English 'camb', a crest. For the first six months of the year 1840, Branwell Brontë lived at Broughton-in-Furness, as tutor

to the sons of Mr Postlethwaite of Broughton House, from which village he
would have a fine view of Black Combe in all weathers.

Far off, and half revealed, 'mid shade and light,
Black Comb half smiles, half frowns; his mighty form
Scarce bending into peace, more formed to fight
A thousand years of struggles with a storm
Than bask one hour subdued by sunshine warm
To bright and breezeless rest; yet even his height
Towers not o'er this world's sympathies; he smiles –
While many a human heart to pleasure's wiles
Can bear to bend, and still forget to rise –
As though he, huge and heath-clad on our sight,
Again rejoices in his stormy skies.
Man loses vigour in unstable joys.
Thus tempests find Black Comb invincible,
While we are lost, who should know life so well.

Branwell Brontë (1817–1848)

Written with a Slate Pencil on a Stone, on the Side of the Mountain of Black Combe

Stay, bold Adventurer; rest awhile thy limbs
On this commodious Seat! for much remains
Of hard ascent before thou reach the top
Of this huge Eminence, – from blackness named,
And, to far-travelled storms of sea and land,
A favourite spot of tournament and war!
But thee may no such boisterous visitants
Molest; may gentle breezes fan thy brow;
And neither cloud conceal, nor misty air
Bedim, the grand terraqueous spectacle,

From centre to circumference, unveiled!
Know, if thou grudge not to prolong thy rest,
That on the summit whither thou art bound,
A geographic Labourer pitched his tent,
With books supplied and instruments of art,
To measure height and distance; lonely task,
Week after week pursued! – to him was given
Full many a glimpse (but sparingly bestowed
On timid man) of Nature's processes
Upon the exalted hills. He made report
That once, while there he plied his studious work
Within that canvass Dwelling, colours, lines,
And the whole surface of the out-spread map,
Became invisible: for all around
Had darkness fallen – unthreatened, unproclaimed –
As if the golden day itself had been
Extinguished in a moment; total gloom,
In which he sate alone, with unclosed eyes,
Upon the blinded mountain's silent top.

William Wordsworth

Bowfell

Bowfell is undoubtedly one of the finest mountains in Lakeland – a shy but shapely pyramid, without notoriety or glamour, stuck right in the centre of some of the best country in England. An honest mountain quite devoid of guile, you might say – unless you happen to be using a compass near Ore Gap.

Bowfell is one of the easiest mountains in the Lake District to recognize and is visible, unmasked by other peaks, from almost all sides. You can see it from the fell at the back of my house – a shapely cone at the end of a ridge – and it is equally visible from mountain tops, from many of the valleys, from many places around the coast, and even from some of the towns . . .

The mountain is easy to recognize because, unlike most Lakeland peaks, its summit has the traditional shape – an equilateral triangle. If you ask a child to draw a mountain it will show you something like the top of Bowfell. Stickle Pike in Dunnerdale has much the same shape, so have two or three mountains in North Wales, so – much more dramatically – has the Matterhorn, but not very many Lakeland mountain tops are so traditional in shape. Grisedale Pike might sometimes qualify, but as often as not, is hidden by other tops.

The best-known mountain shape in Lakeland – the Langdale Pikes – is unrecognizable from 'the back' to the uninitiated, while the sugar-loaf shape of Great Gable is lost when not seen end-on. Scafell Pike, the highest mountain in England, has no real characteristic shape; Harter Fell in Cumberland often looks a better peak. But Bowfell looks properly conical from all directions, even if the cone appears stuck on the end of a ridge. It is a big mountain – not far short of three thousand feet – and a mountain with a shape you can recognize from most parts of Lakeland.

Almost the only thing some guide-books say about Bowfell is that there is magnetic rock on the summit, so that compasses are unreliable, but this is more confusing than helpful. The facts are that minor variations of one or two degrees may be found at a number of points between Crinkle Crags and Esk Pike and about three degrees near Shelter Crags, but in every case you have to hold your compass close to the rock for the deviation to be observed. But on the northwest side of Ore Gap you can get deviations of up to 170 degrees on certain rocks if you place your compass in the right place, so that compasses used in this way could send you back the way you had come. It was the Brathay Exploration Group who reached these conclusions after a most detailed survey carried out several years ago, and it seems clear from their report that all you have to do to avoid being misled by your compass on Bowfell is simply to make sure you don't place the thing on a rock or very close to one.

Otherwise Bowfell is a perfectly straightforward mountain with crags where you'd expect to find them – on the north and east sides – and well sculptured, easily identified shoulders. Ore Gap, where the highly magnetized rocks appear to be, has probably been in use as a pass for at least two thousand years – the stone-axes from Pike o'

Stickle probably went this way – and Three Tarns (there are five of them, really) are difficult to mistake.

Bowfell, like most good mountains, is a rock mountain in its upper tiers and the rock runs to crags in many places. Over the years I have spent dozens of happy hours on the climbs on Bowfell Buttress and elsewhere and many a winter's day in the ice packed gullies in its north-east corner. The Great Slab on Flat Crags is quite unlike anything seen anywhere else in Lakeland and walkers anxious to get the feel of the mountain can traverse it quite easily. Not far away from the summit plateau, perhaps three hundred yards north-east of the cairn and between the crag of the Cambridge Climb and Hanging Knotts, there used to be, crouched among the rocks, a crudely built stone hut about eight feet square with a stone roof. It commanded a splendid view down Mickleden, and I have heard it suggested that it might have been a smugglers' hut, perched in this rather inaccessible place so that the men could watch the valleys and the passes for signs of the excisemen . . .

As a mountain of character Bowfell rightly lords it over two Lakeland counties, for the summit ridge lies on the Cumberland-Westmorland boundary. It rises at the head of three of the finest valleys in Lakeland – Langdale, Eskdale and Langstrath – and its waters run down these valleys into Windermere, Derwentwater and the sea. Below the terraced cliffs of Hanging Knotts, in a dark hollow, is the finely situated Angle Tarn, where I once enjoyed a 6 a.m. bathe. We had camped the previous night by the shore of the tarn in heavy, driving rain and had spent most of the night in sodden sleeping bags, trying to stop the tent from being blown away. But the dawn was sheer magic. Gone was the gloom so often associated with this dark hollow, for instead the morning sunlight was sparkling across the waters and our figures cast long shadows across the turf. After our weary night a bathe was irresistible and we were splashing in even before we had put out the sleeping bags to dry. And after that the bacon and eggs, on the morning of a day that turned out to be one of the hottest of the year, tasted quite wonderful.

If you pick the right day the view from the summit of Bowfell can be unequalled in Lakeland. Scotland can sometimes be seen and often the Solway Firth, the estuaries of the Esk and the Duddon, the

Northern Pennines and the Yorkshire hills and almost all the mountains in Lakeland. There is a splendid close-up view of the Scafells, and if there is snow about and the skies have their winter clarity the effect of airy isolation above a great white world is magical.

Although Bowfell can be ascended from all directions, including Hell Gill out of Oxendale, I have never found the mountain so swarming with hordes of people as Helvellyn, Gable and Scafell Pike so often are, nor is it unduly littered with cairns. And it is a friendly mountain with a low accident rate. Rock-climbers, tired of queuing up for the climbs on Gimmer or Raven Crag find the rocks on Bowfell a pleasant change – not very sunny and often wet, but never crowded and always with a considerable character of their own. And it is often worth the extra walk to get well away, out of sight and sound of the cars roaring up and down the Blea Tarn road . . .

A. H. Griffin (1910–   )
The Roof of England

Descent of Langdale Pikes

Captain John Budworth, who later took the name of Palmer, made two visits to the Lakes: the first in the summer of 1792 and the second in the winter of 1797–8. The first two editions of his book, appearing in 1792 and 1795, were attributed to 'A. Rambler', the third, in 1810, to 'Jos. Budworth'. He was accompanied, on his climb at Langdale, by Paul Postlethwaite, a boy of fifteen, and some of the peculiar difficulties he experienced on his descent may be due to the fact that he had only one arm.

On our preparing to descend, he [Paul] said, 'Wad naw you loike a nearer weay whoam agen, tan th'road we cum up?' On my approving of his proposal, we began our descent opposite from our ascent; we were obliged to be very cautious, and cling close to the rocks; and when we had got a good way down, we came to a part where we had to pass over a large bulging part of the mountain, across a sward nearly perpendicular, and of an immoderate height: he was going unconcernedly to cross by a sheep-track; I checked him, and asked him what he meant by bringing me into such a situation? I looked up to return to the summit again, but it had too laborious an appearance, and the distance was great; and knowing that taking to resolve when danger is near ever increases it, I tied up my right eye, which could not have borne the vast precipice almost under me. I laid hold of one end of his pole, cautioned him as to his pace, and with my left eye on the sheep-walk, not more than three inches broad, my head almost close to the mountain, and thus piloted, we were in about eight minutes safe moored; and when I looked back I had reason to be thankful. Paul said, he had crossed it hundreds a times, or he must have gone a great round; and he literally said what I had remarked of Bob Partridge, to the effect that 'a man moight surely goa wheor a sheop cud'.

Joseph Budworth (later Palmer) (1756–1815)
A Fortnight's Ramble to the Lakes (third edition, 1810)

Castlerigg Remembered

. . . like a dismal cirque
Of Druid stones, upon a forlorn moor,
When the chill rain begins at shut of eve,
In dull November, and their chancel vault,
The Heaven itself, is blinded throughout night.

John Keats (1795–1821)
From *Hyperion*, Book 2

Wall

The wall walks the fell –
Grey millipede on slow
Stone hooves;
Its slack back hollowed
At gulleys and grooves,
Or shouldering over
Old boulders
Too big to be rolled away.
Fallen fragments
Of the high crags
Crawl in the walk of the wall.

A dry-stone wall
Is a wall and a wall,
Leaning together
(Cumberland-and-Westmorland
Champion wrestlers),
Greening and weathering,
Flank by flank,
With filling of rubble
Between the two –
A double-rank
Stone dyke:
Flags and through-
stones, jutting out side-ways,
Like the steps of a stile.

A wall walks slowly.
At each give of the ground,
Each creak of the rock's ribs,
It puts its foot gingerly,
Arches its hog-holes,
Lets cobble and knee-joint
Settle and grip.
As the slipping fellside

Erodes and drifts,
The wall shifts with it,
Is always on the move.

They built a wall slowly,
A day a week;
Built it to stand,
But not stand still.
They built a wall to walk.

Norman Nicholson

Dales

Grasmere, 1

From hence the road led us into another amphitheatre, wild and immense like the former, but varied greatly in the shapes of the mountains, which were here more broken and irregular, shooting, in many places, into craggy summits, and broken points . . .

At the conclusion of this immense amphitheatre . . . we found an exit, equal to the scene – another grand mountain-gap, or portal, through which the road carried us up another steep mountain. – At the top we paused, and looking back on the scenes we had left, were presented with a view, which wholly filled the imagination.

It was a *retrospect* of the amphitheatre we had passed; but in a style still grander, than the prospect of it. It was more strongly marked with the great out-lines of composition; and was, of course, more a whole.

A wide vale, thrown by perspective into a circular form, lay before the eye. Here also the distant part seemed occupied by the lake of Grasmere; but a greyish mist left the idea ambiguous. Beyond the lake arose various mountains, which bounded it: and still beyond these, appeared the blue heads of other mountains. Those, which formed the side-screens of the vale, advancing forward from the distant mountains beyond the lake, approached the eye in a grand sweep, by the easy gradations of perspective. The promontories, and recesses, of the more removed parts were marked by a faint shadow; till by degrees both the side-screens, growing boldly on the eye, were lost behind the two cheeks of the craggy portal, which, with the road between them, formed a fore-ground equal to the scene. The whole view is entirely of the horrid kind. Not a tree appeared to add the least chearfulness to it.

With regard to the adorning of such a scene with figures, nothing could suit it better than a group of banditti. Of all the scenes I ever saw, this was the most adapted to the perpetration of some dreadful deed.

William Gilpin
Observations . . . [on] the Mountains and Lakes of Cumberland and Westmorland

The Lake District

Grasmere, 2

Saturday 12th [December 1801]. Snow upon the ground . . . All looked cheerful and bright. Helm Crag rose very bold and craggy, a Being by itself, and behind it was the large ridge of mountain, smooth as marble and snow white. All the mountains looked like solid stone, on our left, going from Grasmere, i.e. White Moss and Nab Scar. The snow hid all the grass, and all signs of vegetation, and the rocks showed themselves boldly everywhere, and seemed more stony than rocks or stone. The birches on the crags beautiful, red brown and glittering. The ashes glittering spears with their upright stems. The hips very beautiful, and so good!! and, dear Coleridge! I ate twenty for thee, when I was by myself. I came home first. They walked too slow for me. Wm went to look at Langdale Pikes. We had a sweet invigorating walk. Mr Clarkson came in before tea. We played at cards. Sate up late. The moon shone upon the waters below Silver How, and above it hung, combining with Silver How on one side, a bowl-shaped moon, the curve downwards, the white fields, glittering roof of Thomas Ashburner's house, the dark yew tree, the white fields gay and beautiful. Wm lay with his curtains open that he might see it.

Dorothy Wordsworth (1771–1855)
Grasmere Journal

Slater's Bridge

This famous so-called 'pack-horse' bridge spans the River Brathay in Little Langdale. It takes its name from the fact that it was used by the men working in the slate quarries.

A man drinking brandy at Candlemas, and tossing cards
from one hand to the other, thought of this
exercise in hanging circularity, toppling stress.

The rough slate wedges carry their own likeness
on the belly of each, with the grass springing sidewise
at the joins. The bare arch links two valley sides
as though by a handclasp across the sky's reflection.

J. D. Marshall (1919–   )

Approach to the Duddon

The traveller would be most gratified who should approach this beautiful Stream, neither at its source . . . nor from its termination; but from Coniston over Walna Scar; first descending into a little circular valley [i.e. the valley of Tarn Beck, which flows out of Seathwaite Tarn], a collateral compartment of the long winding vale through which flows the Duddon. This recess, towards the close of September, when the after-grass of the meadows is still of a fresh green, with the leaves of many of the trees faded, but perhaps none fallen, is truly enchanting. At a point elevated enough to show the various objects in the valley, and not so high as to diminish their importance, the stranger will instinctively halt. On the foreground, a little below the most favourable station, a rude footbridge is thrown over the bed of the noisy brook foaming by the way-side. Russet and craggy hills, of bold and varied outline, surround the level valley, which is besprinkled with grey rocks plumed with birch trees. A few homesteads are interspersed, in some places peeping out from among the rocks like hermitages, whose site has been chosen for the benefit of sunshine as well as shelter; in other instances, the dwelling-house, barn, and byre, compose together a cruciform structure, which, with its embowering trees, and the ivy clothing part of the walls and roof like a fleece, call to mind the remains of an ancient abbey. Time, in most cases, and nature everywhere, have given a sanctity to the humble works of man, that are scattered over this peaceful retirement. Hence a harmony of tone and colour, a consummation and perfection of beauty, which would have been marred had aim or purpose interfered with the course of convenience, utility, or necessity. This unvitiated region stands in no need of the veil of twilight to soften or disguise its features. As it glistens in the morning sunshine, it would fill the spectator's heart with gladsomeness. Looking from our chosen station, he would feel an impatience to rove among its pathways, to be greeted by the milkmaid, to wander from house to house, exchanging 'goodmorrows' as he passed the open doors; but, at evening, when the sun is set, and a pearly light gleams from the western quarter of the sky, with an answering light from the smooth surface of the meadows; when the trees are dusky, but each kind still distinguishable; when the cool air has condensed the blue smoke rising from the cottage chimneys; when the dark mossy stones seem to sleep in the bed of the foaming brook; *then*, he would be unwilling to move forward, not less from a reluctance to relinquish what he beholds, than from an apprehension of disturbing, by his approach, the quietness beneath him. Issuing from the plain of this valley, the brook descends in a rapid torrent passing by the churchyard of Seathwaite ... From the point where the Seathwaite brook joins the Duddon, is a view upwards, into the pass through which the river makes its way into the plain of Donnerdale. The perpendicular rock on the right bears the ancient British name of THE PEN; the one opposite is called WALLA-BARROW CRAG ... The *chaotic* aspect of the scene is well marked by the expression of a stranger, who strolled out while dinner was preparing, and at his return, being asked by his host, 'What way he had been wandering?' replied, 'As far as it is finished!'

William Wordsworth
Notes to *The River Duddon, A Series of Sonnets*

To the River Duddon

I wonder, Duddon, if you still remember
An oldish man with a nose like a pony's nose,
Broad bones, legs long and lean but strong enough

To carry him over Hard Knott at seventy years of age.
He came to you first as a boy with a fishing-rod
And a hunk of Ann Tyson's bread and cheese in his pocket,
Walking from Hawkshead across Walna Scar;
Then as a middle-aged Rydal landlord,
With a doting sister and a government sinecure,
Who left his verses gummed to your rocks like lichen,
The dry and yellow edges of a once-green spring.
He made a guide-book for you, from your source
There where you bubble through the moss on Wrynose
(Among the ribs of bald and bony fells
With screes scratched in the turf like grey scabs),
And twist and slither under humpbacked bridges –
Built like a child's house from odds and ends
Of stones that lie about the mountain side –
Past Cockley Beck Farm and on to Birk's Bridge,
Where the rocks stride about like legs in armour,
And the steel birches buckle and bounce in the wind
With a crinkle of silver foil in the crisp of the leaves;
On then to Seathwaite, where like a steam-navvy
You shovel and slash your way through the gorge
By Wallabarrow Crag, broader now
From becks that flow out of black upland tarns
Or ooze through golden saxifrage and the roots of rowans;
Next Ulpha, where a stone dropped from the bridge
Swims like a tadpole down thirty feet of water
Between steep skirting-boards of rock; and thence
You dribble into lower Dunnerdale,
Through wet woods and wood-soil and woodland flowers,
Tutsan, the St John's-wort with the single yellow bead,
Marsh marigold, creeping jenny and daffodils.
Here from hazel islands in the late spring
The catkins fall and ride along the stream
Like little yellow weasels, and the soil is loosed
From bulbs of the white lily that smells of garlic,
And dippers rock up and down on rubber legs,
And long-tailed tits are flung through air like darts;

The Lake District

By Foxfield now you taste the salt in your mouth,
And thrift mingles with the turf, and the heron stands
Watching the wagtails. Wordsworth wrote:
'Remote from every taint of sordid industry.'
But you and I know better, Duddon.
For I, who've lived for nearly thirty years
Upon your shore, have seen the slagbanks slant
Like screes into the sand, and watched the tide
Purple with ore back up the muddy gullies,
And wiped the sinter dust from the farmyard damsons.
A hundred years of floods and rain and wind
Have washed your rocks clear of his words again,
Many of them half-forgotten, brimming the Irish Sea;
But that which Wordsworth knew, even the old man
When poetry had failed like desire, was something
I have yet to learn, and you, Duddon,
Have learned and re-learned to forget and forget again.
Not the radical, the poet and heretic,
To whom the water-forces shouted and the fells
Were like a blackboard for the scrawls of God,
But the old man, inarticulate and humble,
Knew that eternity flows in a mountain beck –
The long cord of the water, the shepherd's numerals
That run upstream through the singing decades of dialect.
He knew, beneath mutation of year and season,
Flood and drought, frost and fire and thunder,
The blossom on the rowan and the reddening of the berries,
There stands the base and root of the living rock,
Thirty thousand feet of solid Cumberland.

Norman Nicholson

Valley

The poet refers to Eskdale.

Valley of rock and snow,
The coarse grass burned yellow.

Hide, rib-cage, a hollow
Ram's horn. Here eagles flew.

The white ropes of water
Dangle from a black scar.

That road leads to the sea
Where ships in harbour lay.

The Roman tuba blew,
Glinted. An echo here.

David Wright (1920–   )

Ennerdale

E. Lynn Linton, who was born at Crosthwaite Vicarage, near Keswick, was the wife of W. J. Linton, a well-known printer and engraver, and lived with him at Brantwood on the banks of Coniston Water. It was Linton who later sold the house to John Ruskin. Mrs Linton is remarkable among the Lake writers of her time for a quite outstanding clarity and shrewdness of observation, together with a realistic attitude to the working people of the district, which she may have owed to the fact that her husband was a chartist and republican. Her account of Ennerdale is particularly interesting because it depicts the dale before the extensive afforestation of this century. In some ways Ennerdale is not greatly changed, for, though the level of the water has been raised to provide water for Whitehaven, it is still without 'the benefit of carriage ways along its banks'.

From Egremont down to Ennerdale, the road passes over the fell, rich in gorse and bramble and great bunches of yellow ragwort, with splashes of bronzed and blood-red bracken and purple tufts of vetch for compensating colours, till it comes down to Ennerdale Bridge, and thence on to the foot of the lake. The square top of Herdhouse stands well forward as you round the common road or go down the steep hill which leads to the boathouse; whence the Ennerdale valley is at its best. At the head of the dale stands the Pillar, the steepest and craggiest of all the mountains, till one thousand eight hundred and twenty-six deemed the English Jungfrau, our maiden mountain in-accessible, but now owning to nearly a dozen conquerors; each traveller who has actually reached the top writing his name on a slip of paper which he places in a bottle left in the crevice of a rock for the purpose. So at least goes the story, which we could not verify by personal observation. It is a magnificent-looking mountain; the crowning rock, a great grey striated column which fires all one's ambition to surmount . . .

All the Ennerdale mountains are of the same nature; a kind of craggy moorland, capital for sportsmen; but, save in the sheltered nooks at the foot, where are patches of forward land and good crops enough, no cultivation anywhere. The place is wilder even than Wastdale; more lonely and austere if less sublime; at the head wonderfully noble, with a majesty of mountain unusual. But it is not lovely, taking that word to mean an admixture of softness with the grandeur: not even when 'on the lake', which is such a soft and lovely experience everywhere else . . .

The whole land hereabouts being more or less impregnated with iron ore, even Revelin [one of the fells beside the lake] has had its secret chambers rifled with the rest, and has been forced to give up its treasures. Lately, they have begun to work for iron ore on Bowness Knot – the yield in Revelin failing, or the directors quarrelling among themselves, or some other of the many casualties of mining property having befallen both works and yield, so that it has returned to its earlier and humbler function – that of feeding bees. Every summer and autumn hundreds of hives are brought up to Ennerdale and set on Revelin, for the bees to get strength and sustenance before winter time.

Carts come in the early morning laden with beehives, and 'a vast o' good honey gets shakt oot ont'road' . . .

The head of the dale flows up into the old closed barren sweep, with the Liza running through; the pretty, clear, bright little Liza starting with a laugh from her birthplace on Great Gable, and laughing to the end, where she loses herself on the Big Water . . . More stories are told of travellers lost about the Ennerdale paths and passes than in any other part of the country, the distances between point and point not being long – which is a temptation; and the ways apparently easy – which is another temptation; but under any obliteration, or disguisement by storm, proving utterly unreliable and destructive.

Ennerdale is the least known, and, at the present time, the least likely to be visited of all the lakes. Indeed, it can only have its own special sifting of visitors, for the carriage-road to the foot goes no further than the Boat-House; at least what follows is very indifferent and leads nowhere; and the Boat-House itself, the only place of accommodation, cannot house many visitors at a time, and has no attractions for the fine folks at all. The other approaches to the lake are either severe pony roads, as the Black Sail and Scarf Gap passes, impossible to all save good walkers and hardy riders; or mere mountain paths, like the Bannerdale Fell way over to Floutern, or by Iron Crag and Tong Fell down to Scalderskew and Calder. So that until Ennerdale has the benefit of carriage ways along its banks, it will remain comparatively a terra incognita to the tourist world, save those who can brave a rough pass, and those who care only to gape away an hour at the foot while their horses are baiting at the inn. And this is what butterfly people generally do; driving over from Lowes Water through Lamplugh to Ennerdale Bridge, or from Wastwater by Egremont, or the fell road [i.e. Cold Fell] higher up; to be for ever after quite contented with the belief that they have seen Ennerdale, and have 'done' the lake effectively.

E. Lynn Linton (1822–1898)
The Lake Country (1864)

The Derwent at Cockermouth

'Grunsel' is the Cumbrian pronunciation of 'groundsel' **by which, as can be** *seen from the version of 1850, Wordsworth meant 'ragwort'.*

When, having left his Mountains, to the Towers
Of Cockermouth that beauteous River came,
Behind my Father's House he pass'd, close by,
Along the margin of our Terrace Walk.
Oh! many a time have I, a five years' Child,
A naked Boy, in one delightful Rill,
A little Mill-race sever'd from his stream,
Made one long bathing of a summer's day,
Bask'd in the sun, and plung'd, and bask'd again
Alternate all a summer's day, or cours'd
Over the sandy fields, leaping through groves,
Of yellow grunsel, or when crag and hill,
The woods, and distant Skiddaw's lofty height,
Were bronz'd with a deep radiance, stood alone
Beneath the sky, as if I had been born
On Indian Plains, and from my Mother's hut
Had run abroad in wantonness, to sport,
A naked savage, in the thunder shower.

William Wordsworth
From *The Prelude*, Book 1 (1805–6 version)

Cockermouth

The 'assassinated politician' is the sixth Earl of Mayo.

Past castle, brewery, over a sandstone bridge,
A Midland Bank, 'Fletcher's Fearless Clothing',
And huge effigy of an assassinated politician,
You come upon a Georgian grand frontage,

Still the town's 'big house', built for a Sheriff,
Not long ago ransomed from demolition
(The site an ideal one for the new bus-station)
And looked at, now, by a small bust of Wordsworth.

Turn down its by-lane, leading to the river,
You'll see, fenced like a POW camp, reached by
An iron footbridge, the town's factory;
There ran a mill-race, where was once a meadow,

And Derwent shuffles by it, over stones.
And if you look up the valley toward Isel
With Blindcrake to the north, cloudcatcher fells,
Whose waters track past here to Workington.

Eighteenth-century, like some town of Portugal;
Doorways faced with stone, proportionate windows,
And painted black and white, or gayer colours;
A scale perfectly kept, appropriately small.

Born here or hereabouts then: John Dalton,
Propounder of atomic theory; Fletcher
Christian; and, juxtaposing that Bounty mutineer,
Wordsworth the poet, of all unlikely men.

Tombs of shipmasters on the hill overlook
Town roofs, the valley where the river slips away
Toward the dead ports and the Irish Sea,
Dowsed furnaces, closed mines of haematite

And coal, fortunes of Lowther and Curwen,
Slagheaps, the mansions of industrialists
Shuttered and rotting, burned or derelict,
Where a prosperity of impoverishment

Flourished, and now stands memorial
There, and in small classic façades of this town,
To the era designated Augustan;
Brown leaves about the baroque headstones fall.

The Lake District

On one side foundries; and the other way
Those frugal, delectable mountains
Where the smallholder yeoman, an anachronism,
Hung on into the nineteenth century.

So set, equidistant between past and future,
What more likely than, just here and then,
Should have been born that Janus-headed man,
A conservator and innovator,

As the machine began to gather power,
Menacing nature to smile, because subdued?
The walled garden of his childhood
Stands as it was, pondering the river.

David Wright

Which Way to Watendlath?

'*Watendlath*' *is the accepted modern spelling.*

Watenlath is that tract of mountainous country (itself surrounded by mountains still higher) which coming boldly forward, breaks down abruptly from the south upon the vale of Keswick. The stream, which forms the fall of Lodoar, adorns first the scenes of Watenlath.

'Which way to Watenlath?' said one of our company to a peasant, as we left the vale of Borrodale. 'That way,' said he, pointing up a lofty mountain, steeper than the tiling of a house.

To those who are accustomed to mountains these perpendicular motions may be amusing: but to us, whose ideas were less elevated, they seemed rather peculiar. And yet there is something unmanly in conceiving a difficulty in traversing a path which, we were told, the women of the country would ascend on horseback with their panniers of eggs, and butter, and return in the night. To move upwards, keeping a steady eye on the objects before us, was no great exercise to the brain; but it rather gave it a rotation to look back on what was past – and to see our companions below *clinging*, as it appeared, to the mountain's side; and the rising breasts and bellies of their horses, straining up a path so steep, that it seemed as if the least false step would have carried them rolling many hundred yards to the bottom.

We had another apprehension; that of mistaking our way. If a mist had suddenly overspread the mountain, which is a very common incident, we might have wandered all night: for we had not the precaution to take a guide. The question we asked of the peasant, at the bottom of the mountain, 'Which *way* to Watenlath?' we found was a very improper one. We should have asked in what *direction* we were to seek it? For *way* there was none; except here and there a blind path; which being itself often bewildered, of course, served only to bewilder us. The inhabitants pay little attention to *paths*: they steer along these wilds by *landmarks*, which to us were unknown . . .

It was our business now to get out of this unpleasant scene as soon as we could, which was a matter of no great difficulty. An easy and short descent, on the other side of the mountain, brought us quickly to Watenlath. Here our labours were amply rewarded. We fell into a piece of scenery which for beauty, and grandeur, was equal, if not superior, to any thing we had yet seen.

> William Gilpin
> *Observations . . . [on] the Mountains and Lakes of
> Cumberland and Westmorland*

Cottages

To begin with the COTTAGES. They are scattered over the valleys, and under the hill-sides, and on the rocks; and, even to this day, in the more retired dales, without any intrusion of more assuming buildings:

> Cluster'd like stars some few, but single most,
> And lurking dimly in their shy retreats,
> Or glancing on each other cheerful looks,
> Like separated stars with clouds between.   M.S.

The dwelling houses, and contiguous outhouses, are, in many instances of the colour of the native rock, out of which they have been built; but, frequently, the Dwelling or Fire-house, as it is ordinarily called, has been distinguished from the barn or byre by rough-cast and whitewash, which, as the inhabitants are not hasty in renewing it, in a few years acquires, by the influence of weather, a tint at once sober and variegated. As these houses have been, from father to son, inhabited by persons engaged in the same occupations, yet necessarily with changes in their circumstances, they have received without incongruity additions and accommodations adapted to the needs of each successive occupant, who, being for the most part proprietor, was at liberty to follow his own fancy: so that these humble dwellings remind the contemplative spectator of a production of Nature, and may (using a strong expression) rather be said to have grown than to have been erected; – to have risen, by an instinct of their own, out of the native rock – so little is there in them of formality, such is their wildness and beauty. Among the numerous recesses and projections in the walls and in the different stages of their roofs, are seen bold and harmonious effects of contrasted sunshine and shadow. It is a favourable circumstance, that the strong winds, which sweep down the valleys, induced the inhabitants, at a time when the materials for building were easily procured, to furnish many of these dwellings with substantial porches; and such as have not this defence, are seldom unprovided with a projection of two large slates over their thresholds. Nor will the singular beauty of the chimneys escape the eye of the attentive traveller. Sometimes a low chimney, almost upon a level with the roof, is overlaid with a slate, supported upon four slender pillars, to prevent the wind from driving the smoke down the chimney. Others are of a quadrangular shape, rising one or two feet above the roof; which low square is often surmounted by a tall cylinder, giving to the cottage chimney the most beautiful shape in which it is ever seen. Nor will it be too fanciful or refined to remark, that there is a pleasing harmony between a tall chimney of this circular form, and the living column of smoke, ascending from it through the still air. These dwellings mostly built, as has been said, of rough unhewn stone, are roofed with slates, which were rudely taken from the quarry before the present art of splitting them was understood, and are, therefore, rough and uneven in their surface, so that both the coverings and sides of the houses have furnished places of rest for the seeds of lichens, mosses, ferns, and flowers. Hence buildings, which in their very form call to mind the processes of Nature, do thus, clothed in part with a vegetable garb, appear to be received into the bosom of the living principle of things, as it acts and exists among the woods and fields; and, by their colour and their shape, affectingly direct the thoughts to that tranquil course of Nature and simplicity, along which the humble-minded inhabitants have, through so many generations, been led. Add the little garden with its shed for bee-hives, its small bed of pot-herbs, and its borders and patches of flowers for Sunday posies, with sometimes a choice few too much prized to be plucked; an orchard of proportioned size; a cheese-press, often supported by some tree near the door; a cluster of embowering sycamores for summer shade; with a tall fir, through which the winds sing when other trees are leafless; the little rill or household spout murmuring in all seasons; – combine these incidents and images together, and you have the representative idea of a mountain-cottage in this country so beautifully formed in itself, and so richly adorned by the hand of Nature.

William Wordsworth
Guide to the Lakes

Winter Colouring of Woods

I will take this opportunity of observing, that they who have studied the appearances of Nature feel that the superiority, in point of visual interest, of mountainous over other countries – is more strikingly displayed in winter than in summer. This, as must be obvious, is partly owing to the forms of the mountains, which, of course, are not affected by the seasons; but also, in no small degree, to the greater variety that exists in their winter than their summer *colouring*. This variety is such, and so harmoniously preserved, that it leaves little cause of regret when the splendour of autumn is passed away. The oak-coppices, upon the sides of the mountains, retain russet leaves; the birch stands conspicuous with its silver stem and puce-coloured twigs; the hollies, with green leaves and scarlet berries, have come forth to view from among the deciduous trees, whose summer foliage had concealed them; the ivy is now plentifully apparent upon the stems and boughs of the trees, and upon the steep rocks. In place of the deep summer-green of the herbage and fern, many rich colours play into each other over the surface of the mountains; turf (the tints of which are interchangeably tawny-green, olive, and brown), beds of withered fern, and grey rocks, being harmoniously blended together. The mosses and lichens are never so fresh and flourishing as in winter, if it be not a season of frost; and their minute beauties prodigally adorn the foreground. Wherever we turn, we find these productions of Nature, to which winter is rather favourable than unkindly, scattered over the walls, banks of earth, rocks, and stones, and upon the trunks of trees, with the intermixture of several species of small fern, now green and fresh; and, to the observing passenger, their forms and colours are a source of inexhaustible admiration.

William Wordsworth
Guide to the Lakes

A Night Walk

Wilkinson does not tell us the location of the woods in which he carried out his curious experiment. The passage occurs in his account of a crossing of Shap Fells, but it seems more likely that the woods were those along the banks of the River Eamont near the author's home at Yanwath.

On entering a thick and solitary wood the night was uncommonly dark; and though I was well accustomed to the way, I was soon out of my path, and found myself entangled in the bushes; when, partly to make an experiment, and partly to amuse myself with my forlorn situation, I formed the resolution to make my way through the wood (between half a mile and a mile) with my eyes closed. Accordingly I winked and went on, with my staff in my hand, enjoying my fancy, and met with no interruption, save once coming down on a knee, till I nearly got through the wood; when, lo! I suddenly heard the tread of a man's foot, which instantly occasioned a singular sensation, and threw my musing tranquillity into a kind of thrill, or even a chill. I instantly opened my eyes, and saw the man and I were passing one another. I spoke to him: – he replied; – and I found by his accent he was an Irishman. I before mentioned I wanted to make an experiment; which was to ascertain the difference, if any, in perception between a very dark night, and having one's eyes fully closed. I now found the difference was most manifest. I clearly distinguished the trees around me, as by a faint moonlight, and had not the least difficulty the rest of my way home. Since the above I have found it of advantage, in going from candlelight into a dark night, to shut my eyes for a few minutes.

Another powerful instance of the effects of darkness occurred nearly in the same place. I was making my way through the same wood in darkness and in silence, when I suddenly heard above my head a sound like a very mournful human voice. This threw an instant horror through my frame; which, was, however, but of short continuance, for I instantly heard above my head the flapping of a prodigious number of wings. The fact was, at certain times of the year many thousand crows roost in this wood; and I believe the sound I heard was one of the crows on watch, giving the alarm; so I went on smiling at my fright. If I had not made the discovery, I should not have been well off with my imagination the rest of my way home.

Thomas Wilkinson (1751–1836)
Tours of the British Mountains (1824)

Living in the Woods

John Wyatt is now Head Warden for the Lake District National Park. This book tells of his experiences, some years ago, when he worked as a forester in Southern Westmorland. The location of the woodland is not specifically given in the book, but it lies in the hilly country to the east of the lower reaches of Windermere.

All wood-burning pundits have their prejudices and the commonest one is against elm. It will not burn, they say; or it 'burns cold'. Only wych elm grew in the wood, and it burned for me quite well when dry. For common elm I cannot speak, but the age-old superstition that elm 'loveth not mankind' persists. Does it not, without warning, drop its boughs? It does. And is it not the best wood for coffins? It is. Yet I knew a Wiltshire man who said that he burned hardly anything else; and it was very fine, he said, when well seasoned.

Ash is the darling of the wood-burners. It cuts well, and splits beautifully, and burns even when it is green; and it is a fast grower. Alder burns well, dry; but if you use it exclusively you will be sawing all day. Sycamore and birch, too, burn fast; so for long-lasting stuff you need oak, beech and, best of all hawthorn: all splendid when well seasoned. But holly logs are in a class of their own. Yew, too – but this wood is like iron and will break or blunt your axe, your saw, and your spirit. Of the soft woods pine is good, and larch as well if you are in a hurry for a blaze and prepared to roll back the hearth-rug in preparation for the spectacular fusillade.

Wood burning is so aesthetically pleasing. Every log, as it is picked up, can be examined as an individual work of art – shape, grain, colour, weight – before being placed carefully on the fire in the correct position, to give its own artistic display of pyrotechnics. And in an idle moment by the fire's warmth you can take a knife and improve on the art of nature, carving into the wood, or cutting designs into the bark. Or you can play building or balancing games.

I had to gather kindling too, for storing in a dry place. Larch and pine logs could be split small and dried by the fire; or kindling could be gathered 'raw'. Holly again would be my first choice. The thin dead twigs from a holly tree will start a fire even if gathered wet and then merely shaken. But hollies are rather miserly with their dead twigs, and the only worthy substitute, with a generous yield, is birch. I have won several bets in my time from workmates, by starting a fire outdoors, in heavy rain, without the use of any dry medium such as paper. The trick is easy if there are birch trees about; then there is always an abundance of dead twigs which can be snapped easily off the trunks. From these can be gathered a handful of needle-thin stuff that can be pushed into a pocket while you collect slightly thicker material. A good pile is made of the birch twigs; then, when all is ready, the handful of needle-thins is taken from the pocket (where they have left much of their moisture), put into the fire centre, and carefully lit with a match. The wood contains sufficient natural oil to start the fire well.

Once kindled, stoking the fire can be a work of art. A large back-log is necessary; it should be heavy hardwood – fresh-cut green stuff will do at a pinch – and this acts as a reflector. Holly is the best, and a good log will burn for two days; a really good green one will last for several days. The morning fire should be re-kindled from the back-log of the previous day: a smart blow with a poker to break off its embers, small kindling on top of these, a puff with the bellows or breath and she is away.

In winter, fuel was my first chore. Cooking was another necessary routine. I soon learned to be miserly with the gas, for the heavy steel cylinders had to be lugged up from the entrance gate on my back. There was an iron kettle which could be slung over the fire. I pre-ferred therefore to use one of the iron hooks in the chimney, and stews could be made on the fire if the pan was stood on the iron pan stand close by. An occasional roast was possible if I noosed the meat in a rabbit snare and hung it on the roasting hook at the chimney front. But this meant turning and basting – demanding constant attention; and if one is really hungry after a day outdoors – watching a sizzling, fragrant morsel turning before one's eyes is a long agony of mouth-watering suspense. Far better to clap the meat in a closed pot with onions and carrots and think of other things for an hour.

I have never found cooking an unpleasant task. I had some cookery books to help out; one was a battered gem which included wild foods and flavourings with its ingredients. A stew for instance, with jack-by-the-hedge (or garlic-mustard) leaves to give a subtle country flavour. Tansy pudding: made with bread-crumbs, milk and eggs, and chopped tansy leaves. And a traditional dish of the Lake District: 'Easter ledgers', a tasty physic for the countryman of the pre-can and freezer days, who lived on a winter diet of salt pork, bacon and cereals. This was made from any of the first spring greens such as cabbage leaves, cauliflower or broccoli sprigs, or brussel sprouts tops; and to these were added first and foremost the fresh green leaves of ledgers (bistort) which gave the fine subtle flavour; young nettle leaves, watercress; gooseberry and raspberry leaves new-burst; mint, sour docks, jack-by-the-hedge, and a few dandelion leaves. These should be washed and chopped finely, a handful of barley added; and the whole tied into a cloth to simmer in a pan until the liquid is nearly gone. Turn out, add a nob of butter, salt and pepper, and you have a rich dish to make you fighting fit!

John Wyatt (1925–   )
The Shining Levels

Lakes and Waterfalls

The Wind on the Water

In clear, and windy weather, the *breezy ruffled* lake, as Thomson calls
it, is a shattered mirror: It reflects the serenity; but reflects it partially.
The hollow of each wave is commonly in shadow, the summit is
tipped with light. The light or shadow therefore prevails, according
to the position of the waves to the eye: and at a distance, when the
summits of the waves, agreeably to the rules of perspective, appear in
contact, the whole surface in that part will be light . . .

Sometimes also, when the *whole* lake is tranquil, a gentle pertur-
bation will arise in some distant part, from no apparent cause, from a
breath of air, which nothing else can feel, and creeping softly on,
communicate the tremulous shudder with exquisite sensibility over
half the surface . . .

No pool, no river-bay, can present this idea in its utmost purity. In
them every crystalline particle is set, as it were, in a socket of mud.
Their lubricity is lost. More or less, they all flow *cum gurgite flavo*. But
the lake, like Spencer's fountain, which sprang from the tears of a
nymph,

> . . . is chast, and pure, as purest snow,
> He lets her waves with any filth be dyed.

Refined thus from every obstruction, it is *tremblingly alive* all over:
the merest trifle, a striking fly, a falling leaf, almost a sound alarms it,

> . . . that sound,
> Which from the mountain, previous to the storm,
> Rolls o'er the muttering earth, disturbs the flood,
> And shakes the forest-leaf without a breath.

This tremulous shudder is sometimes even still more partial: It will
run in lengthened parallels, and separate the reflections upon the
surface, which are lost on one side, and taken up on the other. This is
perhaps the most picturesque form, which water assumes; as it
affords the painter an opportunity of throwing in those lengthened
lights and shades, which give the greatest variety and clearness to
water.

There is another appearance on the surface of lakes, which we cannot account for on any principle either of optics, or of perspective. When there is no apparent cause in the *sky*, the *water* will sometimes appear dappled with large spots of shade. It is possible these patches may have connection with the bottom of the lake; as naturalists suppose, the shining parts of the sea are occasioned by the spawn of fish: but it is more probable, that in some way, they are connected with the sky, as they are generally esteemed in the country to be a weather-gage. The people will often say, 'It will be no hay-day to-day, the lake is full of shades'. – I never myself saw this appearance; or I might be able to give a better account of it: but I have heard it so often taken notice of that I suppose there is at least some ground for the observation.

> William Gilpin
> *Observations . . . [on] the Mountains and Lakes of Cumberland and Westmorland*

Light and Shade at Grasmere and Rydal

Monday [2nd June 1800]. I went to Ambleside after tea, crossed the stepping-stones at the foot of Grasmere, and pursued my way on the other side of Rydale and by Clappergate. I sate a long time to watch the hurrying waves, and to hear the regularly irregular sound of the dashing waves. The waves round about the little Island seemed like a dance of spirits that rose out of the water, round its small circumference of shore.

Saturday [21st June]. Walked up the hill to Rydale lake. Grasmere looked so beautiful that my heart was almost melted away. It was quite calm, only spotted with sparkles of light; the church visible. On our return all distant objects had faded away, all but the hills. The reflection of the light bright sky above Black Quarter was very solemn.

Friday Night [31st October]. A very fine moonlight night. The moon shone like herrings in the water.

Tuesday [*4th November*]. Tremendous wind. The snow blew from Helvellyn horizontally like smoke.

Sunday [*31st January 1802*]. Wm had slept very ill. He was tired. We walked round the two lakes. Grasmere was very soft, and Rydale was extremely beautiful from the western side. Nab Scar was just topped by a cloud which, cutting it off as high as it could be cut off, made the mountain look uncommonly lofty. We sate down a long time in different places. I always love to walk that way, because it is the way I first came to Rydale and Grasmere, and because our dear Coleridge did so.

When I came with Wm, 6 and ½ years ago, it was just at sunset. There was a rich yellow light on the waters, and the islands were reflected there. To-day it was grave and soft, but not perfectly calm. William says it was much such a day as when Coleridge came with *him*. The sun shone out before we reached Grasmere. We sate by the roadside at the foot of the Lake, close to Mary's dear name, which she had cut herself upon the stone. Wm cut at it with his knife to make it plainer. We amused ourselves for a long time in watching the breezes, some as if they came from the bottom of the lake, spread in a circle, brushing along the surface of the water, and growing more delicate as it were thinner, and of a *paler* colour till they died away. Others spread out like a peacock's tail, and some went right forward this way and that in all directions. The lake was still where these breezes were not, but they made it all alive. I found a strawberry blossom in a rock. The little slender flower had more courage than the green leaves, for *they* were but half expanded and half grown, but the blossom was spread full out. I uprooted it rashly, and felt as if I had been committing an outrage, so I planted it again. It will have but a stormy life of it, but let it live if it can.

Tuesday 23rd [*February*]. We sate a little while looking at the fading landscape. The lake, though the objects on the shore were fading, seemed brighter than when it is perfect day, and the island pushed itself upwards, distinct and large. All the shores marked. There was a sweet, sea-like sound in the trees above our heads.

Tuesday 13th April. I walked along the lake side. The air becoming still, the lake was a bright slate colour, the hills darkening. The bays shot into the low fading shores. Sheep resting. All things quiet.

Tuesday [1st June, 1802]. It was a lovely night. The clouds of the western sky reflected a saffron light upon the upper end of the lake. All was still. We went to look at Rydale. There was an Alpine, fire-like red upon the tops of the mountains. This was gone when we came in view of the lake. But we saw the lake from a new and most beautiful point of view, between two little rocks, and behind a small ridge that had concealed it from us. This White Moss, a place made for all kinds of beautiful works of art and nature, woods and valleys, fairy valleys and fairy tarns, miniature mountains, alps above alps.

Dorothy Wordsworth
Grasmere Journal

Blea Tarn

There are two Blea Tarns in the Lake District; Wordsworth here describes the one which lies between the upper reaches of the two Langdales. The tarn now has a backing of rhododendrons, which would not have been there in Wordsworth's time.

We scaled, without a track to ease our steps,
A steep ascent; and reached a dreary plain,
With a tumultuous waste of huge hill tops
Before us; savage region! which I paced
Dispirited: when, all at once, behold!
Beneath our feet, a little lowly vale,
A lowly vale, and yet uplifted high
Among the mountains; even as if the spot
Had been from eldest time by wish of theirs
So placed, to be shut out from all the world!

Urn-like it was in shape, deep as an urn;
With rocks encompassed, save that to the south
Was one small opening, where a heath-clad ridge
Supplied a boundary less abrupt and close;
A quiet treeless nook, with two green fields,
A liquid pool that glittered in the sun,
And one bare dwelling; one abode, no more!

William Wordsworth
From *The Excursion*

Windermere, 1

There was a Boy: ye knew him well, ye cliffs
And islands of Winander! – many a time
At evening, when the earliest stars began
To move along the edges of the hills,
Rising or setting, would he stand alone
Beneath the trees or by the glimmering lake,
And there, with fingers interwoven, both hands
Pressed closely palm to palm, and to his mouth
Uplifted, he, as through an instrument,
Blew mimic hootings to the silent owls,
That they might answer him; and they would shout
Across the watery vale, and shout again,
Responsive to his call, with quivering peals,
And long halloos and screams, and echoes loud,
Redoubled and redoubled, concourse wild
Of jocund din; and, when a lengthened pause
Of silence came and baffled his best skill,
Then sometimes, in that silence while he hung
Listening, a gentle shock of mild surprise
Has carried far into his heart the voice
Of mountain torrents; or the visible scene

Would enter unawares into his mind,
With all its solemn imagery, its rocks,
Its woods, and that uncertain heaven, received
Into the bosom of the steady lake.

William Wordsworth
From *The Prelude*, Book 5

Windermere, 2

The 'bay' is Bowness Bay, and the 'large island', Belle Isle, named after Isabella Curwen, whose grand-daughter, also named Isabella Curwen, was later to marry Wordsworth's son, John, Rector of Moresby.

Midway on long Winander's eastern shore,
Within the crescent of a pleasant bay,
A tavern stood; no homely-featured house,
Primeval like its neighbouring cottages,
But 'twas a splendid place, the door beset
With chaises, grooms, and liveries, and within
Decanters, glasses, and the blood-red wine.
In ancient times, and ere the Hall was built
On the large island, had this dwelling been
More worthy of a poet's love, a hut
Proud of its one bright fire and sycamore shade.
But – though the rhymes were gone that once inscribed
The threshold, and large golden characters,
Spread o'er the spangled sign-board, had dislodged
The old Lion and usurped his place, in slight
And mockery of the rustic painter's hand –
Yet to this hour, the spot to me is dear
With all its foolish pomp. The garden lay
Upon a slope surmounted by a plain
Of a small bowling-green; beneath us stood

A grove, with gleams of water through the trees
And over the tree-tops; nor did we want
Refreshment, strawberries and mellow cream.
There, while through half the afternoon we played
On the smooth platform, whether skill prevailed
Or happy blunder triumphed, bursts of glee
Made all the mountains ring. But, ere nightfall,
When in our pinnace we returned at leisure
Over the shadowy lake, and to the beach
Of some small island steered our course with one,
The Minstrel of the Troop, and left him there,
And rowed off gently, while he blew his flute
Alone upon the rock – oh, then, the calm
And dead still water lay upon my mind
Even with a weight of pleasure, and the sky,
Never before so beautiful, sank down
Into my heart, and held me like a dream!

William Wordsworth
From *The Prelude*, Book 2

A Boat on Windermere

'*Christopher North*' – *the pen-name of Prof. John Wilson* – *is little read today, but he was greatly admired in his life-time, as can be seen from Harriet Martineau's tribute on page 239, and any anthology of Lake literature would be incomplete without at least one example of his opulent and over-blown prose.*

So let us descend to the White Lion [at Bowness] – and inquire about Billy Balmer. Honest Billy has arrived from Waterhead – seems tolerably steady – Mr Ullock's boats may be trusted – so let us take a voyage of discovery on the lake. Let those who have reason to think that they have been born to die a different death from drowning, hoist a sail. We today shall feather an oar. Billy takes the stroke – Mr William Garnet's at the helm – and 'row, vassals, row, for the pride of the Lowlands,' is the choral song that accompanies the Naiad out of the bay, and round the north end of the Isle called Beautiful [i.e. Belle Isle], under the wave-darkening umbrage of that ancient oak. And now we are in the lovely straits between that Island and the mainland of Furness Fells. The village has disappeared, but not melted away; for hark! the Church-tower tolls ten – and see the sun is high in heaven. High, but not hot – for the first September frosts chilled the rosy fingers of the morn as she bathed them in the dews, and the air is cool as a cucumber. Cool but bland – and as clear and transparent as a fine eye lighted up by a good conscience. There were breezes in Bowness Bay – but here there are none – or, if there be, they but whisper aloft in the tree-tops, and ruffle not the water, which is calm as Louisa's breast. The small isles here are but few in number – yet the best arithmetician of the party cannot count them – in confusion so rich and rare do they blend their shadows with those of the groves on the Isle called Beautiful, and on the Furness Fells. A tide imperceptible to the eye drifts us on among and above those beautiful reflections – that downward world of hanging dreams! and ever and anon we beckon unto Billy gently to dip his oar, that we may see a world destroyed and recreated in one moment of time. Yes, Billy! thou art a poet – and canst work more wonders with thine oar than could he with his pen who painted 'heavenly Una with her milk-white lamb,' [i.e. Spenser] wandering by herself in Fairy-land. How is it, pray, that our souls are satiated with such beauty as this? Is it because 'tis unsubstantial all – senseless, though fair – and in its evanescence unsuited to the sympathies that yearn for the permanencies of breathing life? Dreams are delightful only as delusions within the delusion of this our mortal waking existence – one touch of what we call reality dissolves them all; blissful though they may have been, we care not when the bubble bursts – nay, we are glad again to return to our own natural world, care-haunted though in its happiest moods it be – glad as if we had escaped from glamoury; and, oh! beyond expression sweet it is once more to drink the light of living eyes – the music of living lips – after that preternatural hush that steeps the shadowy realms of the imagination, whether stretching along a sunset-heaven or the mystical imagery of earth and sky floating in the lustre of lake or sea.

Therefore 'row, vassals, row, for the pride of the Lowlands;' and as rowing is a thirsty exercise, let us land at the Ferry, and each man refresh himself with a horn of ale.

John Wilson (1785–1854)
The Recreations of Christopher North

Drowned in Esthwaite

The 'valley' is that of Hawkshead where Wordsworth began to attend the Grammar School in 1778.

Well do I call to mind the very week
When I was first intrusted to the care
Of that sweet Valley; when its paths, its shores,
And brooks were like a dream of novelty
To my half-infant thoughts; that very week,
While I was roving up and down alone,
Seeking I knew not what, I chanced to cross
One of those open fields, which, shaped like ears,
Make green peninsulas on Esthwaite's Lake:
Twilight was coming on, yet through the gloom
Appeared distinctly on the opposite shore
A heap of garments, as if left by one
Who might have been there bathing. Long I watched,
But no one owned them; meanwhile the calm lake
Grew dark with all the shadows on its breast,
And, now and then, a fish up-leaping snapped
The breathless stillness. The succeeding day,
Those unclaimed garments telling a plain tale
Drew to the spot an anxious crowd; some looked
In passive expectation from the shore,

The Lake District

While from a boat others hung o'er the deep,
Sounding with grappling irons and long poles.
At last, the dead man, 'mid that beauteous scene
Of trees and hills and water, bolt upright
Rose, with his ghastly face, a spectre shape
Of terror.

William Wordsworth
From *The Prelude*, Book 5

Coniston from the Station

West's Guide to the Lakes, *was of special importance in its time because of his detailed instructions on the merits and location of particular viewpoints, or, as he called them, 'stations'. The 'station' described below is now part of the property of the National Trust. Thomas West was a Catholic priest who lived at Tytup Hall, near Lindal-in-Furness, and was perhaps better-known locally for his book on the Antiquities of Furness.*

STATION I. A little above the village of Nibthwaite, the lake opens in full view. From the rock, on the left of the road, you have a general prospect of the lake, upwards. This station is found by observing where you have a hanging rock over the road, on the east, and an ash-tree on the west side of the road. On the opposite shore, to the left, and close by the water's edge, are some stripes of meadow and green ground, cut into small inclosures, with some dark coloured houses under aged yew trees. Two promontories project a great way into the lake; the broadest is finely terminated by steep rocks, and crowned with wood; and both are insulated when the lake is high. Upwards, over a fine sheet of water, the lake is again intersected by a far-projecting promontory, that swells into two eminences, and betwixt them the lake is again caught, with some white houses at the feet of the mountains. And more to the right, over another headland, you catch a fourth view of the lake, twisting to the north-east. Almost opposite to this station, stands a house on the crown of a rock,

88

covered with ancient trees, that has a most romantic appearance.

The noble scenery increases as you ride along the banks. In some places, bold rocks (lately covered with wood) conceal the lake entirely, and when the winds blow, the beating of surges is heard just under you. In other places, abrupt openings shew the lake anew, and there, when calm, its limpid surface, shining like a chrystal mirror, reflects the azure sky, or its dappled clouds, in the finest mixture of nature's clare-obscure. On the western side, the shore is more variegated with small inclosures, scattered cots, groves, and meadows.

The road continues along the eastern banks of the lake; here bare, there sweetly fringed with a few tall trees, the small remains of its ancient woods, that till lately cloathed the whole.

Thomas West (1717–1779)
A Guide to the Lakes in Cumberland, Westmorland, and Lancashire
By the Author of *The Antiquities of Furness*

Wastwater, 1

Thomas Wilkinson, a Quaker who lived at Yanwath, near Penrith, was honoured by Wordsworth in the verses beginning with the notorious line: 'Spade! with which Wilkinson hast tilled his lands'. The poet paid his friend a more lasting compliment, however, in the famous poem The Solitary Reaper, *based on an incident in Wilkinson's* Tour *which he had read in manuscript.*

When people go forth to see the world, they are sometimes in search of beauty. If beauty is the leading object of their search, they need not go to Wast Water. The prominent features round Wast Water are sternness and sterility. Unlike the mountains of Borrowdale, no climbing groves wave on the first stages of these mountains. The mountains of Wast Water are naked to their base: – their sides and their summits are uniform: their summits shoot up into lofty points, and end in the form of pyramids. We have heard of the Pyramids of

Egypt, built by the hand of man; but these are the Pyramids of the world, built by the Architect of the universe.

Thomas Wilkinson
Tours to the British Mountains

Wastwater, 2

The Lake is wholly hidden 'till your very Feet touch it,' as one may say, and to a Stranger the Burst would be almost overwhelming. The Lake itself seen from its Foot appears indeed of too regular shape; exactly like the sheet of Paper on which I am writing, except it is still narrower in respect of its length. (In reality however the Lake widens as it ascends and at the head is very considerably broader than at the foot.) But yet, in spite of this it is a marvellous sight: a sheet of water between 3 and 4 miles in length, the whole or very nearly the whole of its right Bank formed by the Screes, or facing of bare Rock of enormous Height, two-thirds of its height downwards absolutely perpendicular; and then slanting off in *Screes*, or Shiver, consisting of fine red Streaks running in broad Stripes thro' a stone colour – slanting off from the Perpendicular, as steep as the meal newly ground from the Miller's spout. So it is at the foot of the Lake; but higher up this streaky Shiver occupies two-thirds of the whole height, like a pointed Decanter in shape, or an out-spread Fan, or a long-waisted old maid with a fine prim Apron, or – no, other things that would only fill up the paper. When I first came the Lake was a perfect Mirror; and what must have been the Glory of the reflections in it! This huge facing of Rock *said* to be half a mile in perpendicular height, with deep Ravines, the whole *wrinded* and torrent-worn, except where the pink-striped Screes come in, as smooth as Silk, all this reflected, turned into Pillars, dells, and a whole new-world of Images in the water!

S. T. Coleridge
Tour in the Lake Country, 1802

Bassenthwaite Lake

Parties of pleasure at Keswick neglect this water, they seldom think it worth while to navigate it; – its beauties indeed are very different from those of the lake above [i.e. Derwentwater]; but that is the very cause from whence they become more pleasing. To enjoy the scenes properly, the visitant should navigate these lakes alternately. – This affords many bays, where you may in some parts push under the cover of a lofty overhanging grove, and in others rocky coves, where you find the gentler echo, favourable to music and a song. The painter has tamer landscapes here, but they are warmer and more serene than those of Keswick. – Soft pastoral scenes margin the lake on the eastern side, over which Skiddaw lifts an august brow, to give the boldest contrast to the green and gently rising eminences, the scattered coppices, the velvet-dressed lawn, the rich verdure of the mead, the tranquil cottage, and the serene and shining mirror which the lake expands. The boldest landscape found here consists of irregular eminences cloathed with oaks, at whose feet a grassy margin lies to the water's brink, and holds some farmhold; whilst the sublimer mountains, pile upon pile, lift up their heads, and, from the western sun, cast long shades upon the lake, whose distant shores catch the surpassing beams, and glow with additional beauty from the contrasting shades: over which the distant eminences mix their brows with the azure of the atmosphere. – Such are the beauties of Bassenthwaite Water.

William Hutchinson (1732–1814)
The History of the County of Cumberland (1793–6)

Keswick and Dovedale Compared

Dr John Brown's 'Description of the Lake and Vale of Keswick', printed at Newcastle in 1767, played a most important part in the discovery of the Lakes by the people of the rest of England. Together with Dr Dalton's

'Descriptive Poem' – see overleaf – it helped to persuade both Thomas Gray and Arthur Young to visit the Lakes and so started a new fashion in picturesque travel. Eleven years after its first publication, it became familiar to many tourists as an appendix to Father Thomas West's anonymous Guide to the Lakes.

Instead of the narrow slip of valley which is seen at Dovedale, you have at Keswick a vast amphitheatre, in circumference above twenty miles. Instead of a meagre rivulet, a noble living lake, ten miles round, of an oblong form, adorned with a variety of wooded islands. The rocks indeed of Dovedale are finely wild, pointed and irregular; but the hills are both little and unanimated; and the margin of the brook is poorly edged with weeds, morass, and brushwood. – But at Keswick, you will on one side of the lake, see a rich and beautiful landscape of cultivated fields, rising to the eye, in fine inequalities, with noble groves of oak, happily dispersed, and climbing the adjacent hills, shade above shade, in the most various and picturesque forms. On the opposite shore you will find rocks and cliffs of stupendous height, hanging broken over the lake in horrible grandeur, some of them a thousand feet high, the woods climbing up their steep and shaggy sides, where mortal foot never yet approached. On these dreadful heights the eagles build their nests; a variety of water-falls are seen pouring from their summits, and tumbling in vast sheets from rock to rock in rude and terrible magnificence: while on all sides of this immense amphitheatre the lofty mountains rise round, piercing the clouds in shapes as spiry and fantastic as the very rocks of Dovedale. – To this I must add the frequent and bold projection of the cliffs into the lake, forming noble bays and promontories: in other parts they finely retire from it, and often open in abrupt chasms or cliffs, thro' which at hand, you see rich and cultivated vales, and beyond these at various distances, mountain rising over mountain, among which, new prospects present themselves in mist, till the eye is lost in an agreeable perplexity:

> Where active fancy travels beyond sense,
> And pictures things unseen. –

Were I to analyse the two places into their constituent principles,

I should tell you, that the full perfection of Keswick, consists of three circumstances, *beauty*, *horror*, and *immensity* united; the second of which alone is found in Dovedale . . . But to give you a complete idea of these three perfections, as they are joined in Keswick, would require the united powers of Claude, Salvator, and Poussin. The first should throw his delicate sunshine over the cultivated vales, the scattered cots, the groves, the lake, and wooded islands. The second should dash out the horror of the rugged cliffs, the steeps, the hanging woods, and foaming water-falls; while the grand pencil of Poussin should crown the whole with the majesty of the impending mountains.

John Brown (1715–1766)
Description of the Lake and Vale of Keswick

Dr Dalton's descriptive poem, enumerating the beauties of the Vale of Keswick

John Dalton, D.D., who was born at Dean, near Cockermouth, should not be confused with the scientist of the same name, born only a few miles away at Eaglesfield, who became a pioneer in atomic physics. This extract from Dr Dalton's poem, together with the title, is taken from West's Guide.

Horrors like these at first alarm,
But soon with savage grandeur charm,
And raise to noblest thoughts the mind:
Thus by thy fall, Lowdore, reclin'd,
The craggy cliff, impendent wood,
Whose shadows mix o'er half the flood,
The gloomy clouds, which solemn sail,
Scarce lifted by the languid gale,
O'er the capp'd hill, and dark'ned vale;
The rav'ning kite, and bird of Jove,
Which round the aerial ocean rove,

93

And, floating on the billowy sky,
With full expanded pinions fly,
Their flutt'ring or their bleating prey
Thence with death-dooming eye survey;
Channels by rocky torrents torn,
Rocks to the lake in thunders borne,
Or such as o'er our heads appear
Suspended in their mid career,
To start again at his command
Who rules fire, water, air, and land,
I view with wonder and delight,
A pleasing, though an awful sight:
For, seen with them, the verdant isles
Soften with more delicious smiles,
More tempting twine their op'ning bow'rs,
More lively glow the purple flow'rs,
More smoothly slopes the border gay,
In fairer circles bend the bay.
And last, to fix our wand'ring eyes,
Thy roofs, O Keswick, brighter rise,
The lake, and lofty hills between,
Where giant Skiddaw shuts the scene.

> John Dalton
> From *Descriptive Poem Addressed to Two Young Ladies at their
> Return from Viewing the Mines near Whitehaven* (1755)

Derwentwater

*Of Thomas Pennant, Dr Johnson said: 'He's a Whig, sir, a sad dog. But
he's the best traveller I have ever read; he observes more things than anyone
else does.' Pennant visited the Lakes twice – in 1769, on his way back from
Scotland, and in 1772, on his way up to Scotland. His real interest was not
in the picturesque, but in industry, trade, antiquities and any meteorological*

*or scientific curiosity that came his way, yet his descriptions of the Lake
scene were quoted over and over until at least the end of the eighteenth
century. I include his account of Derwentwater as typical of his somewhat
unimaginative, though – in comparison with others – restrained style.*

The two extremities of the lake afford most discordant prospects: the
southern is a composition of all that is horrible; an immense chasm
opens in the midst, whose entrance is divided by a rude conic hill,
once topped with a castle, the habitation of the tyrant of the rocks;
beyond, a series of broken mountainous crags, now patched with
snow, soar one above the other, overshadowing the dark winding
deeps of Borrowdale. In these black recesses are lodged variety of
minerals, the origin of evil by their abuse, and placed by nature, not
remote from the fountain of it . . . But the opposite or northern view
is in all respects a strong and beautiful contrast: Skiddaw shews its
vast base, and bounding all that part of the vale, rises gently to a
height that sinks the neighbouring hills; opens a pleasing front, smooth
and verdant, smiling over the country like a gentle generous lord,
while the fells of Borrowdale frown on it like a hardened tyrant.
Skiddaw is covered with grass to within half a mile of the summit,
after which it becomes stony. The view from the top extends north-
ward over Solway firth and various of the Scottish mountains; to the
west the sea and the isle of Man; while the interjacent country exhibits
a flatter variety, no bad contrast to the rude and exalted fells of
Borrowdale: finally, to the east appear the dreary mountains of
Westmoreland, less interesting than the rest of the scenery.

Each boundary of the lake seems to take part with the extremities,
and emulates their appearance: the southern varies in rocks of different
forms, from the tremendous precipices of the Lady's-leap, the broken
front of the Falcon's-nest, to the more distant concave curvature of
Lowdore, an extent of precipitous rock, with trees vegetating from
the numerous fissures, and the foam of a cataract precipitating amidst.

Thomas Pennant (1726–1798)
A Tour in Scotland and Voyage to the Hebrides in 1772

Friar's Crag, Derwentwater

Part of this quotation is engraved on the Ruskin Memorial, set up on Friar's Crag.

The first thing which I remember, as an event in life, was being taken by my nurse to the brow of Friar's Crag on Derwentwater; the intense joy, mingled with awe, that I had in looking through the mossy roots, over the crag, into the dark lake, has associated itself more or less with all twining roots of trees ever since.

John Ruskin (1819–1900)
Modern Painters

Red Tarn on Helvellyn

The 'enormous barrier' is, of course, Striding Edge.

It was a cove, a huge recess,
That keeps, till June, December's snow;
A lofty precipice in front,
A silent tarn below!
Far in the bosom of Helvellyn,
Remote from public road or dwelling,
Pathway, or cultivated land;
From trace of human foot or hand.

There sometimes doth a leaping fish
Send through the tarn a lonely cheer;
The crags repeat the raven's croak,
In symphony austere;
Thither the rainbow comes – the cloud –
And mists that spread the flying shroud;
And sunbeams; and the sounding blast,

That, if it could, would hurry past;
But that enormous barrier holds it fast.

William Wordsworth
From *Fidelity*

Ullswater in Autumn

Oct. 1 [1769]. A grey autumnal day, the air perfectly calm, and mild, went to see Ulls-water, five miles distant . . . Walked over a spongy meadow or two, and began to mount the hill through a broad straight green alley among the trees, and with some toil gained the summit. From hence saw the lake opening directly at my feet, majestic in its calmness, clear and smooth as a blue mirror, with winding shores and low points of land covered with green inclosures, white farm houses looking out among the trees, and cattle feeding. The water is almost every where bordered with cultivated lands, gently sloping upwards from a mile to a quarter of a mile in breadth, till they reach the feet of the mountains which rise very rude and awful with their broken tops on either hand. Directly in front, at better than three miles distance, Place-fell, one of the bravest among them, pushes its bold broad breast into the midst of the lake, and forces it to alter its course, forming first a large bay to the left, and then bending to the right. I descended Dunmallet again by a side avenue, that was only not perpendicular, and came to Barton-bridge, over the Emont [Eamont]; then walking through a path in the wood round the bottom of the hill, came forth where the Emont issues out of the lake, and continued my way along its western shore, close to the water, and generally on a level with it. Saw a cormorant flying over it and fishing. The figure of the lake nothing resembles that laid down in our maps: It is nine miles long; and at widest under a mile in breadth. After extending itself three miles and a half in a line to south west, it turns at the foot of Place-fell almost due west, and is here not twice the breadth of the Thames at London. It is soon again interrupted by the root of

97

The Lake District

Helvellyn, a lofty and very rugged mountain, and spreading again turns off to the south-east, and is lost among the deep recesses of the hills. To this second turning I pursued my way about four miles along its border beyond a village scattered among trees and called Wattermillock, in a pleasant grave day, perfectly calm and warm, but without a gleam of sunshine; then the sky seeming to thicken, and the valley to grow more desolate, and the evening drawing on, I returned by the way I came to Penrith.

Thomas Gray (1716–1771)
Journal in the Lakes

A Boat on Ullswater

One summer evening . . . I found
A little boat tied to a willow tree
Within a rocky cave, its usual home.
Straight I unloosed her chain, and stepping in
Pushed from the shore. It was an act of stealth
And troubled pleasure, nor without the voice
Of mountain-echoes did my boat move on;
Leaving behind her still, on either side,
Small circles glittering idly in the moon,
Until they melted all into one track
Of sparkling light. But now, like one who rows,
Proud of his skill, to reach a chosen point
With an unswerving line, I fixed my view
Upon the summit of a craggy ridge,
The horizon's utmost boundary; for above
Was nothing but the stars and the grey sky.
She was an elfin pinnace; lustily
I dipped my oars into the silent lake,
And, as I rose upon the stroke, my boat
Went heaving through the water like a swan;

When, from behind that craggy steep till then
The horizon's bound, a huge peak, black and huge,
As if with voluntary power instinct
Upreared its head. I struck and struck again,
And growing still in stature the grim shape
Towered up between me and the stars, and still,
For so it seemed, with purpose of its own
And measured motion like a living thing,
Strode after me. With trembling oars I turned,
And through the silent water stole my way
Back to the covert of the willow tree;
There in her mooring-place I left my bark, –
And through the meadows homeward went, in grave
And serious mood; but after I had seen
That spectacle, for many days, my brain
Worked with a dim and undetermined sense
Of unknown modes of being; o'er my thoughts
There hung a darkness, call it solitude
Or blank desertion. No familiar shapes
Remained, no pleasant images of trees,
Of sea or sky, no colours of green fields;
But huge and mighty forms, that do not live
Like living men, moved slowly through the mind
By day, and were a trouble to my dreams.

William Wordsworth
From *The Prelude*, Book 1

Waterfalls from a Side Saddle

From these great fells there are severall springs out of the rock that
trickle down their sides, and as they meete with stones and rocks in
the way when something obstructs their passage and so they come
with more violence that gives a pleaseing sound and murmuring

noise; these descend by degrees, at last fall into the low grounds and fructifye it which makes the land soe fruit full in the valleys.

Celia Fiennes (1662–1741)
Through England on a Side Saddle in the time of William and Mary (first published, 1888)

Waterfall at Buttermere

The waterfall is Moss Force on Buttermere, or, as it is now more often called, Newlands Hause. Scale Force lies on the opposite, i.e. western, side of the Buttermere-Crummock valley.

It is a great Torrent from the Top of the Mountain to the Bottom; the lower part of it is not the least Interesting, where it is beginning to slope to a level. The mad water rushes thro' its *sinuous* bed, or rather prison of Rock, with such rapid Curves as if it turned the Corners not from mechanic force but with foreknowledge, like a fierce and skilful Driver: great Masses of Water, one after the other, that in twilight one might have feelingly compared them to a vast crowd of huge white Bears, rushing, one over the other, against the wind – their long white hair scattering abroad in the wind. The remainder of the Torrent is marked out by three great Waterfalls, the lowermost Apron-shaped, and though the Rock down which it rushes is an inclined Plane, it shoots off in such an independence of the Rock as shews that its direction was given it by the force of the Water from above. The middle which in peaceable times would be two tinkling Falls formed in this furious Rain one great *Water-wheel* endlessly revolving and double the size and height of the lowest. The third and highest is a mighty one indeed. It is twice the height of both the others added together, nearly as high as Scale Force, but it rushes down an inclined Plane, and does not *fall*, like Scale Force; however, if the Plane had been smooth, it is so near a Perpendicular that it would have *appeared* to fall, but it is indeed so fearfully savage, and black, and jagged, that it tears the flood to pieces. And one great black Outjutment divides the water, and overbrows and keeps uncovered a long slip of jagged black Rock beneath, which gives a marked *Character* to the whole force. What a sight it is to look down on such a Cataract! The wheels, that circumvolve it, the leaping up and plunging forward of that infinity of Pearls and Glass Bulbs, the continual *change* of the *Matter*, the perpetual *Sameness* of the *Form* – it is an awful Image and Shadow of God and the World.

S. T. Coleridge
Tour in the Lake Country, 1802

The Cataract of Lodore

Described in Rhymes for the Nursery

'How does the Water
Come down at Lodore?'
My little boy ask'd me
Thus, once on a time;
And moreover he task'd me
To tell him in rhyme.
Anon at the word,
There first came one daughter
And then came another,
To second and third
The request of their brother,
And to hear how the water
Comes down at Lodore,
With its rush and its roar,
As many a time
They had seen it before.
So I told them in rhyme,
For of rhymes I had store:

And 'twas in my vocation
  For their recreation
That so I should sing;
Because I was Laureate
  To them and their King.

From its sources which well
  In the Tarn on the fell;
    From its fountains
    In the mountains,
Its rills and its gills;
Through moss and through brake,
  It runs and it creeps
  For a while, till it sleeps
In its own little Lake.
And thence at departing,
  Awakening and starting,
It runs through the reeds
  And away it proceeds,
Through meadow and glade,
  In sun and in shade,
And through the wood-shelter,
  Among crags in its flurry,
    Helter-skelter,
    Hurry-scurry.
Here it comes sparkling,
And there it comes darkling—
Now smoking and frothing
Its tumult and wrath in,
  Till in this rapid race
  On which it is bent,
  It reaches the place
  Of its steep descent.

  The Cataract strong
  Then plunges along,
  Striking and raging

As if a war waging
Its caverns and rocks among:
Rising and leaping,
Sinking and creeping,
Swelling and sweeping,
Showering and springing,
Flying and flinging,
Writhing and ringing,
Eddying and whisking,
Spouting and frisking,
Turning and twisting,
Around and around
With endless rebound!
Smiting and fighting,
A sight to delight in;
Confounding, astounding,
Dizzying and deafening the ear with its sound.

Collecting, projecting,
Receding and speeding,
And shocking and rocking,
And darting and parting,
And threading and spreading,
And whizzing and hissing,
And dripping and skipping,
And hitting and splitting,
And shining and twining,
And rattling and battling,
And shaking and quaking,
And pouring and roaring,
And waving and raving,
And tossing and crossing,
And flowing and going,
And running and stunning,
And foaming and roaming,
And dinning and spinning,
And dropping and hopping,

> And working and jerking,
> And guggling and struggling,
> And heaving and cleaving,
> And moaning and groaning;
>
> And glittering and frittering,
> And gathering and feathering,
> And whitening and brightening,
> And quivering and shivering,
> And hurrying and skurrying,
> And thundering and floundering;
>
> Dividing and gliding and sliding,
> And falling and brawling and sprawling,
> And driving and riving and striving,
> And sprinkling and twinkling and wrinkling,
> And sounding and bounding and rounding,
> And bubbling and troubling and doubling,
> And grumbling and rumbling and tumbling,
> And clattering and battering and shattering;
>
> Retreating and beating and meeting and sheeting,
> Delaying and straying and playing and spraying,
> Advancing and prancing and glancing and dancing,
> Recoiling, turmoiling and toiling and boiling,
> And gleaming and streaming and steaming and beaming,
> And rushing and flushing and brushing and gushing,
> And flapping and rapping and clapping and slapping,
> And curling and whirling and purling and twirling,
> And thumping and plumping and bumping and jumping,
> And dashing and flashing and splashing and clashing;
> And so never ending, but always descending,
> Sounds and motions for ever and ever are blending,
> All at once and all o'er, with a mighty uproar,
> And this way the Water comes down at Lodore.

Robert Southey (1774–1843)

Aira Force Valley

          Not a breath of air
Ruffles the bosom of this leafy glen.
From the brook's margin, wide around, the trees
Are steadfast as the rocks; the brook itself,
Old as the hills that feed it from afar,
Doth rather deepen than disturb the calm
Where all things else are still and motionless.
And yet, even now, a little breeze, perchance
Escaped from boisterous winds that rage without,
Has entered, by the sturdy oaks unfelt,
But to its gentle touch how sensitive
Is the light ash! that, pendant from the brow
Of yon dim cave, in seeming silence makes
A soft eye-music of slow-waving boughs,
Powerful almost as vocal harmony
To stay the wanderer's steps and soothe his thoughts.

                                                 William Wordsworth

Stockgill Force, Ambleside

Before breakfast we went to see the Ambleside waterfall. The morning beautiful – the walk early among the hills. We, I may say, fortunately, missed the direct path, and after wandering a little, found it out by the noise – for, mark you, it is buried in trees, in the bottom of the valley – the stream itself is interesting throughout with 'mazy error over pendant shades'. Milton meant a smooth river – this is buffeting all the way on a rocky bed ever various – but the waterfall itself, which I came suddenly upon, gave me a pleasant twinge. First we stood a little below the head about half way down the first fall, buried deep in trees, and saw it streaming down two more descents to the depth of near fifty feet – then we went on a jut of rock nearly level with the second fall-head, where the first fall was above us, and the third below our feet still – at the same time we saw that the water was divided by a sort of cataract island on whose other side burst out a glorious stream – then the thunder and the freshness. At the same time, the different falls have as different characters; the first darting down the slate rock like an arrow; the second spreading out like a fan – the third dashed out into a mist – and the one on the other side of the rock a sort of mixture of all these. We afterwards moved away a space, and saw nearly the whole more mild, streaming silverly through the trees. What astonishes me more than anything is the tone, the colouring, the slate, the stone, the moss, the rock-weed; or, if I may so say, the intellect, the countenance of such places. The space, the magnitude of mountains and waterfalls are well imagined before one sees them; but this countenance or intellectual tone must surpass every imagination and defy any remembrance. I shall learn poetry here and shall henceforth write more than ever, for the abstract endeavour of being able to add a mite to that mass of beauty which is harvested from these grand materials, by the finest spirits, and put into ethereal existence for the relish of one's fellows.

John Keats (1795–1821)
Letters

At the Waterfall

Touching the mantle of the empty sky
with a clear sound on a canvas of silence
the stream flows out of the clouds,

And on a rock, high on Place Fell
a gust of wind sounds
with a noise almost animal.

So much nearer than stillness they speak to me!
I have heard too much silence,
listened too long to the mute sky.

Kathleen Raine (1908–   )

The Lake Coast

Crossing the Bay, 1

A RECONCILING VIEW

Mrs Radcliffe's visit was made in 1794.

We took the early part of the tide, and entered these vast and desolate plains before the sea had entirely left them, or the morning mists were sufficiently dissipated to allow a view of distant objects; but the grand sweep of the coast could be faintly traced, on the left, and a vast waste of sand stretching far below it, with mingled streaks of gray water, that heightened its dreary aspect. The tide was ebbing fast from our wheels, and its low murmur was interrupted, first, only by the shrill small cry of sea-gulls, unseen, whose hovering flight could be traced by the sound, near an island that began to dawn through the mist; and then, by the hoarser croaking of sea-geese, which took a wider range, for their shifting voices were heard from various quarters of the surrounding coast. The body of the sea, on the right, was still involved, and the distant mountains on our left, that crown the bay, were also viewless; but it was sublimely interesting to watch the heavy vapours beginning to move, then rolling in lengthening volumes over the scene, and, as they gradually dissipated, discovering through their veil the various objects they had concealed – fishermen with carts and nets stealing along the margin of the tide, little boats putting off from the shore, and, the view still enlarging as the vapour expanded, the main sea itself softening into the horizon, with here and there a dim sail moving in the hazy distance. The wide desolation of the sands, on the left, was animated only by some horsemen riding remotely in groups towards Lancaster, along the winding edge of the water, and by a muscle-fisher in his cart trying to ford the channel we were approaching ...

We set out rather earlier than was necessary, for the benefit of the guide over part of these trackless wastes, who was going to his station on a sand near the first ford, where he remains to conduct passengers across the united streams of the rivers Crake and Leven, till the returning tide washes him off. He is punctual to the spot as the tides themselves, where he shivers in the dark comfortless midnights of winter, and is scorched on the shadeless sands, under the noons of summer, for a stipend of ten pounds a year! and he said that he had fulfilled the office for thirty years . . .

Near the first ford is Chapel Isle, on the right from Ulverston, a barren sand, where are yet some remains of a chapel built by the monks of Furness, in which divine service was daily performed at a certain hour, for passengers, who crossed the sands with the morning tide. The ford is not thought dangerous, though the sands frequently shift, for the guide regularly tries for, and ascertains, the proper passage. The stream is broad and of formidable appearance, spreading rapidly among the sands and, when you enter it, seeming to bear you away in its course to the sea. The second ford is beyond the peninsula of Cartmel, on the Lancaster sands, and is formed by the accumulated waters of the rivers, Ken [kent] and Winster, where another guide waits to receive the traveller.

The shores of the Lancaster sands fall back to greater distance and are not so bold, or the mountains beyond so awful, as those of Ulverston; but they are various, often beautiful, and Arnside-fells have a higher character. The town and castle of Lancaster, on an eminence, gleaming afar over the level sands and backed by a dark ridge of rocky heights, look well as you approach them. Thither we returned and concluded a tour, which had afforded infinite delight in the grandeur of its landscapes and a reconciling view of human nature in the simplicity, integrity, and friendly disposition of the inhabitants.

Anne Radcliffe (1764–1823)
*Observations During a Tour to The Lakes
of Lancashire, Westmoreland, and Cumberland*

Crossing the Bay, 2

Oct. 11 [1769]. I crossed the river and walked over a peninsula, three miles, to the village of Poulton, which stands on the beach. An old fisherman mending his nets (while I enquired about the danger of passing those sands) told me in his dialect, a moving story; how a brother of the trade, a *Cockler*, as he stiled him, driving a little cart with two daughters (women grown) in it, and his wife on horseback following, set out one day to pass the seven mile sands, as they had been frequently used to do: (for nobody in the village knew them better than the old man did) when they were about half-way over, a thick fog rose, and as they advanced they found the water much deeper than they had expected: the old man was puzzled; he stopped, and said he would go a little way to find some mark he was acquainted with; they staid a while for him, but in vain; they called aloud, but no reply: at last the young women pressed their mother to think where they were, and go on; she would not leave the place; she wandered about forlorn and amazed; she would not quit her horse and get into the cart with them: they determined after much time wasted, to turn back, and give themselves up to the guidance of their horses. The old woman was soon washed off, and perished; the poor girls clung close to their cart, and the horse, sometimes wading and sometimes swimming, brought them back to land alive, but senseless with terror and distress, and unable for many days to give any account of themselves. The bodies of their parents were found the next ebb: that of the father a very few paces distant from the spot where he had left them.

Thomas Gray
Journal in the Lakes

Crossing the Bay, 3

Adam Walker, from whose work the following extract is taken, published his Tour under the name of 'A. Walker', which had led many people into thinking that it was a pseudonym, after the style of James Budworth's 'A Rambler'.

Having passed this Peninsula [i.e. Cartmel], ate flounders (called *flooks*) at Flookborough, we again enter the Sands, and ride three miles over them before we arrive at Ulverstone. In crossing each of these Sands, we cross also two rivers, each sometimes more than half a mile wide. This sounds alarmingly! but it is seldom they are more than a foot deep. Indeed, I have crossed them when we were obliged to open the two doors of the chaise, and let the water run through; but this is seldom the case.

Fatal accidents sometimes happen, and sometimes ludicrous ones. A Gentleman's horse was some time ago drowned in crossing one of these rivers too late. The horse floated, and the Gentleman stuck to him, as a wrecked seaman would to a plank. The Man and Horse were carried up by the tide a considerable way inland, and so near the shore that he tried by the long tail of the Horse if he could touch the bottom. No bottom was to be found! The tide turned, and the Man and Horse began to move towards the main sea! His heart sunk within him, though he still swam by the assistance of the Horse's tail. Several miles was he carried by this uncouth navigation, when once more he was determined to try if he was within soundings. Having fastened one hand in the Horse's tail, he plunged into the sea, and think what must have been his feelings when he felt the bottom! Providence had placed him on a sand-bank! He stood up to the chin – the waves went over him – he disengaged himself from his good friend the dead Horse, and waited there till the tide forsook the Sands, and got safe home.

Adam Walker (*c.* 1731–1821)
Remarks Made in a Tour from London to the Lakes (1792)

Guides to the Sands

Before the railway was made, the old way of crossing the sands from Lancaster to Ulverstone must have been very striking, both from the character of the scenery around and a sense of danger, which cannot but have given something of the piquancy of adventure to the journey. The channels are constantly shifting, particularly after heavy rains, when they are perilously uncertain. For many centuries past, two guides have conducted travellers over them. Their duty is to observe the changes, and find fordable points. In all seasons and states of the weather this was their duty, and in times of storm and fog it must have been fraught with danger. The office of guide has been so long held by a family of the name of Carter, that the country people have given that name to the office itself. A gentleman, crossing from Lancaster, once asked the guide if 'Carters' were never lost on the sands. 'I never knew any lost,' said the guide; 'there's one or two drowned now and then, but they're generally found somewhere i'th bed when th'tide goes out.'

Edwin Waugh (1817–1890)
Over Sands to the Lakes

On Duddon Marsh

This is the shore, the line dividing
The dry land from the waters, Europe
From the Atlantic; this is the mark
That God laid down on the third day.
Twice a year the high tide sliding,
Unwrapping like a roll of oil-cloth, reaches
The curb of the mud, leaving a dark
Swipe of grease, a scaled-out hay

Of wrack and grass and gutterweed. Then
For full three hundred tides the bare
Turf is unwatered except for rain;
Blown wool is dry as baccy; tins
Glint in the sedge with not a sight of man
For two miles round to drop them there.
But once in spring and once again
In autumn, here's where the sea begins.

Norman Nicholson

Seagulls at St Bees

Hardwicke Drummond Rawnsley began his ministry in the Lake District in 1877, at Wray on Windermere. In 1883 he moved to Crosthwaite, near Keswick, was appointed Canon of Carlisle Cathedral in 1909, and, on his retirement in 1917, settled at Allan Bank, Grasmere, the former home of Wordsworth. Canon Rawnsley was one of the founders of the National Trust and a voluminous writer on local topics, being best remembered for his Literary Associations of the English Lakes. *He also produced a vast number of sonnets, seeming to write them as one might make entries in a diary. 'Sea-Gulls at St Bees' comes from a series of well over two hundred, depicting the coastline of England and Wales.*

Moveless of wing, as if by spell suspended,
About the ledges where their eggs are laid
The sea-mews hung, of no alarms afraid,
So well had height and depth their home defended.
Yet with a wailing that was never ended
Far out to sea was lamentation made,
And, trembling up the cliffs, shade after shade
Like ghosts in grief ascended and descended.
It seemed as if the cries of all the pain
The travailing earth has felt, were there expressed;
The tortured rocks were vocal with dismay:
As if all storms that ever wracked the main
Were finding utterance in the sea-bird's breast,
And sudden sorrow had possessed the bay.

H. D. Rawnsley (1851–1920)

Fleswick Bay – A Victorian Engraving

There is a choice of pleasant ways about St Bees. One carries you by the breezy downs, where the elastic grass is beaded with white mush-

room balls, and starred with flowers – sea-pinks and thrift and laven-
der and rest-harrow and countless others – whence you look over to
the sea dotted with ships, some standing close in shore, their white
sails looking like large wings, and others gliding noiselessly away over
the edge of creation, bound one knows not for what distant port;
through heath and pleasant pasturage, down to the head of that
strange red rift gemmed with agates and pretty pebbles, called
Fleswick Bay. . .

The way off the cliffs is down a true gipsy lane, where you have to
do a little scrambling: not more than is good for you, but still at one
point, rather a pinch for the stately and many-fleshed; the red walls of
rock on either side are covered with a small fine green bordering of
moss, and flowers grow on the ledges – chamomile with its hair-like
leaves, samphire, and thrift. The cows, pasturing on the uplands,
come down the red glen to drink at the sweet streamlet of fresh
water, and to stand knee-deep in the warm, smooth sea; and you have
to drive them boisterously before you when you go back, if you
return by the way of the downs, for the rift is too narrow for you and
those four-footed beasts, in comfortable intermingling together. The
stones are water-worn and ribbed and channelled, and you can see
where the waves have washed up in their remorseless strength for
centuries past, and how the once sharp ribs of the earth are worn away
under that incessant sweep; and you can learn, if you will, something
of the law of wave force, which is the same, with a difference, as what
you have learnt in the lake wave; with a difference: for the sea wave
is a long, steady, and incessant sweep, regular and rhythmic, and the
lake wave is irregular and interrupted – partial in its flow and of
uncertain boundary – so that lake rocks, though they get worn and
channelled too, do not show such persistent action as either river
stones or sea-side rocks.

From Fleswick you may go back either by the road or the downs,
or, at low tide, by the rocks and the sea-shore; or you may go farther
on the Whitehaven side, to the lighthouse, and see what fine arrange-
ments they have there for the guidance into safety of the ships wan-
dering in fog or darkness about the pathless dangers of the St Bees
headland, and how the very perfection of cleanliness is attained in
that tall, chimney-looking building – a cleanliness almost approaching

to genius, it is so full of watchfulness and thought. The road and the downs are both delightful ways, but by the sea-shore is the best of the three; for there you not only pass under magnificent cliffs, where the sea birds are sitting in the sun or wheeling round in heavy flight screaming to their young within their nests, where you have the sensation of being at the roots of creation, and under the shadow of the remorseless grandeur of Nature; but you also come upon a bed of rocks, where you may lose yourself for as many hours as the tide will give you free-warren and the right of search. And how many soever these hours may be, you will not have seen half the wonders of that marvellous world.

Limpets and periwinkles, and small gray cirrhipeds and great yellow whelks and deep blue mussels – some of them of singular smallness – with their long beards like slender rootlets beaded with fragments of stone and seaweed, cling all about; some fastened to the lifeless rock with a look of ancient holding as if they had sat there since before the flood, and some entangled in among the ulva – that fine green weed hanging down from the rocks like hair newly smoothed and combed, as if those great round stones were the heads of enchanted mermen, and that smooth growth of weed their comely locks . . . And there are grapes, which, however, are nothing but cuttle-fish eggs; and sea barberries, which are the eggs of the purpura whelk; and mermaid's purses, which, if not empty, hold a very ugly creature as their treasure; and masses of bladder wrack, which you pop with a sounding noise and great squirt of sea water; and balls of honey-combed froth like dessicated sponges or consolidated foam, which are the worn-out egg clusters of the whelk; and other wonderful things to be picked up and studied by those caring to know what lies about them . . .

These, and many more than these, you will find among those green and black-haired rocks by the bluff headland; there where the escarpment, split into great parallel blocks of the richest red, wears such a different aspect to the sea-beach pavement smoothed and rounded into gigantic pebbles; yet both are of the same formation; only the one shows the varied action of the wind and rain and frost, and the other the uniform sweep and swell of wave, for ever and ever repeated.

When the tide has run down the sands are ribbed and channelled in the old form, like the markings on the Screes at Wastwater; and you see again the leaf, both the coralline growth and the fan shape, which the downward pour of water on a yielding surface always gives. And farther on, you most likely fall against a thick length of iron cable, now bent and twisted like a doll's wire, telling its sad tale of wreck and disaster, and noble lives entombed and lost to humanity for ever. Nothing gives a more vivid idea of the tremendous force of the waves than a cast-up iron cable, not one strand of which you can bend, now all twisted and unravelled as if it had been made of thread.

E. Lynn Linton
The Lake Country

Nature's Plan

Lines Written in Early Spring

I heard a thousand blended notes,
While in a grove I sate reclined,
In that sweet mood when pleasant thoughts
Bring sad thoughts to the mind.

To her fair works did Nature link
The human soul that through me ran;
And much it grieved my heart to think
What man has made of man.

Through primrose tufts, in that green bower,
The periwinkle trailed its wreathes;
And 'tis my faith that every flower
Enjoys the air it breathes.

The birds around me hopped and played,
Their thoughts I cannot measure: –
But the least motion which they made,
It seemed a thrill of pleasure.

The budding twigs spread out their fan,
To catch the breezy air;
And I must think, do all I can,
That there was pleasure there.

If this belief from heaven be sent,
If such be Nature's holy plan,
Have I not reason to lament
What man has made of man?

                                        William Wordsworth

The Green Linnet

*The bird to which Wordsworth refers is now more usually known as the
greenfinch.*

Beneath these fruit-tree boughs that shed
Their snow-white blossoms on my head,
With brightest sunshine round me spread
  Of spring's unclouded weather,
In this sequestered nook how sweet
To sit upon my orchard-seat!
And birds and flowers once more to greet,
  My last year's friends together.

One have I marked, the happiest guest
In all this covert of the blest:
Hail to Thee, far above the rest
  In joy of voice and pinion!
Thou, Linnet! in thy green array,
Presiding Spirit here today,
Dost lead the revels of the May;
  And this is thy dominion.

While birds, and butterflies, and flowers,
Make all one band of paramours,
Thou, ranging up and down the bowers,
  Art sole in thy employment:
A Life, a Presence like the Air,
Scattering thy gladness without care,
Too blest with any one to pair;
  Thyself thy own enjoyment.

Amid yon tuft of hazel trees,
That twinkle to the gusty breeze,
Behold him perched in ecstasies,
  Yet seeming still to hover;
There! where the flutter of his wings

Upon his back and body flings
Shadows and sunny glimmerings,
    That cover him all over.

My dazzled sight he oft deceives,
A Brother of the dancing leaves;
Then flits, and from the cottage eaves
    Pours forth his song in gushes;
As if by that exulting strain
He mocked and treated with disdain
The voiceless Form he chose to feign,
    While fluttering in the bushes.

William Wordsworth

To the Cuckoo

O blithe New-comer! I have heard,
I hear thee and rejoice.
O Cuckoo! shall I call thee Bird,
Or but a wandering Voice?

While I am lying on the grass
Thy twofold shout I hear;
From hill to hill it seems to pass
At once far off, and near.

Though babbling only to the Vale,
Of sunshine and of flowers,
Thou bringest unto me a tale
Of visionary hours.

Thrice welcome, darling of the Spring!
Even yet thou art to me
No bird, but an invisible thing,
A voice, a mystery;

The same whom in my schoolboy days
I listened to; that Cry
Which made me look a thousand ways
In bush, and tree, and sky.

To seek thee did I often rove
Through woods and on the green;
And thou wert still a hope, a love;
Still longed for, never seen.

And I can listen to thee yet;
Can lie upon the plain
And listen, till I do beget
That golden time again.

O blessèd Bird! the earth we pace
Again appears to be
An unsubstantial faery place;
That is fit home for Thee!

William Wordsworth

Swallows

Wednesday, 16th [June 1802]. I wrote to Mary after dinner, while
William sate in the orchard ... I spoke of the little birds keeping us
company, and William told me that that very morning a bird had
perched upon his leg. He had been lying very still, and had watched
this little creature. It had come under the bench where he was sitting
... He thoughtlessly stirred himself to look further at it, and it flew
on to the apple tree above him. It was a little young creature that had
just left its nest, equally unacquainted with man, and unaccustomed
to struggle against the storms and winds. While it was upon the apple
tree the wind blew about the stiff boughs, and the bird seemed
bemazed, and not strong enough to strive with it. The swallows come

to the sitting-room window as if wishing to build, but I am afraid they will not have courage for it; but I believe they will build in my room window. They twitter, and make a bustle, and a little cheerful song, hanging against the panes of glass with their soft white bellies close to the glass and their forked fish-like tails. They swim round and round, and again they come. . .

Friday, 25th June. I went, just before tea, into the garden. I looked up at my swallow's nest, and it was gone. It had fallen down. Poor little creatures, they could not themselves be more distressed than I was. I went upstairs to look at the ruins. They lay in a large heap upon the window ledge; these swallows had been ten days employed in building this nest, and it seemed to be almost finished. I had watched them early in the morning, in the day many and many a time, and in the evenings when it was almost dark. I had seen them sitting together side by side in their unfinished nest, both morning and night. When they first came about the window they used to hang against the panes, with their white bellies and their forked tails, looking like fish; but then they fluttered and sang their own little twittering song. As soon as the nest was broad enough, a sort of ledge for them, they sat both mornings and evenings, but they did not pass the night there. I watched them one morning, when William was at Eusemere, for more than an hour. Every now and then there was a motion in their wings, a sort of tremulousness, and they sang a low song to one another.

[*A page is missing at this point in the* Journal *and the swallows must have rebuilt their nest between 25th June and 29th June, the date of the next surviving entry.*]

Tuesday, 29th June. It is now eight o'clock; I will go and see if my swallows are on their nest. Yes! there they are, side by side, both looking down into the garden. I have been out on purpose to see their faces. I knew by looking at the window that they were there. . .

Dorothy Wordsworth
Grasmere Journal

The Lake District

Stonechats

Friday Morning, [*16th May 1800*]. Warm and mild, after a fine night of rain . . . The woods extremely beautiful with all autumnal variety and softness. I carried a basket for mosses, and gathered some wild plants. Oh! that we had a book of botany. All flowers now are gay and deliciously sweet. The primrose still pre-eminent among the later flowers of the spring. Foxgloves very tall, with their heads budding. I went forward round the lake at the foot of Loughrigg Fell. I was much amused with the busyness of a pair of stone-chats; their restless voices as they skimmed along the water, following each other, their shadows under them, and their returning back to the stones on the shore, chirping with the same unwearied voice. Could not cross the water, so I went round by the stepping-stones . . . Rydale was very beautiful, with spear-shaped streaks of polished steel . . . Grasmere very solemn in the last glimpse of twilight. It calls home the heart to quietness. I had been very melancholy in my walk back. I had many of my saddest thoughts, and I could not keep the tears within me. But when I came to Grasmere I felt that it did me good. I finished my letter to M.H. . . .

Dorothy Wordsworth
Grasmere Journal

Robin Redbreast

When winter winds blow strang and keen,
   An' neets are lang an' cauld,
An' flocks o' burds, wi' famine team't,
   Come flutteren into t'fauld;
I hev a casement, just ya pane,
   'At Robin kens reet weel,
An' pops in menny a time i 't'day,
   A crumb or two to steal.

At furst he's shy an' easy flay't,
   Bit seunn he bolder gits,
An' picks aboot quite unconsarn't.
   Or here an' theer he flits.
An' when he gits his belly full,
   An's tir't o' playin' pranks,
He'll sit quite still, on t'auld chair back,
   An' sing his simple thanks.

Bit when breet spring comes back ageann,
   An' fields ur growen green,
He bids good day, an' flees away,
   An' than na mair he's seen;
Till winter comes ageann wi' frost,
   An' driften snow, an' rain,
An' than he venters back ageann,
   To leuk for t'oppen pane.

Noo, burds an' fwok ur mickle t'seamm,
   If they be i' hard need;
An' yan hes owt to give, they'll come,
   An' be girt frinds indeed.
Bit when theer nowt they want to hev,
   It's nut sa lang they'll stay,
Bit just as Robin does i' t' spring,
   They'll seun aw flee away.

John Richardson (1817–1886)

Green Woodpecker

Was't at us thoo brast oot laughan
On that breet October day,
When we walk't bih Darrenwatter's
Nabs an neuks teh Barrow Bay?
Darrenwater: Derwentwater

The Lake District

Er was't at that woman-body
Brummelan near Ashness yat,
Coz thoo knew 'twes said Ole Horny
On October fruit hed spat?

Anywazes, when thoo gliff't us
Off thoo skifted – gone like t'win',
Fer whor angels might ev tip-tee'd
We hed gawkishly rushed in.

Hoo we wish thoo'd stopp't a minute,
Just teh let us feast oor eyes
On thih cwoat o' many colours,
Fit fer Bird ev Paradise! –

Reed es ripened holly-berries,
Breetest green like young spring grass,
Wid't wil'-mustard's sulpha-yalla,
Aw es glassy es a glass.

Flate er some fwoaks they'll be laugh't at,
But we'll risk it any day,
If't's a popinjay 'ats yafflen★
'Mang them trees bih Barrow Bay.

William Sanderson (1887–*c.* 1970)
Dialect and other Verse (Keswick, 1956)

brummelan: blackberrying   *gliff't:* spied, noticed
yat: gate   *flate:* scared
★ The green woodpecker is called the 'yaffle' in some parts of England.

Bubblen Ower

(Curlew)
Com a sang like watter bubblen
Frae an uplan' rwoadside fiel',
Marra teh mih own heart's lowpen,
Smittle in its gay appeal.

Just a curlew back frae t'Solway,
Owerjoyed coz Spring's abroad;
It, abeun a green hill-paster,
Me, on t'dusty, steanny rwoad.

William Sanderson

T' Watter Pyat

*The name 'water-pyat' seems to be applied to several black and white
waterside birds, but here it undoubtedly means the dipper. A 'pyat' is
a magpie.*

Bonnie laal hanter o' t' moontan becks,
Wid breest as white as t'feddery flecks
O' floatin foam 'at santer an' run
Past t'eller shaddas, oot inta t'sun.
Piebald piper wid silvery tongue,
Creunan the' sang nar t'hezzeks hung
Wid tosselt gowld, in t'days o'March
Fooer t'buds hev brussen on t'breet'nin' larch:
Singin' for joy 'fooer t'woods ur sturred
Be t'double nwotes o' t'cuckoo burd;

marra: companion   hanter: haunter
lowpen: leaping   eller: elder
smittle: infectious   hezzeks: hazels
hill-paster: pasture   brussen: burst

The Lake District

'Fooer t'millary comes ta t'lonnin' neuks,
Or t'jacks hev partit fra t'nestin' reuks:
'Fooer t'furst wild sangs o' t'throssels hard,
Or t'fwoal-feut flooers in t'gurse ur starred.
Many a time wid brudders o'mine
In thur sunbreet days o'life's lang syne,
Ah've ran het-feut on Cocker broos,
Or stop't annunder t'beck side bews,
Ta watch the' dook or ta lissen the' sing,
Day in, day oot, frae Spring ta Spring:
Lontert ta watch the' nestin' on t'rocks
Whoar t'dark moss droops in wattery locks,
Buildin', hoddenly, leat an' seun,
While t'beck ron by wid a merry teun.
But life hes brong tull t'lads an' me,
Sen we furst hard the' chirp an' flee,
Changes leetsome, an' changes sair,
Some glints o' joy, some cloods o'care:
Yit, though we're change't wid t'passin' 'eears,
Thy seam oald sang still soothes an' cheers.
Soo teutal on fra t'spring ta t'Fa',
An' on throo t'months when t'winter's snaw
Dapples aw t'fells wid gleamin' specks,
Bonnie laal hanter o' t'moontan becks.

John Denwood, Junior (1871–1917)

On Meeting Sheep

A sudden start and the group
stiffened momentarily
like ten-pins waiting.

jacks: jack-daws   *hoddenly:* persistently
lontert: loitered   *'eears:* years

Then their eyes drifted
in heads heavy with
their green looking.

And they moved on
silently as ghosts
in their own mists,

floating away with walls
into distant skies,
slowly melting to stones.

David Watkin Price (1932–   )

The Faithful Dog, 1

*The story of Charles Gough and his faithful dog was, of course, the subject
of the well-known poem by Wordsworth, two stanzas of which are quoted
on page 96. Wilkinson's suggestion that the dog 'eat grass' was made in
answer to the accusation that it fed on the corpse of its master. It is more
probable, however, that it fed on carrion, such as that of dead lambs and sheep,
which is often to be found among the mountain precipices. Wilkinson, as
can be seen from his use of the second person singular, was a Quaker.*

First I shall mention to thee an affecting interment that took place
lately in our graveyard at Tirril. 'Twas of the bare skeleton of a young
man of the name of Gough (Charles Gough) of Manchester, a
relation of the Goughs of Ireland, who, fourteen weeks ago, had
fallen from the heights of Helvellyn (one of the highest mountains in
Westmoreland), down a precipice 600 feet high.

He had attained the summit of the mountain (where his staff was
found) in his passage out of our parish to another valley, but it was
apprehended the mist had struck in, and he had fallen down as just
described. His bones were bleached white though covered with his

clothes, and his skull was separated and found at a distance from the rest. His pocket-book, with his Disownment therin for becoming a volunteer, being shown to Thomas Clarkson [Clarkson, the opponent of the Slave Trade, lived at Eusemere, near Pooley Bridge] as he was passing the village whither they were bringing his remains, led to the discovery who he was. His faithful little dog had attended his relics between three and four months, but how it had subsisted itself is difficult to suppose, though it appeared to the people who collected his remains that it eat grass.

Thomas Wilkinson
Letter – quoted from H. D. Rawnsley's
Literary Associations of the English Lakes

The Faithful Dog, 2

I clim'd the dark brow of the mighty Helvellyn,
    Lakes and mountains beneath me gleam'd misty and wide;
All was still, save by fits, when the eagle was yelling,
    And starting around me the echoes replied.
On the right, Striden-edge round the Red-tarn was bending,
And Catchedicam its left verge was defending,
One huge nameless rock in the front was ascending,
    When I mark'd the sad spot where the wanderer had died.

Dark green was that spot 'mid the brown mountain-heather,
    Where the Pilgrim of Nature lay stretch'd in decay,
Like the corpse of an outcast abandon'd to weather,
    Till the mountain winds wasted the tenantless clay.
Nor yet quite deserted, though lonely extended,
For, faithful in death, his mute favourite attended,
The much-loved remains of her master defended,
    And chased the hill-fox and the ravens away.

How long didst thou think that his silence was slumber?
   When the wind waved his garment, how oft didst thou start?
How many long days and long weeks didst thou number,
   Ere he faded before thee, the friend of thy heart?
And, oh, was it meet, that – no requiem read o'er him –
No mother to weep, and no friend to deplore him,
And thou, little guardian, alone stretch'd before him –
   Unhonour'd the Pilgrim from life should depart?

When a Prince to the fate of the Peasant has yielded,
   The tapestry waves dark round the dim-lighted hall;
With scutcheons of silver the coffin is shielded,
   And pages stand mute by the canopied pall:
Through the courts, at deep midnight, the torches are gleaming,
In the proudly-arch'd chapel the banners are beaming,
Far adown the long aisle sacred music is streaming,
   Lamenting a Chief of the people should fall.

But meeter for thee, gentle lover of nature,
   To lay down thy head like the meek mountain lamb,
When, wilder'd, he drops from some cliff huge in stature,
   And draws his last sob by the side of his dam.
And more stately thy couch by this desert lake lying,
Thy obsequies sung by the grey plover flying,
With one faithful friend but to witness thy dying,
   In the arms of Helvellyn and Catchedicam.

Walter Scott (1771–1832)

The Wild Dog of Ennerdale

A recent occurrence recalled to my memory the misdeeds of the
Ennerdale Dog. These were so numerous and audacious, and so
unusual, that whatsoever mischief other dogs might have done in

other years, their deeds of destruction were all greatly overshadowed by the doings of this animal in the year 1810. 'T'girt dog' was talked about, and dreamt about, and written about, to the utter exclusion of nearly every other topic in Ennerdale and Kinniside, and all the vales round about there; for the number of sheep he destroyed was amazing, and the difficulties experienced in taking him were beyond belief . . .

No one knew to whom the dog had belonged, or whence he came; but being of a mongrel breed, and excessively shy, it was conjectured he had escaped from the chain of some gypsy troop. He was a smooth haired dog, of a tawny mouse-colour, with dark streaks, in tiger-fashion, over his hide; and appeared to be a cross between mastiff and greyhound. Strongly built and of good speed, being both well fed and well exercised, his endurance was very great. His first appearance in the district was on or about the 10th May, 1810, when he was seen by Mr Mossop of Thornholme [a farm in the upper Calder Valley], who was near, and noticed him as a stranger. His worrying exploits followed soon after; and from that time till his being shot in September following, he was not known to have fed on anything but living mutton, or, at least, the flesh of lambs and sheep before the carcases had time to cool. From one sheep he was scared during his feast, and when the shepherd examined the carcase, the flesh had been torn from the ribs behind the shoulder, and the *still beating* heart was laid bare and visible. He was once seen to run down a fine ram at early dawn; and, without killing it, to tear out and swallow lumps of living flesh from the hind quarters of the tortured animal while it stood on its feet, without the power to resist or flee, yet with sufficient life to crawl forward on its fore legs. He would sometimes wantonly destroy seven or eight sheep in one night; and all his work was done so silently that no one ever heard him either bark or growl . . .

At other times, when a lazy fit came over him, or when he had been fatigued by a long chase, a single life and the tit-bits it afforded would satisfy him for the time – taking his epicurean meals from a choice part of the carcase. He seldom fed during the day; and his cunning was such that he did not attack the same flock or sport on the same ground on two successive nights, often removing two or three miles for his next meal . . . Various schemes were tried to entice him within shooting range, such as tethering bitches in heat on his domain; and though the cunning brute was often seen to hover about them, yet he took especial care to keep out of harm's way. Poison was tried, but soon abandoned, on account of the risk of injury to other dogs . . .

As the summer advanced, and the crops got full on the ground, it was useless to continue chasing the dog; for . . . he got so well acquainted with the country for many miles around the district chosen as his home, that, after leading his pursuers many a long and weary chase, he always threw the hounds off the scent by some clever manoeuvre; often gliding from one cornfield to another, where the hunters would not go in to injure the growing crops in assisting the hounds . . .

At last it was thought better to waste less time over him till some of the crops were cut, and then one available source, at least, of his deceptions, would be taken away. . .

A chance incident soon over-ruled this determination; for on the 12th of September, the dog was seen by Jonathan Patrickson to go into a cornfield.

Jonathan Patrickson said, 'Aa'l let ta lig theer a bit, me lad, but aa'l want to see tha just noo.'

Away went the old man, and, without the usual noise, soon raised men enow to surround the field; and as some in their haste came unprovided with guns, a halt was whispered round to wait till more guns were brought and the hounds collected. When a good muster of guns, and men with dogs were got together, the wild dog was disturbed out of the corn; and only the old man who had seen him go into the field was lucky enough to get a shot at him, and to wound him in the hind quarters. This took a little off his speed, and enabled the hounds to keep well up to him, but none durst engage him. And, though partly disabled, he kept long on his legs, and was often headed and turned by the numerous parties of pursuers, several of whom met him in his circuitous route from the upper side of Kinniside, by Eskat, Arlecdon, and Asby, by Rowrah and Stockton Hall, to the River Ehen. Each of these parties he shied, and turned in a new direction till he got wearied. He was quietly taking a cold bath in the river, with the hounds as quietly looking on, when John Steel came up with his gun laden with small bullets, but durst not shoot, lest he injured some of the hounds. When the dog caught sight of him it made off to Eskat Woods, with the hounds and John on its track, and after a few turnings in the wood, amid the greatest excitement of dogs and men, a fair chance offered, and the fatal discharge was made by John Steel, when the destroyer fell to rise no more; and the marksman received his well-earned reward of ten pounds, with the hearty congratulations of all assembled.

William Dickinson
Cumbriana (1875)

Glow-Worms

Among all lovely things my Love had been;
Had noted well the stars, all flowers that grew
About her home; but she had never seen
A Glow-worm, never one, and this I knew.

While riding near her home one stormy night
A single Glow-worm did I chance to espy;
I gave a fervent welcome to the sight,
And from my Horse I leapt; great joy had I.

Upon a leaf the Glow-worm did I lay,
To bear it with me through the stormy night:
And, as before, it shone without dismay;
Albeit putting forth a fainter light.

When to the Dwelling of my Love I came,
I went into the Orchard quietly;
And left the Glow-worm, blessing it by name,
Laid safely by itself, beneath a Tree.

The whole next day I hoped, and hoped with fear;
At night the Glow-worm shone beneath the Tree:
I led my Lucy to the spot, 'Look here!'
Oh! joy it was for her, and joy for me!

William Wordsworth

Daffodils at Gowbarrow Park

Thursday 15th [April 1802]. It was a threatening, misty morning, but mild. We set off after dinner from Eusemere. Mrs Clarkson went a short way with us, but turned back. The wind was furious, and we thought we must have returned. We first rested in the large boat-house, then under a furze bush opposite Mr Clarkson's. Saw the plough going in the field. The wind seized our breath. The lake was rough. There was a boat by itself floating in the middle of the bay below Water Millock. We rested again in the Water Millock Lane. The hawthorns are black and green, the birches here and there greenish, but there is yet more of purple to be seen on the twigs. We got over into a field to avoid some cows – people working. A few primroses by the roadside – woodsorrel flower, the anemone, scentless violets, strawberries, and that starry, yellow flower which Mrs C. calls pile wort [i.e. the lesser celandine]. When we were in the woods beyond Gowbarrow Park, we saw a few daffodils close to the water-side. We fancied that the lake had floated the seeds ashore, and that the little colony had so sprung up. But as we went along there were more and yet more; and at last, under the boughs of the trees, we saw that there was a long belt of them along the shore, about the breadth of a country turnpike road. I never saw daffodils so beautiful. They grew among the mossy stones about and about them; some rested their heads upon these stones, as on a pillow, for weariness; and the rest tossed and reeled and danced, and seemed as if they verily laughed with the wind, that blew upon them over the lake; they looked so gay, ever glancing, ever changing. This wind blew directly over the lake to them. There was here and there a little knot, and a few stragglers higher up; but they were so few as not to disturb the simplicity, unity, and life of that one busy highway. We rested again and again. The bays were stormy, and we heard the waves at different distances, and in the middle of the water, like the sea.

Dorothy Wordsworth
Grasmere Journal

Daffodils

It should be remembered that this poem was not given a title by the poet.

I wandered lonely as a cloud
That floats on high o'er vales and hills,
When all at once I saw a crowd,
A host, of golden daffodils;
Beside the lake, beneath the trees,
Fluttering and dancing in the breeze.

Continuous as the stars that shine
And twinkle on the milky way,
They stretched in never-ending line
Along the margin of a bay:
Ten thousand saw I at a glance,
Tossing their heads in sprightly dance.

The waves beside them danced; but they
Out-did the sparkling waves in glee:
A poet could not but be gay,
In such a jocund company:
I gazed – and gazed – but little thought
What wealth the show to me had brought.

For oft, when on my couch I lie
In vacant or in pensive mood,
They flash upon that inward eye
Which is the bliss of solitude;
And then my heart with pleasure fills,
And dances with the daffodils.

William Wordsworth

Swans Don't Eat Daffodils

Surely Wordsworth must be as mad as was ever the poet Lee. Those volumes of his, which you were so good as to give me, have excited, by turns, my tenderness and warm admiration, my contemptuous astonishment and disgust. The two latter rose to their utmost height while I read about his dancing daffodils, ten thousand, as he says, in high dance in the breeze beside the river, whose waves dance with them, and the poet's heart, we are told, danced too. Then he proceeds to say, that in the hours of pensive or of fancied contemplation, these same capering flowers flash on his memory, and his heart, losing its cares, dances with them again.

Surely if his worst foe had chosen to caricature this too egotistic manufacturer of metaphysic importance upon trivial themes, he could not have done it more effectively.

Anna Seward, 'The Swan of Litchfield' (1747–1809)
Letter to Sir Walter Scott

Sleea-Bleum

Its strange hoo laal oor poyets sing –
Nut caren, nut a streea –
Aboot that bonny flooer o'Spring
Et pooders t'boos o' t'sleea!

Theh sing ev peer-trees aw a-blow
Like full-rigged sailen-ships,
Ev plum an' churry, white es snow,
An' apples blush't teh t'tips,

Bet when it cums teh t'sleea-bleum
Nee win's left i' their lungs;
Theh're ayder struckken codfish-dumb
Er fin' theh've lost ther tongues.

Sih just a wurd fer Cinderella,
T'rich plum tree's poor relation –
Bet oh that some big poyet-fella
Wad feel its inspiration!

Yance t'darkest thing ther was bih t'way,
Noo t'welcomest o'seets,
White-hung, es if t'wes weshin-day
Fer t'countrywoman's sheets . . .

When Winter ling-ers, ling-ers lang,
T'sleea cums, a heartsom thing,
Tells Winter's en' – an, nivver wrang,
Lifts t'hesp on t'dooar ev Spring.

William Sanderson

streea: straw   *hesp:* latch
sleea: sloe or blackthorn

Wind and Weather

Skiey Influences

It may now be proper to say a few words respecting climate, and 'skiey influences', in which this region, as far as the character of its landscapes is affected by them, may, upon the whole, be considered fortunate. The country is, indeed, subject to much bad weather, and it has been ascertained that twice as much rain falls here as in many parts of the island; but the number of black drizzling days, that blot out the face of things, is by no means *proportionally* great. Nor is a continuance of thick, flagging, damp air so common as in the West of England and Ireland. The rain here comes down heartily, and is frequently succeeded by clear, bright weather, when every brook is vocal, and every torrent sonorous; brooks and torrents, which are never muddy, even in the heaviest floods, except, after a drought, they happen to be defiled for a short time by waters that have swept along dusty roads, or have broken out into ploughed fields. Days of unsettled weather, with partial showers, are very frequent; but the showers, darkening, or brightening, as they fly from hill to hill, are not less grateful to the eye than finely interwoven passages of gay and sad music are touching to the ear. Vapours, exhaling from the lakes and meadows after sunrise, in a hot season, or in moist weather, brooding upon the heights, or descending towards the valleys with inaudible motion, give a visionary character to everything around them; and are in themselves so beautiful as to dispose us to enter into the feelings of those simple nations (such as the Laplanders of this day) by whom they are taken for guardian deities of the mountains; or to sympathize with others who have fancied these delicate apparitions to be the spirits of their departed ancestors. Akin to these are fleecy clouds resting upon the hill-tops; they are not easily managed in picture, with their accompaniments of blue sky; but how glorious are they in Nature! how pregnant with imagination for the poet! and the height of the Cumbrian mountains is sufficient to exhibit daily and hourly instances of those mysterious attachments. Such clouds, cleaving to their stations, or lifting up suddenly their glittering heads from behind rocky barriers, or hurrying out of sight with speed of the sharpest edge – will often tempt an inhabitant to congratulate himself on belonging to a country of mists and clouds and storms, and make

The Lake District

him think of the blank sky of Egypt, and of the cerulean vacancy of
Italy, as an unanimated and even a sad spectacle.

William Wordsworth
Guide to the Lakes

Summer Rain

Thick lay the dust, uncomfortably white,
In glaring mimicry of Arab sands.
The woods and mountains slept in hazy light;
The meadows look'd athirst and tawny tann'd;
The little rills had left their channels bare,
With scarce a pool to witness what they were;
And the shrunk river gleam'd 'mid oozy stones,
That stared like any famish'd giant's bones.

Sudden the hills grew black, and hot as stove
The air beneath; it was a toil to be.
There was a growling as of angry Jove,
Provoked by Juno's prying jealousy –
A flash – a crash – the firmament was split,
And down it came in drops – the smallest fit
To drown a bee in fox-glove bell concealed;
Joy fill'd the brook, and comfort cheer'd the field.

Hartley Coleridge (1796–1849)

The Beauty of Fog

Among the beautiful appearances of fogs, and mists, their *gradually
going off* may be observed. A landscape takes a variety of pleasing

hues, as it passes, in a retiring fog, through the different modes of obscurity into full splendour.

There is great beauty also in a fog's *partially clearing up at once*, as it often does; and presenting some distant piece of landscape under great radiance, when all the surrounding parts are still in obscurity. The curtain is not intirely drawn up; it is only just raised, to let in some beautiful, transient view; and perhaps falling again, while we admire, leaves us that ardent relish, which we have for pleasing objects suddenly removed. – Some very beautiful ideas of this kind were displayed on the summits of Gascadale [Keskadale or Newlands Valley]. Tho the mountains around us, and the contracted vallies in our neighbourhood, were all so much absorbed in the dark atmosphere of clouds and vapours, we could discover, in catches, through their thinner skirts, the vale of Keswick, at a distance, overspread with serenity and sunshine.

William Gilpin
Observations . . . [on] the Mountains, and Lakes of Cumberland, and Westmorland

New Moon at Keswick

This poem was written at a time when Coleridge was in love with Sara Hutchinson, Wordsworth's sister-in-law.

Late, late yestreen I saw the new Moon,
With the old Moon in her arms:
And I fear, I fear, my Master dear!
We shall have a deadly storm.

Ballad of Sir Patrick Spence

Well! if the Bard was weather-wise, who made
   The grand old ballad of Sir Patrick Spence,
   This night, so tranquil now, will not go hence
Unroused by winds, that ply a busier trade
Than those which mould yon clouds in lazy flakes,

Or the dull sobbing draught, that moans and rakes
Upon the strings of this Aeolian lute,
    Which better far were mute.
  For lo! the New-moon winter-bright!
  And overspread with phantom light,
  (With swimming phantom light o'erspread
  But rimmed and circled by a silver thread)
I see the old Moon in her lap, foretelling
  The coming-on of rain and squally blast.
And oh! that even now the gust were swelling,
  And the slant night-shower driving loud and fast!
Those sounds which oft have raised me, whilst they awed,
    And sent my soul abroad,
Might now perhaps their wonted impulse give,
Might startle this dull pain, and make it move and live!

A grief without a pang, void, dark, and drear,
  A stifled, drowsy, unimpassioned grief,
  Which finds no natural outlet, no relief,
    In word, or sigh, or tear –
O Lady! in this wan and heartless mood,
To other thoughts by yonder throstle woo'd,
  All this long eve, so balmy and serene,
Have I been gazing on the western sky,
  And its peculiar tint of yellow green:
And still I gaze – and with how blank an eye!
And those thin clouds above, in flakes and bars,
That give away their motion to the stars;
Those stars, that glide behind them or between,
Now sparkling, now bedimmed, but always seen:
Yon crescent Moon, as fixed as if it grew
In its own cloudless, starless lake of blue;
I see them all so excellently fair,
I see, not feel, how beautiful they are!

        S. T. Coleridge
        From *Dejection: An Ode* (written 4 April 1802)

New Moon at Grasmere

Monday morning [*8th March 1802*]. On Friday evening the moon hung over the northern side of the highest point of Silver How, like a gold ring snapped in two, and shaven off at the ends. Within this ring lay the circle of the round moon, as distinctly to be seen as ever the enlightened moon is. William had observed the same appearance at Keswick, perhaps at the very same moment, hanging over the Newland Fells.

Dorothy Wordsworth
Grasmere Journal

The Young Moon Seen as a Circle

Under the above title in Vols. 28 and 29 of this *Journal* are a number of notes and observations of the slightly brighter rim that is sometimes seen along the dark limb of the crescent moon, thus making the earth-lit portion of the disk appear as if outlined by a silver thread. The phenomenon does not seem to have been very frequently observed or reported, and the suggestion, even, has been made that it is perhaps of comparatively recent date ... It is gratifying to find that one, at any rate, of our great poets is not silent on the subject, and ... attention may appropriately be drawn to Coleridge's beautiful description of the young moon in the first stanza of his ode, 'Dejection' ...

The sight of the earth-lit moon recalled to the poet's mind 'The grand old ballad of Sir Patrick Spence', four lines from which quoted rather from memory than with strict accuracy from the version in Percy's *Reliques*, 1765, are prefixed to the ode. From the Oxford Dictionary, s.v. new-moon, it would appear that this ballad of uncertain date affords the earliest-known example of our popular term for the earthshine – 'the old moon in the new moon's arms'. It is possible that Coleridge was indebted to his remembrance of the ballad both for the suggestion of the corresponding expression in the ode and for the significance, real or supposed, of the phenomenon as a weather portent. But his precise and vivid description of the earth-lit moon, more especially the line – 'But rimmed and circled by a silver thread', – must surely have been the result of personal and minute observation on some particular occasion, which it may be interesting to attempt to identify . . .

Calculation shows that the moon was new on April 2, about 3h 20m G.M.A.T., so that on April 4, at Keswick (long. 12N 4W), about 7h 56m p.m., L.M.T. the moon would be 2.20 days old. As this appears to be about the optimum age for observing the 'silver thread', there is a strong presumption that the observation was made on the evening of the day on which the ode was written, as indeed the poet's use of the present tense in referring to the earthshine would also suggest. But it may be well to consider the matter more closely. Now at Keswick (lat. 54° 36'N) on 1802 April 4, apparent sunset ($z = 90°$ 50') was at 6h 41m, and moonset ($z = 90°$ 50'-58' $= 89°$ 52'), at 9h 56m p.m., L.M.T. If the observation was made on that day, it must, therefore, have been made between those times, though both would be somewhat accelerated by the mountainous nature of the terrain. The references in stanza ii of the ode to the western sky, 'And its peculiar tint of yellow green' (1.29); the stars 'Now sparkling, now bedimmed, but always seen' (1.34), and the crescent moon 'In its own cloudless, starless lake of blue' (1.36), all suggest that twilight, though still present, was well advanced. The earlier and lighter part of twilight is usually regarded as coming to an end with the appearance of the brighter stars when the sun's zenith-distance is about 96°, and the later and darker part, with the appearance of the smaller stars when the sun's zenith-distance is about 108°. The L.M.T.s at Keswick corresponding to those zenith-distances on the day in question were 7h 18m and 8h 53m p.m., respectively. The mean of those times, 8h 6m, is within a few minutes of the time when the moon was 2.20 days old. The convergence of these various indications seems, therefore, to point with some probability to the observation having been made about 8 o'clock in the evening of 1802 April 4. Internal evidence shows that the eighth and last stanza was composed at or near midnight on that day (cf 1.126). Hence, if the time here deduced for the observation be correct, the first seven stanzas, comprising 137 lines in the earliest draft . . . as compared with 125 lines in the final draft, . . . must have been written in about four hours.

S. B. Gaythorpe
Papers Communicated to the Royal Astronomical Association
(published December 1934)

Stars at Mid-day

Under mount Skiddaw is the head of the river Caldew; it issues through a narrow trough, and takes its winding course with great rapidity to Mosedale, where it turns northward for Carlisle. Near two miles above that village it receives a small rivulet from Bouscale [Bowscale] Tarn, a lake near a mile in circumference, on the side of a high mountain, so strangely surrounded with a more eminent amphitheatrical ridge of quarry rocks, that it is excluded the benefit of the sun for at least three months in the middle of winter; but this is not its only singularity. Several of the most credible inhabitants thereabouts affirming, that they frequently see the stars in it at mid-day; but, in order to discover that phenomenon, the firmament must be perfectly clear, the air stable, and the water unagitated. These circumstances not occurring at the time I was there, deprived me of the pleasure of that sight, and of recommending it to the naturalists upon my own occular evidence, which I regret the want of, as I question if the like has been any where else observed. The spectator must be situated at least 200 yards above the lake, and as much below the summit of the semi-ambient ridge; and, as there are other high mountains, which, in that position, may break and deaden the solar rays, I can only give an implicit credit to the power of their agency, till I am convinced of their effects, and am qualified to send it better recommended to the public.

William Hutchinson
The History of the County of Cumberland

Cloud on the Old Man

John Ruskin visited the Lakes many times in the course of his life, but when at last he settled there, in 1871, his work was largely over, and he was famous, worn-out and profoundly unhappy. Brantwood, the house which he bought from the wood-engraver, W. J. Linton, stands on the eastern shore of Coniston Water, looking across the lake to Coniston Old Man.

This second diagram is from my sketch of the sky in the afternoon of the 6th of August, 1880, at Brantwood, two hours before sunset. You are looking west by north, straight towards the sun, and nearly straight towards the wind. From the west the wind blows fiercely towards you out of the blue sky. Under the blue space is a flattened dome of earth-cloud clinging to, and altogether masquing the form of, the mountain, known as the Old Man of Coniston.

The top of that dome of cloud is two thousand eight hundred feet above the sea, the mountain two thousand six hundred, the cloud lying two hundred feet deep on it. Behind it, westward and seaward, all's clear; but when the wind out of that blue clearness comes over the ridge of the earth-cloud, at that moment and that line, its own moisture congeals into these white – I believe, *ice*-clouds; threads, and meshes, and tresses, and tapestries, flying, failing, melting, reappearing; spinning and unspinning themselves, coiling and uncoiling, winding and unwinding, faster than eye or thought can follow: and through all their dazzling maze of frosty filaments shines a painted window in palpitation; its pulses of colour interwoven in motion, intermittent in fire, – emerald and ruby and pale purple and violet melting into a blue that is not of the sky, but of the sunbeam; – purer than the crystal, softer than the rainbow, and brighter than the snow.

> John Ruskin
> *The Storm-Cloud of the Nineteenth Century*
> Two Lectures delivered at the London Institution,
> 4 and 11 February 1884

Thunder at Coniston

22nd June 1876. Thunderstorm; pitch dark, with no *blackness*, – but deep, high, *filthiness* of lurid, yet not sublimely lurid, smoke-cloud; dense manufacturing mist; fearful squalls of shivery wind, making Mr Severn's sail quiver like a man in a fever fit – all about four, afternoon – but only two or three claps of thunder, and feeble, though near, flashes. I never saw such a dirty, weak, foul storm. It cleared suddenly, after raining all afternoon, at half-past eight to nine, into pure, natural weather, – low rain-clouds on quite clear, green, wet hills.

Brantwood 13th August, 1879. The most terrific and horrible thunderstorm, this morning, I ever remember. It waked me at six, or a little before – then rolling incessantly, like railway luggage trains, quite ghastly in its mockery of them – the air one loathsome mass of sultry and foul fog, like smoke; scarcely raining at all, but increasing to heavier rollings, with flashes quivering vaguely through all the air, and at last terrific double streams of reddish-violet fire, not forked or zig-zag, but rippled rivulets – two at the same instant some twenty to thirty degrees apart, and lasting on the eye at least half a second, with grand artillery-peals following, not rattling crashes, or irregular cracklings, but delivered volleys. It lasted an hour, then passed off, clearing a little, without rain to speak of, – not a glimpse of blue, – and now, half-past seven, seems settling down again into Manchester devil's darkness.

Quarter to eight, morning. – Thunder returned, all the air collapsed into one black fog, the hills invisible, and scarcely visible the opposite shore; heavy rain in short fits, and frequent, though less formidable, flashes, and shorter thunder. While I have written this sentence the cloud has again dissolved itself, like a nasty solution in a bottle, with miraculous and unnatural rapidity, and the hills are in sight again; a double-forked flash – rippled, I mean, like the others – starts into its frightful ladder of light between me and Wetherlam, as I raise my eyes. All black above, a rugged spray cloud on the Eaglet. (The 'Eaglet' is my own name for the bold and elevated crag to the west of the little lake above Coniston mines. It had no name among the country people, and is one of the most conspicuous features of the mountain chain, as seen from Brantwood.)

Half-past eight. – Three times light and three times dark since last I wrote, and the darkness seeming each time as it settles more loathsome, at last stopping my reading in mere blindness. One lurid gleam of white cumulous in upper lead-blue sky, seen for half a minute through the sulphurous chimney-pot vomit of blackguardly cloud beneath, where its rags were thinnest.

Thursday, 22nd Feb. 1883. Yesterday a fearfully dark mist all afternoon, with steady, south plague-wind of the bitterest, nastiest, poisonous blight, and fretful flutter. I could scarcely stay in the wood for the horror of it. To-day, really rather bright blue, and bright semi-cumuli, with the frantic Old Man blowing sheaves of lancets and chisels across the lake – not in strength enough, or whirl enough, to raise it in spray, but tracing every squall's outline in black on the silver grey waves, and whistling meanly, and as if on a flute made of a file.

Sunday, 17th August, 1879. Raining in foul drizzle, slow and steady; sky pitch-dark, and I just get a little light by sitting in the bow-window; diabolic clouds over everything: and looking over my kitchen garden yesterday, I found it one miserable mass of weeds gone to seed, the roses in the higher garden putrefied into brown sponges, feeling like dead snails; and the half-ripe strawberries all rotten at the stalks.

John Ruskin
The Storm-Cloud of the Nineteenth Century
Quoted from *Queen of the Air*

The Thunderstorm

When Coniston Old Man was younger
And his deep-quarried sides were stronger,
Goats may have leapt about Goat's Water;

But why the tarn that looks like its young daughter
Though lying high under the fell
Should be called Blind Tarn, who can tell?

For from Dow Crag, passing it by,
I saw it as a dark presageful eye;
And soon I knew that I was not mistaken
Hearing the thunder the loose echoes waken
About Scafell and Scafell Pike
And feeling the slant raindrops strike.

And when I came to Walna Pass
Hailstones hissing and hopping among the grass,
Beneath a rock I found a hole;
But with sharp crack and rumbling roll on roll
So quick the lightning came and went
The solid rock was like a lighted tent.

Andrew Young (1885–1971)

Storm

The occasion of this poem was the cloud-burst which fell on the central parts of the Lake District in August 1966; the beck is Coledale Beck, a tributary of Newlands, and the village is Braithwaite, near Keswick.

That Saturday evening I was at the pub
When it began – an exhilaration of lightning
As floury water like meal from a split sack
Stammered and slatted on slate roofs in our valley.
Other phenomena played up – thunder sledded
From rock to rock, hurrahing, grumbling with solid

Devotion to the increment of hubbub
While wind helped water to flog the trees again.

The Lake District

Every ditch and gutter aroar, each conduit choked,
The most alterable of elements at play
Footballing with boulders, boxing caryatid
Mountains until their entablature tottered.

Water fell like a wall or the blows of a club.
Whatever it was you could not call it rain.
I left my beer in a hurry and waded back
To see if the house where I lived were tight and dry
As overhead the elements shook and glittered
Underfoot my road already was a river.

Yet I didn't expect the animal under our bridge.
Familiar with the conversation of our stream
Below the garden wall, or sometimes, when in spate,
Its rougher habit, burlier and free,
I did not recognize the livid rapid
That lipped the bank and, reared on hind legs, battered

The stone arch, hurtling missiles – e.g. a tree-stub,
A concrete slab, and, once, a huge black oil-drum
Aimed slap at the bridge, travelled like a rocket.
The beck had its dander up, and wonderfully.
Three hours it went on. The village shop got flooded,
But the bridge held till the rain at last abated.

The catchment saved us and there was no landslip.
Nonetheless we agreed it had been a near thing –
What fool called out the fire-brigade, in that wet?
Still, they had worse than us up the next valley:
Breached walls and broken bridges, rivers gutted,
No lives lost though, just a farm or two bankrupted.

Today the light syllables at our doorstep
Recreate their bucolic, but I am not won,
Having seen the rocks gouged from a mountain slope
Witness that language, what it means to say,

And by what sufference I have inhabited
These aspects, neither loved by them nor hated.

David Wright

The Inundation at St John's-in-the-Vale

In the Second Edition of the Survey, *Clarke prefaces his account with the following comment: 'Travellers have been amused with various fictitious accounts of the innundation ... and exaggerated circumstances have crept into the productions of hasty writers, who thought proper to describe their journeys of pleasure to the public.'*

This rivulet [i.e. Mosedale Beck] is remarkable for having been the scene of the most dreadful and destructive innundation ever remembered in this country, and of which many awful vestiges may to this hour be traced; this happened on the 22nd of August 1749. All the evening of that day, horrid, tumultuous noises were heard in the air; sometimes a puff of wind would blow with great violence, then in a moment all was calm again. The inhabitants, used to bosom-winds, whirlwinds, and the howling of distant tempests among the rocks, went to bed as usual, and from the fatigues of the day were in a sound sleep when the innundation awoke them. About one in the morning rain began to fall, and before four such a quantity fell as covered the face of the country below with a sheet of water many feet deep: several houses were filled with sand to the first storey, many more driven down; and among the rest Legberthwate Mill, of which not one stone was left upon another; even the heavy millstones were washed away; one was found at a considerable distance, but the other was never discovered. Several persons were obliged to climb to the tops of the houses to escape instantaneous death; and there many (particularly those who were either worn out with age, or too weak to attempt a removal) were obliged to remain, in a situation of the most dreadful suspense, till the waters abated. Mr Mounsey of Wallthwaite says, that when he came down the stairs in the morning, the first sight he saw was a gander belonging to one of his neighbours, and several planks and kitchen-utensils, which were floating about his lower apartments, the violence of the waters having forced open the doors on both sides of the house. The most dreadful vestiges of this innundation, or water-spout, are at a place called *Lob-wath*, a little above *Wallthwaite*: here thousands of prodigious stones are piled upon each other, to the height of eleven yards; many of these stones are upward of 20 ton weight each, and are thrown together in such a manner as to be at once the object of curiosity and horror. Those who wish to see this place must turn in a gate which leads towards *Wallthwaite*, and is just before you arrive at the eleventh-mile post: it is necessary, however, to inform travellers, that they must proceed either on horseback or on foot to visit it, as a carriage will hardly be able to pass this road.

The quantity of water which had fallen here is truly astonishing, more particularly considering the small place it had to collect in. The distance from *Lob-wath* to *Wolf-Cragg* is not more than a mile and a half, and there could none collect much above Wolf-Cragg; nor did the whole rain extend more than eight miles in any direction . . . At *Melfell* (only three miles distant) the farmers were leading corn all night (as is customary when they fear ill weather) and no rain fell there; yet such was the fury of the descending torrent, that the fields at *Fornside* exhibited nothing but devastation. Here a large tree broken in two, there one torn up by the roots, and the ground every where covered with sand and stones.

Many falsehoods are related of this innundation; as, that a large stone came rolling from the mountains and rested a little above the school-house where the master and his scholars then were; and that this stone broke the force of the water, which would otherwise have carried away both the pedagogue and his pupils, together with their college. This story, tho' commonly told and believed, is a mere fiction, and no tradition of the kind is preserved in the neighbourhood.

James Clarke
A Survey of the Lakes (first edition, 1787)

The Helm Wind

The *helm-wind* . . . which frequently affects this tract of mountains [i.e. the Crossfell range], nearly forty miles in extent, is now to be considered. These heights are supposed to affect the weather, in a manner somewhat similar to what the inhabitants of the Malabar and Coromandel coasts experience; and what are called in this country *shedding-winds*, generally blow on the contrary sides of Cross-fell, from opposite quarters to the *helm-winds*; and the storms which rake the country on one side of the mountain, seldom affect the other. Upon the summits of this lofty ridge of mountains, there frequently hangs a vast volume of clouds, in a sullen and drowsy state, having little movement; this heavy collection of vapours often extends several miles in length, and dips itself from the summit, half way down to the base of those eminences; and frequently, at the same time, the other mountains in view are clear of mist, and shew no signs of rain. This *helm*, or cloud, exhibits an awful and solemn appearance, tinged with white by the sun's rays that strike the upper parts, and spreads a gloom below, over the inferior parts of the mountains, like the shadows of night. When this collection of vapour first begins to gather upon the hills, there is to be observed hanging about it, a black strip of cloud, continually flying off, and fed from the white part, which is the real *helm*; this strip is called the *helm-bar*, as, during its appearance, the winds are thought to be resisted by it; for, on its dispersion, they rage vehemently upon the vallies beneath. The direction of the *helm-bar* is parallel to that part of the main cloud or collection of vapour, that is tinged with white by being struck with the sun's rays; the *bar* appears in continual agitation, as boiling, or struggling with contrary blasts; whilst the *helm* all this time keeps a motionless station. When the *bar* is dispersed, the winds that issue from the *helm* are sometimes extremely violent; but that force seems to be in proportion to the real current of the winds which blow at a distance from the mountains, and which are frequently in a contrary direction, and then the *helm-wind* does not extend above two or three miles; without these impediments it seldom sweeps over a larger track than twelve miles, perhaps from the mere resistance of the lower atmosphere. It is remarkable, that at the base of the mountain the blasts are much less violent than in the middle region; and yet the hurricane is sometimes impetuous even there, bearing every thing before it, when at the distance of a few miles there is a dead calm, and a sunny sky. The spring is most favourable to this phenomenon, the *helm-wind* will sometimes blow for a fortnight, till the air in the lower regions, warmed before by the influence of the sun, is thereby rendered piercing cold.

From William Hutchinson's *The History of the County of Cumberland* (probably by John Housman)

The Irruption of Solway Moss

This singular occurrence took place somewhat outside the main area of the Lakes but the following account, from Pennant's tour of 1772, aroused much interest among the early tourists. It is fortunate that so level-headed a reporter as Thomas Pennant should have visited the district within a year of the disaster, so being able to gather his information at first-hand from the local inhabitants.

Solway Moss consists of sixteen hundred acres; lies some height above the cultivated tract, and seems to have been nothing but a collection of thin peaty mud: the surface itself was always so near the state of a quagmire, that in most places it was unsafe for any thing heavier than a sportsman to venture on, even in the driest summer.

The shell or crust that kept this liquid within bounds, nearest to the valley, was at first of sufficient strength to contain it: but by the imprudence of the peat-diggers, who were continually working on that side, at length became so weakened, as not longer to be able to resist the weight pressing on it . . .

Late in the night of the 17th of November of the last year, a farmer, who lived nearest the moss, was alarmed with an unusual noise. The crust had at once given way, and the black deluge was rolling towards his house, when he was gone out with a lantern to see the cause of his fright: he saw the stream approach him; and first thought that it was his dunghill, that by some supernatural cause, had been set in motion; but soon discovering the danger, he gave notice to his neighbours with all expedition: but others received no other advice but what this Stygian tide gave them: some by its noise, many by its entrance into their houses, and I have been assured that some were surprised with it even in their beds: these passed a horrible night, remaining totally ignorant of their fate, and the cause of their calamity, till the morning, when their neighbours, with difficulty, got them out through the roof. About three hundred acres of moss were thus discharged, and above four hundred of land covered; the houses either overthrown or filled to their roofs; and the hedges overwhelmed; but providentially not a human life lost; several cattle were suffocated; and those which were housed had very small chance of escaping. The case of a cow is so singular as to deserve mention. She was the only one out of eight, in the same cow-house, that was saved, after having stood sixty hours up to the neck in mud and water: when she was relieved, she did not refuse to eat, but would not taste water: nor could even look without shewing manifest signs of horror.

The irruption burst from the place of its discharge, like a cataract of thick ink; and continued in a stream of the same appearance, intermixed with great fragments of peat, with their heathy surface; then flowed like a tide charged with pieces of wreck, filling the whole valley, running up every little opening, and on its retreat, leaving upon the shore tremendous heaps of turf, memorials of the height this dark torrent arrived at. The farther it flowed, the more room it had to expand, lessening in depth, till it mixed its stream with that of the Esk.

Thomas Pennant
A Tour of Scotland and Voyage to the Hebrides in 1772

The Picturesque

Beauty in the Lap of Horrour

The 'ingenious person' was Charles Avison, organist of St Nicholas Church, Newcastle, and a composer whose work is gradually becoming more appreciated.

Of all the lakes in these romantic regions, the lake we are now examining seems to be most generally admired. It was once admirably characterized by an ingenious person, who, on his first seeing it, cryed out, *Here is beauty indeed – Beauty lying in the lap of Horrour!* We do not often find a happier illustration. Nothing conveys an idea of *beauty* more strongly, than the lake; nor of *horrour*, than the mountains; and the former *lying in the lap* of the latter, expresses in a strong manner the mode of their combination.

> William Gilpin
> *Observations . . . [on] the Mountains and Lakes of Cumberland and Westmorland*

Doctor Syntax in the Lakes

William Combe's satirical poem, 'The Tour of Dr Syntax in Search of the Picturesque', published, anonymously, in the Poetical Magazine, *was the first of a series of parodies of the travel books of the day and especially of William Gilpin. The book was illustrated with drawings by Rowlandson and became immensely popular, being reprinted many times, later under the title of 'Dr Syntax's Tour of the Lakes'. In the passage quoted, Dr Syntax has been patronizingly received by one of the gentry in the course of his journey to the Lakes.*

MY LORD
A truce, I pray, to your debate;
The hunters all impatient wait;
And much I hope our learned Clerk
Will take a gallop in the Park.

SYNTAX

Your sport, my Lord, I cannot take,
For I must go and hunt a lake;
And while you chase the flying deer,
I must fly off to *Windermere*.
'Stead of hallooing to a fox,
I must catch echoes from the rocks;
With curious eye and active scent,
I on the *picturesque* am bent.
This is my game, I must pursue it,
And make it where I cannot view it:
Tho' in good truth, but do not flout me,
I bear that self-same thing about me.
If in man's form you wish to see
The *picturesque*, pray look at me;
I am myself without a flaw,
The very *picturesque* I draw.
A Rector, on whose face so sleek
In vain you for a wrinkle seek;
In whose fair form, so fat and round,
No obtuse angle's to be found;
On such a shape no man of taste
Would his fine tints or canvas waste:
But take a Curate who's so thin,
His bones seem peeping thro' his skin;
Make him to stand, or walk or sit,
In any posture you think fit,
And, with all these nice points about him,
No well-taught painter e'er would scout him;
For with his air, and look and mien,
He'd give effect to any scene.
In my poor beast, as well as me,
A fine example you may see:
She's so abrupt in all her parts –
O what fine subjects for the arts!
That thus we travel on together,
With gentle gale or stormy weather;

And, tho' we trot along the plains,
Where one dead level ever reigns,
Or pace where rocks and mountains rise,
Who lift their heads, and brave the skies;
I, Doctor Syntax, and my horse,
Give to the landscape double force.

*

My Lord now sought th' expecting chase,
And Syntax in his usual pace,
When four long tedious days had pass'd,
The town of Keswick reach'd at last,
Where he his famous work prepar'd,
Of all his toil the hop'd reward.

Soon as the morn began to break,
Old Grizzle [i.e. his horse] bore him to the Lake,
Along the banks he gravely pac'd,
And all its various beauties trac'd;
When lo, a threat'ning storm appear'd;
Phoebus the scene no longer cheer'd:
The dark clouds sunk on ev'ry hill:
The floating mists the vallies fill:
Nature, transform'd, began to lour,
And threaten'd a tremendous show'r.
'I love,' he cried, 'to hear the rattle,
When elements contend in battle;
For I insist, tho' some may flout it,
Who write about it, and about it,
That we the *picturesque* may find
In thunder loud, or whistling wind:
And often, as I fully ween,
It may be heard as well as seen;
For, tho' a pencil cannot trace
A sound as it can paint a place,
The pen, in its poetic rage,
Can make it figure on the page.'

A fisherman, who pass'd that way,
Thought it civility to say –
'An' please you, Sir, 'tis all in vain
To take your prospects in the rain;
On horseback too you'll ne'er be able –
'Twere better sure to get a table.' –
'Thanks,' Syntax said, 'for your advice,
And faith, I'll take it in a trice;
For, as I'm moisten'd to the skin,
I'll seek a table at the Inn;' –
But Grizzle, in her haste to pass,
Lur'd by a tempting tuft of grass,
A luckless step now chanc'd to take,
And sous'd the Doctor in the Lake.

William Combe (1741–1823)
From *The Tour of Doctor Syntax in Search of the Picturesque* (1809)
(published anonymously)

Gentleman in a Hurry

It was customary, I am told, to dash by them [i.e. the Lakes] with an exclamation or two of 'Oh, how fine!' &c – or as a gentleman said to Robin Partridge the day after we were upon Windermere, 'Good God! how delightful! – how charming! – I could live here for ever! – Row on, row on, row on, row on;' and, after passing one hour of exclamations upon the Lake, and half an hour at Ambleside, he ordered his horses into his phaeton, and flew off to take (I doubt not) an equalling flying view of Derwentwater. Robin Partridge, when he told us of it, asked us if we thought the gentleman was as 'composed as he sud be?'

Joseph Budworth
A Fortnight's Ramble to the Lakes
From the Preface to the Second Edition (1795)

Ladies at Leisure

Monday 9th [June 1800]. In the morning W. cut the winter cherry tree. I sowed French beans and weeded. A coronetted landau went by, when we were sitting upon the sodded wall. The ladies (evidently tourists) turned an eye of interest upon our little garden and cottage.

Dorothy Wordsworth
Grasmere Journal

Persistence of an Honourable Traveller

Sarah Aust, or the Hon. Mrs Murray, visited the Lakes in 1794 and 1796, and was for many years celebrated as 'The First Lady of Quality to cross Honister Pass'.

The head of Buttermere is close to the village of Gatesgarth, and you will ride very near that lake all the way to the village of Buttermere: where is an alehouse, at which you can get admirable ale, and bread and cheese, perchance a joint of mutton.

Few people will like to sleep at the Buttermere alehouse; but, with the help of my own sheets, blanket, pillows, and counterpane, I lodged there a week very comfortably.

From Buttermere I one day walked to the Wad Mines, or black-lead mines, and returned over the top of Honister Crag. Another day, I walked over the mountains by Gatesgarth into Innerdale [Ennerdale], and through it to Inner Bridge [Ennerdale Bridge], on the whole, sixteen miles. If possible Innerdale should be seen, for it is beautiful, particularly about Gillerthwaite, at the head of the lake: and again at the foot of the lake, looking up the vale towards its head. At the ale-house at Inner Bridge, I was obliged to pass the night in a chair by the kitchen fire, there being not a bed in the house fit to put myself upon.

> Sarah Aust
> *A Companion and Useful Guide to the Beauties of Scotland and the Lakes* (1799)
> (third edition, 1810, under the name of the Hon. Mrs Murray Aust)

Miss Bennet Looks Forward to the Lakes

'We have not quite determined how far it shall carry us,' said Mrs Gardiner, 'but perhaps to the Lakes.'

No scheme could have been more agreeable to Elizabeth, and her acceptance of the invitation was most ready and grateful. 'My dear, dear aunt,' she rapturously cried, 'what delight, what felicity! You give me fresh life and vigour. Adieu to disappointment and spleen. What are men to rocks and mountains? Oh, what hours of transport we shall spend! And when we *do* return, it shall not be like other travellers, without being able to give one accurate idea of anything. We *will* know where we have gone – we *will* recollect what we have seen. Lakes, mountains, and rivers shall not be jumbled together in our imaginations; nor, when we attemp᷄ to describe any particular scene, will we begin quarrelling about its relative situation. Let *our* first effusions be less insupportable than those of the generality of travellers.'

> Jane Austen (1775–1817)
> *Pride and Prejudice*

Echoes on Ullswater

Hutchinson's first 'excursion' to the Lakes was made in 1772.

Whilst we sate to regail, the barge put off from shore, to a station where the finest echoes were to be obtained from the surrounding mountains. – The vessel was provided with six brass cannon, mounted on swivels; – on discharging one of these pieces, the report was echoed from the opposite rocks, where by reverberation it seemed to roll from cliff to cliff, and return through every cave and valley; till the decreasing tumult gradually died away upon the ear.

The instant it had ceased, the sound of every distant water-fall was heard, but for an instant only; for the momentary stillness was interrupted by the returning echo on the hills behind; where the report was repeated like a peal of thunder bursting over our heads, continuing for several seconds, flying from haunt to haunt, till once more the sound gradually declined; – again the voice of water-falls possessed the interval; – till to the right, the more distant thunder arose upon some other mountain, and seemed to take its way up every winding dell and creek, sometimes behind, on this side, or on that, in wondrous speed, running its dreadful course; – when the echo reached the mountains within the line and channel of the breeze, it was heard at once on the right and left, at the extremities of the lake. – In this manner was the report of every discharge re-echoed seven times distinctly.

At intervals we were relieved from this entertainment, which consisted of a kind of wond'rous tumult and grandeur of confusion, by the music of two French horns, whose harmony was repeated from every recess which echo haunted on the borders of the lake; – here the breathings of the organ were imitated, there the bassoon with clarinets; – in this place from the harsher sounding rocks, the cornet; – in that from the wooded creek, amongst the caverns and the trilling water-falls, we heard the soft-toned lute accompanied with the languishing strains of enamoured nymphs; whilst in the copse and grove was still retained the music of the horns. All this vast theatre was possessed by innumerable aerial beings, who breathed celestial harmony.

As we finished our repast, a general discharge of the guns roused us to new astonishment; although we had heard with great surprise the former echoes, this exceeded them so much that it seemed incredible: for on every hand, the sounds were reverberated and returned from side to side, so as to give the semblance of that confusion and horrid uproar, which the falling of these stupendous rocks would occasion, if by some internal combustion they were rent to pieces, and hurled into the lake.

William Hutchinson
An Excursion to the Lakes in Westmorland and Cumberland

The Bowder Stone

Southey's Letter from England appeared in 1807, and purported to be by 'Don Manuel Alvarez Espriella. Translated from the Spanish'. Espriella is, in fact, entirely fictitious, and the nom de plume was used by Southey to allow himself to write a very lively mixture of travelogue, social comment and satire. The Bowder Stone of Borrowdale is the largest glacial erratic in the district. Southey was mistaken in saying that it had 'fallen from the heights'.

Another mile of broken ground, the most interesting which I ever traversed, brought us to a single rock called the Bowder Stone, a fragment of great size which has fallen from the heights. The same person [i.e. Mr Pocklington] who formerly disfigured the island in Keswick Lake with so many abominations, has been at work here also; has built a little mock hermitage, set up a new druidical stone, erected an ugly house for an old woman to live in who is to show the rock, for fear travellers should pass under it without seeing it, cleared away all the fragments round it, and as-it rests upon a narrow base, like a ship upon its keel, dug a hole underneath through which the curious may gratify themselves by shaking hands with the old woman. The oddity of this amused us greatly, provoking as it was to meet with such hideous buildings in such a place, – for the place is as beautiful as eyes can behold or imagination conceive. The river flows immediately below, of that pale green transparency which we sometimes see in the last light of the evening sky; a shelf of pebbles on the opposite shore shows where it finds its way through a double channel when swoln by rains: – the rest of the shore is covered with a grove of young trees which reach the foot of a huge single crag, half clothed with brush-wood: – this crag [i.e. Castle Crag] when seen from Keswick appears to block up the pass. Southward we looked down into Borrowdale, whither we were bound; – a vale which appeared in the shape of a horse-shoe.

> Robert Southey
> *Letters from England: by Don Manuel Alvarez Espriella*

Echoes on Derwentwater

But the pride of the Lake of Keswick is the head, where the mountains of Borrowdale bound the prospect, in a wilder and grander manner than words can adequately describe. The cataract of Lodore thunders down its eastern side through a chasm in the rocks, which are wooded with birch and ash trees. It is a little river, flowing from a small lake upon the mountains about a league distant. The water, though there had been heavy rains, was not adequate to the channel; – indeed it would require a river of considerable magnitude to fill it, – yet it is at once the finest work and instrument of rock and water that I have ever seen or heard. At a little public-house near where the key of the entrance is kept, they have a cannon to display the echo; it was discharged for us, and we heard the sound rolling round from hill to hill, – but for this we paid four shillings, – which are very nearly a peso duro. So that English echoes appear to be the most expensive luxuries in which a traveller can indulge. It is true there was an inferior one which would have cost only two shillings and sixpence; but when one buys an echo, who would be content for the sake of saving eighteen pence, to put up with the second best, instead of ordering at once the super-extra-double-superfine?

Robert Southey
Letters from England: by Don Manuel Alvarez Espriella

A Capital Curiosity

Peter Crosthwaite was as remarkable a curiosity as any in his own collection. He was born near Keswick, and, after serving at sea and as an excise officer, he returned to Cumberland and made detailed surveys of most of the Lakes, published a charming set of maps, and, by reason of his naval experience, was appointed Admiral of Mr Pocklington's 'fleet' on Derwentwater. His museum was fitted with a barrel-organ, the music of which greeted distinguished visitors as they walked down the street. Joseph Budworth claimed to have received this 'acknowledgement' about six times.

KESWICK, August 25, 1792
PETER CROSTHWAITE,
FORMERLY NAVAL COMMANDER IN INDIA,
Surveyor and Seller of the Maps of the Lakes,
MASTER of the Celebrated MUSEUM,
(of eleven years standing)
At the Quadrant, Telescope, and Weathercock,
A little below the MIDDLE OF KESWICK,

RETURNS his most grateful Thanks to the NOBILITY, GENTRY, and OTHERS, for crowning his Labour with Success. His House is the loftiest in *Keswick*, and has the Advantage of most delightful Prospects quite round the Vale.

In 1784, *Sir Ashton Lever*, and several other able Virtuosos, declared his Museum the most capital one *North of Trent*. Since which Time it is improved as Three to One. – It consists of many Hundred Natural

and Artificial Curiosities, from every Quarter of the World; the
Fossils, Spontaneous *Plants*, and *Antiquities* of *Cumberland*; *Coins*,
Medals, *Arms*, *Quadrupeds*, *Birds*, *Insects*, *Shells*, *Landscapes*, *Pictures*,
Grottos, and his much admired *Organ*; together with many Models
and useful Inventions of his own; and if it were not for the low
Cunning, and mischievous Falsehoods continually circulated against
him by an ungrateful Junto of Imposters in the Place, it is thought few
of the Gentry would pass him; but, being covetous to an Extreme,
and much hurt by Envy, they take all Advantages of misleading the
Gentry to this Day; and all this after he has laid out several Hundred
Pounds in the Museum, and spent near Thirteen Years of his Time in
collecting Curiosities, making and repairing roads, Surveying the
Lakes, &c, &c. all which has been done for the better entertainment
of the Gentry, and an honest Livelihood for his Family.

Admittance to LADIES and GENTLEMEN, *One Shilling* each;
COUNTRY PEOPLE, *Sixpence* each. – Open from 7 A.M. till 10 P.M.

He has sold many Thousand Maps of the Lakes, and shews un-
deniable Certificates as to their Accuracy and masterly Engraving.
They are now sold at his MUSEUM, at *Nine Shillings* per Set (single
Maps at *Eighteen-Pence* each) he having made an additional Survey
and added every Thing which could be thought necessary or useful
to the Tourist.

He also sells *Mr Farrington's* Twenty *Landscapes* of the *Lakes*; *Mr
Donald's Map of Cumberland*; his *Map* of the *Environs* of *Keswick*;
West's and *Shaw's* GUIDES; *Gray's* Landscape Glasses; *Claud Lorain's*
Do. Pocket Compasses, Music, Spar, &c. and hopes to merit the
future Favour of the Nobility, Gentry, and Others: having added
several capital Curiosities since last November.

Handbill for Crosthwaite's Museum, 1792

The Lake District

Ups and Downs of Travel

Thence I rode almost all the waye in sight of this great water [i.e. Windermere]; sometymes I lost it by reason of the great hills inter-poseing and so I continu'd up hill and down hill and that pretty steep even when I was in that they called bottoms, which are very rich good grounds, and so I gained by degrees from lower to higher hills which I allwayes went up and down before I came to another hill; at last I attained to the side of one of these hills or fells of rocks which I passed on the side much about the middle; for looking down to the bottom it was at least a mile all full of those lesser hills and inclosures, so looking upward I was as farre from the top which was all rocks and something more barren tho' there was some trees and woods growing in the rocks and hanging over all down the brow of some of the hills.

Celia Fiennes
Through England on a Side Saddle

By Cart over Kirkstone

The party ascended to Kirkstone by the direct route from Ambleside, now known as 'The Struggle'.

On the third morning after my arrival in Grasmere, I found the whole family [i.e. the Wordsworths], except the two children, prepared for the expedition across the mountains. I had heard of no horses, and took it for granted that we were to walk; however, at the moment of starting, a cart – the common farmer's cart of the country – made its appearance; and the driver was a bonny young woman of the vale. Such a vehicle I had never in my life seen used for such a purpose; but what was good enough for the Wordsworths was good enough for me; and, accordingly, we were all carted along to the little town, or large village, of Ambleside – three and a half miles distant. Our style of travelling occasioned no astonishment; on the contrary, we met a smiling salutation wherever we appeared – Miss Wordsworth being, as I observed, the person most familiarly known of our party, and the one who took upon herself the whole expenses of the flying colloquies exchanged with stragglers on the road. What struck me with most astonishment, however, was the liberal manner of our fair driver, who made no scruple of taking a leap, with the reins in her hand, and seating herself dexterously upon the shafts (or, in Westmoreland phrase, the *trams*) of the cart. From Ambleside – and without one foot of intervening flat ground – begins to rise the famous ascent of Kirkstone; after which, for three long miles, all riding in a cart drawn by one horse becomes impossible. The ascent is computed at three miles, but is, probably, a little more. In some parts it is almost frightfully steep; for the road, being only the original mountain track of shepherds, gradually widened and improved from age to age (especially since the era of tourists began), is carried over ground which no engineer, even in alpine countries, would have viewed as practicable. In ascending, this is felt chiefly as an obstruction and not as a peril, unless where there is a risk of the horses backing; but in the reverse order, some of these precipitous descents are terrific; and yet once, in utter darkness, after midnight, and the darkness irradiated only by continual streams of lightning, I was driven down this whole descent, at a full gallop, by a young woman – the carriage being a light one, the horses frightened, and the descents at some critical parts of the road, so literally like the sides of a house, that it was difficult to keep the fore wheels from pressing upon the hind legs of the horses ... The innkeeper of Ambleside, or Lowwood, will not mount this formidable hill without four horses. The leaders you are not required to take beyond the first three miles; but, of course, they are glad if you will take them on the whole stage of nine miles, to Patterdale; and, in that case, there is a real luxury at hand for those who enjoy velocity of motion. The descent into Patterdale is much above two miles; but such is the propensity for flying down hills in Westmoreland, that I have found the descent accomplished in about six minutes, which is at the rate of eighteen miles an hour; the various turnings of the road making the speed much more sensible to the traveller.

Thomas De Quincey (1785–1859)
Recollections of the Lake Poets

The Lake District

By Stage-Coach to Windermere

Hawthorne's visit to the Lakes was made in 1855. He caught a train at Windermere for Lancaster.

We spent the day yesterday at Grasmere, in quiet walks about the hotel; and at a little past six in the afternoon, I took my departure in the stage-coach for Windermere. The coach was greatly overburdened with outside passengers – fifteen in all, besides the four insiders – and one of the fifteen formed the apex of an immense pile of luggage on the top. It seems to me miraculous that we did not topple over, the road being so hilly and uneven, and the driver, I suspect, none the steadier for his visits to all the tap-rooms along the route from Cockermouth. There was a tremendous vibration of the coach now and then; and I saw that, in case of our going over, I should be flung headlong against the high stone fence that bordered most of the road. In view of this I determined to muffle my head in the folds of my thick shawl at the moment of overturn, and as I could do no better for myself, I awaited my fate with equanimity. As far as apprehension goes, I had rather travel from Maine to Georgia by rail, than from Grasmere to Windermere by stage-coach.

Nathaniel Hawthorne (1804–1864)
English Note-Books

Them Ramm'lers: A Cumbrian's Soliloquy

Ay, spooart's awreet – That's if ye've nowte ta de:
Bit wher's t'spooart i' this hiking? Nay, t'caps me!

I'summer, us chaps up on t'fells
Wark leeat, fra early mworn
We're oalas gaan till t'hay's in t'barn,
An' than we start o't'cworn:
cworn: oats

176

Bit any hour, be day, be neet,
Whativver t'wedder's like,
Ah'll gammel we'll see straangers:
'Em 'at gaas oot ta hike.

    Th're toakers, trampers, hikers, woakers,
    Ramm'lers, climmers, guides:
    Ah dun't knaa wh're the' git the're spooart
    I' swammelan' up t'fell-sides.

Th're nut togged up i'city cleas,
The' dun't put on nee swank,
Bit anytime, the're i' the're prime
When scallan' sum brant bank.
An' when the've scraffelt oot at t'top
The' luik on t'rwoad the 've clumb,
An' than, as like as nut, the'll say:
'T's bin wurth oor while ta cum . . .

    'Luiksta: that beck a siller thrid,
    An' t'pas'ter, frush and green,
    That crag (a rock at's cracked an' brock)
    Hoo wunnerful it's bin!
    Noo we moant bide, we med git gaan
    Ta sceeal sum udder heyt' . . .
    Away the' gaa . . . the're lost ta seet
    An' will be until neet.

Us chaps, if we'd sum time ta kill,
We wadn't swammel t'fells:
When we gaa gedderan t'Herdwick tups
We sumhoo cure oorsels –
We med gang theer if t'hoonds led t'way,
When t'air's frost-nipped an' chill . . .

    Bit, what due them fwoak due it fer?
    Nay, man! It caps ma still!

Lance Porter (twentieth century)

Wordsworth Foresees the National Park

It is then much to be wished that a better taste should prevail among these new proprietors; and, as they cannot be expected to leave things to themselves, that skill and knowledge should prevent unnecessary deviations from that path of simplicity and beauty along which, without design and unconsciously, their humble predecessors have moved. In this wish the author will be joined by persons of pure taste throughout the whole island, who, by their visits (often repeated) to the Lakes in the North of England, testify that they deem the district a sort of national property, in which every man has a right and interest who has an eye to perceive and a heart to enjoy.

William Wordsworth
A Guide to the Lakes

Legend and History

The Legend of St Herbert of Derwentwater

There was a certain priest, venerable for the probity of his life and manners, called Herebert, who had long been united with the man of God, Cuthbert [i.e. St Cuthbert of Lindisfarne], in the bonds of spiritual friendship. This man leading a solitary life in the island of that great lake from which the river Derwent flows, was wont to visit him every year, and to receive from him spiritual advice. Hearing that Bishop Cuthbert was come to the city of Lugubalia [i.e. Carlisle], he repaired thither to him, according to custom, being desirous to be still more and more inflamed in heavenly desires through his wholesome admonitions. Whilst they alternately entertained one another with the delights of the celestial life, the bishop, among other things, said, 'Brother Herebert, remember at this time to ask me all the questions you wish to have resolved, and say all you design; for we shall see one another no more in this world. For I am sure that the time of my dissolution is at hand, and I shall speedily put off the tabernacle of the flesh.' Hearing these words, he [i.e. Herebert] fell down at his feet, and shedding tears, with a sigh, said, 'I beseech you, by our Lord, not to forsake me; but that you remember your most faithful companion, and entreat the Supreme Goodness that, as we served Him together upon earth, we may depart together to see his bliss in heaven. For you know that I have always endeavoured to live according to your directions, and whatsoever faults I have committed, either through ignorance or frailty, I have instantly submitted to your correction according to your will.' The bishop applied himself to prayer, and having presently had intimation in the spirit that he had obtained what he asked of the Lord, he said, 'Rise, brother, and do not weep, but rejoice, because the Heavenly Goodness has granted what we desired.'

The event proved the truth of this promise and prophecy, for after their parting at that time, they no more saw one another in the flesh; but their souls quitting their bodies on the very same day, that is, on the 20th of March, they were immediately again united in spirit, and translated to the heavenly kingdom by the ministry of angels. But Herebert was first prepared by a tedious sickness, through the dispensation of the Divine Goodness, as may be believed, to the end that if he was anything inferior in merit to the blessed Cuthbert, the same might be made up by the chastising pain of a long sickness, that being thus made equal in grace to his intercessor, as he departed out of the body at the very same time with him, so he might be received into the same seat of eternal bliss.

> The Venerable Bede (673–735)
> *The Ecclesiastical History of the English Nation*
> (translated from the Latin by John Stevens)

The Legend of St Cuthbert

At the back of the choir stalls in Carlisle Cathedral can be seen several sets of fifteenth-century paintings depicting the lives of St Augustine, St Anthony and St Cuthbert. The following rhymes – based on Bede's Life and Miracles of St Cuthbert – are taken from those dealing with the saint who has a particular link with the diocese, both as the friend of St Herbert of Derwentwater and as the evangelist who was said to have preached the Christian faith in Carlisle, in the seventh century, on the orders of Ecgfrith, King of Northumbria. The pictures and rhymes are in a reasonable state of preservation but the reading of some of the words must be a matter of conjecture.

1. Her Cuthbert was forbid layks and plays
   As Bede in his story says.

2. Her the angel did hym care
   And made his sore to hele.

3. Her saw he Aydan's sawl upgo
   To hevyns bliss wt angels two.

4. Her to hym and hys palfray
   God fand them fude in his journey.

5. Her on Mellrose for to converse.
   Wt h g boisle and laws reherse.

6. The angel he did as geste refreshe
   Wt mete & drynk and his fete weshe.

7. Her Bosel told him yt must die
   And after yt he bysshop should be.

8. Her to his breden & pepyl eke
   He preched God's word mylde & mek.

9. Her stude he nakyd in the se
   Till all David's Psalter sayd had he.

10. He was gedyd by the egle fre
    And fed with the delfyne as ye se.

11. Her by prayers fendys out farn glad
    And with angels hands hys house made.

12. Fresh water God sent out of the ston
    To him in Farne & before was non.

13. The crowys yt did his hous unthek
    Ys for full law fell at hys fete.

14. Consecrate Byshop yai made hy' her
    Of Lyndisfarne both far & nere.

15. To this child Gòd grace
    Thro hys prayers as ye may se.

16. Bisshop two yeares when he had beyn
    In Farne he died both holy & clene.

17. XI yeare after beryd was he
    Yai found hole as red may ye.

Notes:
1. *Layks:* sports
3. St Aidan, Bishop of Lindisfarne
4. God found them food.
5. The Abbey of Melrose
   'Boisil' – a holy man, see stanza 7 – 'was standing before the doors of the monastery, and saw him first. Foreseeing in spirit what an illustrious man the stranger would become, he made this single remark to the bystanders: "Behold a servant of the Lord!".' From Bede's *Life and Miracles of St Cuthbert*.
7. That he must die.
10. He was guided by an eagle to find a fish (delfyne) for his food.
11. He drove the fiends out of the Farne Islands.
    The second line has no basis in Bede.
13. *Unthek:* un-thatch
    Ys for full law fell at hys fete: the crows apologized to him for the harm they had done.
15. He cured a child of the plague by making the sign of the cross over him.
17. They found his body undecayed as you may read (red).

Anonymous (fifteenth century)

The Ballad of Tarn Wadling
or
The Marriage of Sir Gawain

Tarn Wadling, in the parish of Hesket in the Forest, between Penrith and Carlisle, was well-known in medieval times but was drained in the nineteenth century. Close by is the site of Castle Hewin or Ewain, the name of which may be connected with Sir Gawain. There are many sites in Cumberland traditionally associated with King Arthur.

Kinge Arthur lives in merry Carleile,
    And seemely is to see,
And there he hath with him Queene Genever,
    That bride soe bright of blee.
blee: complexion

And there he hath with him Queene Genever,
   That bride soe bright in bower.
And all his barons about him stoode,
   That were both stiffe and stowre.

*The King was riding by Tarn Wadling, in the Forest of Inglewood,
when he was challenged by a fierce giant, armed with a club, who offered him
a choice between fighting and ransom. For ransom, the King must return on
New Year's Day, and answer the giant's riddle.*

'And bring me word what thing it is
   That a woman will most desire;
This shalbe thy ransom, Arthur,' he sayes,
   'For I'le have noe other hier.'

King Arthur then held up his hand,
   According thene as was the law;
He tooke his leave of the baron there,
   And homeward can he draw . . .

*Then King Arthur collected and wrote down many answers to the giant's
riddle, and set off, on New Year's Day, to keep his promise.*

Then King Arthur drest him for to ryde,
   In one soe rich array.
Toward the fore-said Tearne Wadling,
   That he might keepe his day.

And as he rode over a more,
   Hee see a lady where shee sate
Betwixt an oke and a greene hollen;
   She was cladd in red scarlett.

Then thereas shold have stood her mouth,
   Then there was sett her eye;
The other was in her forhead fast,
   The way that she might see.

stowre: strong
hollen: holly-tree

Her nose was crooked and turn'd outward,
  Her mouth stood foule a-wry;
A worse form'd lady than shee was,
  Never man saw with his eye.

To halch upon him, King Arthur,
  This lady was full faine,
But King Arthur had forgott his lesson,
  What he shold say againe.

'What knight art thou,' the lady sayd,
  'That will not speak to me?
Of me be thou nothing desmayd,
  Tho I be ugly to see.

'For I have halched you curteouslye,
  And you will not me againe;
Yett I may happen Sir Knight,' shee said,
  'To ease thee of thy paine.'

'Give thou ease me, lady,' he said,
  'Or helpe me any thing,
Thou shalt have gentle Gawaine, my cozen,
  And marry him with a ring.'

  The hag thereupon gave him the right answer to the riddle and he rode forward.

And when he came to the Tearne Wadling.
  The baron there cold he finde,
With a great weapon on his backe,
  Standing stiffe and stronge.

And then he tooke King Arthur's letters in his hands,
  And away he cold them fling,
And then he puld out a good browne sword,
  And cryd himself a king.

halch: salute

And he sayd, 'I have thee and thy land, Arthur.
   To doe as it pleaseth me,
For this is not thy ransome sure,
   Therfore yeeld thee to me.'

And then bespoke him noble Arthur,
   And bad him hold his hand:
'And give me leave to speake my mind
   In defence of all my land.'

He said, 'As I came over a more,
   I see a lady where shee sate
Between an oke and a green hollen;
   Shee was clad in red scarlett.

'And she says a woman will have her will,
   And this is all her cheef desire:
Doe me right, as thou art a baron of sckill,
   This is thy ransome and all thy hyer.'

He sayes, 'An early vengeance light on her!
   She walkes on yonder more;
It was my sister that told thee this,
   As shee heard it of me before.

'But heer I'le make mine avow to God
   To doe her an evill turne;
Fo an ever I may thate fowle theefe get,
   In a fyer I will her burne.'

   The King, having returned home, told his knights that he had found in the forest a bride for one of them, and they rode out to seek her.

And when he came to the greene forrest,
   Underneath a greene holly tree,
Their sate that lady in red scarlett
   That unseemly was to see.

Sir Kaye beheld this lady's face,
   And looked uppon her swire;
'Whosoever kisses this lady,' he sayes,
   'Of his kisse he stands in feare.'

Sir Kay beheld the lady againe.
   And looked upon her snout;
'Whosoever kisses this lady,' he saies,
   'Of his kisse he stands in doubt.'

'Peace, cozen Kay,' then said Sir Gawaine,
   'Amend thee of thy life;
For there is a knight amongst us all
   That must marry her to his wife.'

'What! wedd her to wiffe!' then said Sir Kay,
   'In the divell's name anon!
Gett me a wiffe where-ere I may,
   For I had rather be slaine!'

Then some tooke up their hawkes in hast,
   And some tooke up their hounds,
And some sware they wold not marry her
   For citty nor for towne.

And then be-spake him noble King Arthur,
   And sware there by this day.
For a little foule sight and misliking
   They shold not say her Nay.

At length Sir Gawaine, for Arthur's sake, consented. The ugly bride was taken home and bedded, when she turned in Gawaine's arms into a beautiful woman. She then offered him the choice, whether he would have her ugly by day and beautiful by night, or beautiful by day and ugly by night.

And then bespake him gentle Gawaine,
   Said, 'Lady, that's but skill;

swire: neck

And because thou art my owne lady,
   Thou shalt have all thy will.'

Then she said, 'Blessed be thou, gentle Gawaine.
   This day that I thee see!
For as thou seest me att this time,
   From henceforth I wilbe.

'My father was an old knight,
   And yett it chancèd soe
That he marryed a younge lady
   That brought me to this woe.

'Shee witched me, being a faire young lady,
   To the greene forrest to dwell,
And there I must walke in woman's likeness,
   Most like a feend of hell.'

*Having thus been given what a woman most desires – that is, her will –
she is released from the spell and becomes beautiful at all times; and Sir
Gawaine leads his lady among the knights, to present her to the King and
Queen.*

Sir Gawaine tooke the lady by the one arme,
   Sir Kay tooke her by the tother,
They led her straight to King Arthur,
   As they were brother and brother.

King Arthur welcomed them there all,
   And soe did Lady Genever his queene,
With all the knights of the Round Table,
   Most seemly to be seene.

King Arthur beheld that lady faire
   That was soe faire and bright,
He thanked Christ in Trinity
   For Sir Gawaine that gentle knight.

Soe did the knights, both more and lesse,
   Rejoyced all that day
For the good chance that hapened was
   To Sir Gawaine and his lady gay.

                Anonymous (perhaps fifteenth century)

The Legend of the Vale of St John

For Hutchinson's comment on the noon-day stars, see page 149.

King Arthur has ridden from merry Carlisle
   When Pentecost was o'er:
He journey'd like errant-knight the while,
And sweetly the summer sun did smile
   On mountain, moss, and moor.
Above his solitary track
Rose Glaramara's ridgy back,
Amid whose yawning gulfs the sun
Cast umber'd radiance red and dun,
Though never sunbeam could discern
The surface of that sable tarn,
In whose black mirror you may spy
The stars, while noontide lights the sky
The gallant King he skirted still
The margin of that mighty hill;
Rock upon rocks incumbent hung,
And torrents, down the gullies flung,
Join'd the rude river that brawl'd on,
Recoiling now from crag and stone,
Now diving deep from human ken,
And raving down its darksome glen.
The Monarch judged this desert wild,
With such romantic ruin piled,

Was theatre by Nature's hand
For feat of high achievement plann'd.

He rode, till over down and dell
The shade more broad and deeper fell;
And though around the mountain's head
Flow'd streams of purple, and gold, and red,
Dark at the base, unblest by beam
Frown'd the black rocks, and roar'd the stream.
With toil the King his way pursued
By lonely Threlkeld's waste and wood,
Till on his course obliquely shone
The narrow valley of SAINT JOHN,
Down sloping to the western sky,
Where lingering sunbeams love to lie.
Right glad to feel those beams again,
The King drew up his charger's rein;
With gauntlet raised he screen'd his sight,
As dazzled with the level light,
And, from beneath his glove of mail,
Scann'd at his ease the lovely vale,
While 'gainst the sun his armour bright
Gleam'd ruddy like a beacon's light.

Paled in by many a lofty hill,
The narrow dale lay smooth and still,
And, down its verdant bosom led,
A winding brooklet found its bed.
But, midmost of the vale, a mound
Arose with airy turrets crown'd,
Buttress, and rampire's circling bound,
    And mighty keep and tower;
Seem'd some primeval giant's hand
The castle's massive walls had plann'd,
A ponderous bulwark to withstand
    Ambitious Nimrod's power.
Above the moated entrance slung,

The balanced drawbridge trembling hung,
  As jealous of a foe;
Wicket of oak, as iron hard,
With iron studded, clench'd, and barr'd,
And prong'd portcullis, join'd to guard
  The gloomy pass below.
But the grey walls no banners crown'd,
Upon the watch-tower's airy round
No warder stood his horn to sound,
No guard beside the bridge was found,
And, where the Gothic gateway frown'd,
  Glanc'd neither bill nor bow.

King Arthur enters the enchanted castle where, beguiled by the beautiful witch, Guendolen, he neglects his royal duties and leaves Britain undefended against the invaders. At last, early in the morning, he decides to break free from the witch's spell, and rides out from the castle walls.

The Monarch gave a passing sigh
To penitence and pleasures by,
When lo! to his astonish'd ken
Appear'd the form of Guendolen.
Beyond the outmost wall she stood,
Attired like huntress of the wood:
Sandall'd her feet, her ankles bare,
And eagle-plumage deck'd her hair;
Firm was her look, her bearing bold,
And in her hand a cup of gold.
'Thou goest!' she said, 'and ne'er again
Must we two meet, in joy or pain.
Full fain would I this hour delay,
Though weak the wish – yet, wilt thou stay?
No! thou look'st forward. Still, attend!
Part we like lover and like friend.'
She raised the cup – 'Not this the juice
The sluggish vines of earth produce;
Pledge we at parting, in the draught

Which Genii love!' She said, and quaff'd;
And strange unwonted lustres fly
From her flush'd cheek and sparkling eye.

The courteous Monarch bent him low,
And, stooping down from saddlebow,
Lifted the cup, in act to drink.
A drop escaped the goblet's brink –
Intense as liquid fire from hell,
Upon the charger's neck it fell.
Screaming with agony and fright,
He bolted twenty feet upright!
The peasant still can show the dint
Where his hoofs lighted on the flint.
From Arthur's hand the goblet flew,
Scattering a shower of fiery dew,
That burn'd and blighted where it fell!
The frantic steed rush'd up the dell,
As whistles from the bow the reed;
Nor bit nor rein could check his speed
    Until he gain'd the hill;
Then breath and sinew fail'd apace,
And, reeling from the desperate race,
    He stood, exhausted, still.
The Monarch, breathless and amazed,
Back on the fatal castle gazed:
Nor tower nor donjon could he spy;
Darkening against the morning sky;
But, on the spot where once they frown'd,
The lonely streamlet brawl'd around
A tufted knoll, where dimly shone
Fragments of rock and rifted stone . . .

Know, too, that when a pilgrim strays,
In morning mist or evening maze,
    Along the mountain lone,
That fairy fortress often mocks

His gaze upon the castled rocks
  Of the Valley of Saint John;
But never man since brave De Vaux
  The charmed portal won.
'Tis now a vain illusive show,
That melts whene'er the sunbeams glow
  Or the fresh breeze hath blown.

> Walter Scott
> From *The Bridal of Triermain*

The Castle Rocks of St John's

We now gained a view of the vale of ST JOHN'S; a very narrow dell, hemmed in by mountains, through which a small brook makes many meanderings, washing little inclosures of grass ground, which stretch up the risings of the hills. – In the widest part of the dale you are struck with the appearance of an ancient ruined castle, which seems to stand upon the summit of a little mount, the mountains around forming an amphitheatre. This massive bulwark shews a front of various towers, and makes an awful, rude, and gothic appearance, with its lofty turrets, and ragged battlements; we traced the galleries, the bending arches, the buttresses; the greatest antiquity stands characterized in its architecture; the inhabitants near it assert it is an antediluvian structure.

The traveller's curiosity is rouzed, and he prepares to make a nearer approach, when that curiosity is put upon the rack, by his being assured, that if he advances, certain genii who govern the place, by virtue of their supernatural arts and necromancy, will strip it of all its beauties, and by inchantment transform the magic walls. The vale seems adapted for the habitation of such beings; its gloomy recesses and retirements look like haunts of evil spirits; there was no delusion in this report, we were soon convinced of its truth; for this piece of antiquity, so venerable and noble in its aspect, as we drew near, changed its figure, and proved no other than a shaken massive pile of rocks, which stand in the midst of this little vale, disunited from the adjoining mountains; and have so much the real form and resemblance of a castle, that they bear the name of THE CASTLE ROCKS OF ST JOHN'S.

William Hutchinson
An Excursion to the Lakes

The Ghostly Bells of Borrowdale

Each matin bell, the Baron saith,
Knells us back to a world of death,
These words Sir Leoline first said,
When he rose and found his lady dead:
These words Sir Leoline will say
Many a morn to his dying day!

And hence the custom and law began
That still at dawn the sacristan,
Who duly pulls the heavy bell
Five and forty beads must tell
Between each stroke – a warning knell,
Which not a soul can choose but hear
From Bratha Head to Wyndermere.

Saith Bracy the bard, So let it knell!
And let the drowsy sacristan
Still count as slowly as he can!
There is no lack of such, I ween,
As well fill up the space between.
In Langdale Pike and Witch's Lair,
And Dungeon-ghyll so foully rent,
With ropes of rock and bells of air
Three sinful sextons' ghosts are pent,

Who all give back, one after t'other,
The death note to their living brother;
And oft too, by the knell offended,
Just as their one! two! three! is ended,
The devil mocks the doleful tale
With a merry peal from Borodale.

S. T. Coleridge
From *Christabel*, Part 2

The Phantoms of Souther Fell

The spelling 'Souther' is more usual today.

On Midsummer eve, 1735, William Lancaster's servant related, that
he saw the east side of Souter-fell, towards the top, covered with a
regular marching army for above an hour together; he said they
consisted of distinct bodies of troops, which appeared to proceed
from an eminence in the north end, and marched over a niche in the
top, . . . but, as no other person in the neighbourhood had seen the
like, he was discredited and laughed at. Two years after, on Mid-
summer eve also, betwixt the hours of eight and nine, William
Lancaster himself imagined that several gentlemen were following
their horses at a distance, as if they had been hunting, and taking them
for such, he paid no regard to it, till about ten minutes after, again
turning his head towards the place, they appeared to be mounted, and
a vast army following, five in rank, crowding over at the same place
where the servant said he saw them two years before. He then called
his family, who all agreed in the same opinion; and, what was most
extraordinary, he frequently observed that some one of the five
would quit rank, and seem to stand in a fronting posture, as if he was
observing and regulating the order of their march, or taking account
of their numbers, and, after some time, appeared to return full
gallop to the station that he had left, which they never failed to do as

often as they quitted their lines; and the figure that did so was generally one of the middlemost men in the rank. As it grew later, they seemed more regardless of discipline, and rather had the appearance of people riding from a market, than an army; though they continued crowding on, and marching off, so long as they had light to see them.

This phaenomenon was no more seen till the Midsummer eve which preceded the rebellion [i.e. that of 1745], when they were determined to call more families to be witness of this sight, and accordingly went to Wilton-hill and Souter-fell side, till they convened about 26 persons, who all affirm they then saw the same appearance, but not conducted with the usual regularity as the preceding ones, having the likeness of carriages interspersed; however, it did not appear to be less real; for some of the company were so affected with it, as, in the morning, to climb the mountain, through an idle expectation of finding horse shoes after so numerous an army; but saw not the vestige or print of a foot . . .

Mr Clarke has corroborated the circumstances of this account, by adding, that Daniel Stricket, who first observed the spectacle, at the time of Mr Clarke's publishing, lived under Skiddaw, and was an auctioneer.

William Hutchinson
The History of the County of Cumberland

An Adventure at Aira Force

'Aira' is now the accepted spelling.

There is, on the western side of Ulleswater, a fine cataract (or, in the language of the country, a *force*), known by the name of Airey Force; and it is of importance enough, especially in rainy seasons, to attract numerous visitors from among 'the Lakers'. Thither, with some purpose of sketching, not the whole scene, but some picturesque features of it, Miss Smith had gone, quite unaccompanied. The road

197

to it lies through Gobarrow Park; and it was usual, at that time, to take a guide from the family of the Duke of Norfolk's keeper, who lived in Lyulph's Tower – a solitary hunting lodge, built by his Grace for the purposes of an annual visit which he used to pay to his estates in that part of England. She, however, thinking herself sufficiently familiar with the localities, had declined to encumber her motions with such an attendant; consequently she was alone. For half an hour or more, she continued to ascend: and, being a good 'cragswoman', she had reached an altitude much beyond what would generally be thought corresponding to the time. The path had vanished altogether; but she continued to pick out one for herself among the stones, sometimes receding from the *force*, sometimes approaching it, according to the openings allowed by the scattered masses of rock. Pressing forward in this hurried way, and never looking back, all at once she found herself in a little stony chamber, from which there was no egress possible in advance. She stopped and looked up. There was a frightful silence in the air. She felt a sudden palpitation at her heart, and a panic from she knew not what. Turning, however, hastily, she soon wound herself out of this aerial dungeon; but by steps so rapid and agitated, that, at length, on looking round, she found herself standing at the brink of a chasm, frightful to look down. That way, it was clear enough, all retreat was impossible; but, on turning round, retreat seemed in every direction alike even more impossible. Down the chasm, at least, she might have leaped, though with little or no chance of escaping with life; but on all other quarters it seemed to her eye that at no price could she effect an exit, since the rocks stood round her in a semi-circus, all lofty, all perpendicular, all glazed with trickling water, or smooth as polished porphyry. Yet how, then, had she reached the point? . . . Finding herself grow more and more confused, and every instant nearer to sinking into some fainting fit or convulsion, she resolved to sit down and turn her thoughts quietly into some less exciting channel. This she did; gradually recovered some self-possession . . . Once again she rose; and, supporting herself upon a little sketching stool that folded up into a stick, she looked upwards, in the hope that some shepherd might, by chance, be wandering in those aerial regions; but nothing could she see except the tall birches growing at the brink of the high summits, and the clouds slowly sailing overhead. Suddenly, however, as she swept the whole circuit of her station with her alarmed eye, she saw clearly, about two hundred yards beyond her own position, a lady in a white muslin morning robe, such as were then universally worn by young ladies until dinner-time. The lady beckoned with a gesture and in manner that, in a moment, gave her confidence to advance – *how* she could not guess; but, in some way that baffled all power to retrace it, she found instantaneously the outlet which previously had escaped her. She continued to advance towards the lady, whom now, in the same moment, she found to be standing on the other side of the *force*, and, also to be her own sister . . . The guiding sister began to descend, and by a few simple gestures, just serving to indicate when Miss Elizabeth was to approach and when to leave the brink of the torrent, she gradually led her down to a platform of rock, from which the further descent was safe and conspicuous. There Miss Smith paused, in order to take breath from her panic, as well as to exchange greetings and questions with her sister. But sister there was none. All trace of her had vanished; and, when, in two hours after, she reached her home, Miss Smith found her sister in the same situation and employment in which she had left her; and the whole family assured her that she had never stirred from the house.

Thomas De Quincey
Recollections of the Lake Poets

Dalehead Park Boggle

Dalehead Park lies close to the lower reaches of Thirlmere.

Aye, I've seen t'Park Boggle different times, an' Armboth Boggle an' aw; bit, what, I mindit nowt aboot them. Theer nowt to be flate [afraid] on; for they nivver mell't o' neah body 'at ivver I hard tell on. I yance spak to t'Park Boggle, bit it ga' me neah answer; an' I'll tell ye hoo it happen't.

We'd hed t'hogs [lambs of the previous year] off winteren doon below Hawkshead. I'd been fetchen them back, an' as it's a gay lang geate, an' I've a canny lock o' aquentance owre that way, 'at keep't me santeren on a langish time, it was rayder darkish afwore I gat ower t'Park. As I'd just gitten ower t'top, an' was beginnen to come doon o' this side, t'hogs aw stop't i't'mid rwoad, an' wadden't gang a step farder. What! I shootit t'dog up to help me on wi' them; bit it wad nowder bark nor nowt, an' keep't creepen in agean me legs, like as if it was hofe freeten't to deith. I began to leuk than if I could see what it was 'at was freetenen beath t'dog an' t'hogs; seah, an' seur eneuf, I saw reet afwore them what leuk't like a girt lime an'mowd [soil] heap, 'at reach't clean across t'rwoad. It went up heigher nor t'wo o' teaa side o' t' rwoad, an' slowp't doon tull aboot hofe a yard hee o' t'udder. Noo, I was seur at neabody wad put a midden across t'rwoad i' that way, an' I thowt 'at it mud be t'Park Boggle. I steud a laal bit consideren what to deu, an' than I shootit an' ax't what was t'reason 'at t'hogs was to gang neah farder; when just wi' that yan o' them gev a girt lowp ower t'low end o' t'heap, an' than t'udder aw went helter-skelter efter 't doon t'rwoad. When that waa ower, I went on til't, an' thowt I wad set me feut on't to see what it was; bit when I sud ha's step't on't theer was nowt, nor could I see nowt. It was gean awtogidder.

Theer was anudder time, teu, 'at I saw t'Park Boggle, in anudder form; bit I wassen't seah nar't that time, as I was when I'd been fetchen t'hogs. I'd been wo-en [walling] a gap 'at hed fawn [fallen] ower o' t'udder side o' t'Park; an' as t'days war nobbut short, I wrout on till it was gitten to be duskish. I happen'd to nwotish 'at some sheep hed gitten intul an'intack [intake – i.e. walled enclosure] 'at we hed away up t'fell side; seeah I thowt I was gang up an' put them oot, an' mebby stop a thorn into t'gap whoar they'd gitten in, if I nobbut could finnd t'spot. Wi' that I clam up, an' bodder't on wi' putten t'sheep oot, an' stoppen t'gap up, an'ya thing or anudder, till it was pitch dark. When I gat to cummin doon agean, I saw sec a fire on t'top o' t'Park, as I nivver saw befwore i' o'my life. It lowe't up sec a heet, an' sparks fell i'shooers o' aw sides on 't! What! I thowt it was varra queer 'at enny body sud kinnel sec a fire as that up theer, seeah I thowt I wad gang an' see what it meant. Bit when I gat to t'pleace, theer was nowder a fire nor enny spot whoar theer hed been yan! Theer was nowder a black pleace, nor a bit o' gurse swing't, nor owt 'at I could see, for aw it wassent a quarter iv an 'oor efter I'd seen t'girt fire blazing away furiously. Noo, ye may mak what ye will on't; ye may believe me or nut, just as ye like; bit nivver neabody 'ill persuade me 'at it was owt bit t'Park Boggle 'at I saw beath times.

John Richardson
Cummerlan' Talk

Westmorland Dobbies

John Briggs, born at Cartmel and the son of a swill or basket maker, was almost entirely self-educated. He became a schoolmaster, published a number of poems, but is remembered chiefly for his editing of The Lonsdale Maga-zine, *published in several annual numbers at Kirkby Lonsdale in the early 1820s.*

According to the ancient sages of Westmorland – the oldest and best acquainted with the philosophy of spirits – no spirit could appear before twilight had vanished in the evening, or after it appeared in the morning. On this account the winter nights were peculiarly dangerous, owing to the long levels which dobbies could keep at that season. Indeed there was one exception to this. If a man had murdered a woman who was with child to him, she had power to haunt him at all hours; and the Romish priests (who alone had the power of laying spirits) could not lay a spirit of this kind with any certainty, as she generally contrived to break loose long before her stipulated time . . . In common cases, however, the priest could 'lay' the ghosts; 'while ivy was green', was the usual term. But in very desperate cases, they were laid in the 'Red Sea', which was accomplished with great difficulty and even danger to the exorcist. In this country, the most usual place to confine spirits was under Haws Bridge [on the River Kent, near Natland], a few miles below Kendal. Many a grim ghost had been chained in that dismal trough. – According to the laws of ghosts, they could only seldom appear to more than one person at once. When these dobbies appeared to the eyes, they had not the power of making a noise; and when they saluted the ear, they could not greet the eyes. To this however there was an exception, when a human being spoke to them in the name of the Blessed Trinity. For it was an acknowledged truth, that however wicked the individual might have been in this world, or however light he might have made of the Almighty's name, he would tremble at its very sound, when separated from his earthly covering.

The causes of spirits appearing after death were generally three. Murdered persons came again to haunt their murderers, or to obtain justice by appearing to other persons, likely to see them avenged. In this, however, the spirit seems generally to have taken a very foolish plan, as they mostly appeared to old women, or young men, with old women's hearts. – Persons who had hid any treasure were doomed to haunt the place where that treasure was hid; as they had made a god of their wealth in this world, the place where their treasure was placed was to be their heaven after death. If any person could speak to them, and give them an opportunity of confessing where their treasure was hid, they could then rest in peace, but not without. – Those who died with any heavy crimes on their conscience, which they had not confessed, were also doomed to wander the earth at the midnight hour. These three causes are all that we have been able to discover among our Westmorland hills, where the laws of spirits seem to have been extremely well understood. Those spirits had no power over those who did not molest them; but if insulted, they seem to have been extremely vindictive, and to have felt little compunction in killing the insulter. They had power to assume any form, and to change that as often as they pleased; but they could neither vanish nor change while a human eye was firmly fixed upon them.

John Briggs (1788–1824)
Notes to *Westmorland As It Was* by the Rev. Mr Hodgson

The Millom Brownie and the Millom Poet

'*Hobthrust*' or (as he was more generally called) *Throb-Thrush* was a being distinct from the fairies. He was a solitary being who resided in Millom, and had his regular range of farm houses. He seems to have been a kind spirit, and willing to do any thing he was required to do. His only reward was a quart of milk porridge in a snipped pot. The servant girls would regularly put the cream in the churn, and say, 'I wish Throb would churn that,' and they regularly found it done. Throb's readiness to fulfil the wishes of his friends was sometimes productive of ludicrous incidents. One evening there was every prospect of rain next day, and a farmer had all his grain out. 'I wish,' said he, 'I had that grain housed.' The next morning Throb had housed every sheaf, but a fine stag that had helped him was lying dead at the barn door. The day, however, became extremely fine, and the farmer thought his grain would have been better in the field. 'I wish,' said he, 'that Throb-Thrush was in the mill-dam,' and next morning all the farmer's grain was in the mill-dam. Such were the tales that were told of the Millom Brownie, and as constantly believed. He left the country at last, through the kindness of a tailor, who left him a coat and a hood to keep him warm during the winter. He was heard at night singing at his favourite haunts,

> Throb-Thrush has got a new coat and a new hood,
> And he'll never do more good.

From this we conclude, that however excellent he might be as a workman, he was but a very indifferent poet.

> John Briggs
> Notes to *Westmorland As It Was* by the Rev. Mr Hodgson

A Skirmish at Swarthmoor – 1643

The turbulent state of Furness, during that period of public calamity [i.e. the Civil War], was too inconsiderable an object for the general historians to notice, yet we may introduce some account of it here, as it will serve to shew how penetrating the spirit of civil discord is, and how dreadful in all its effects; and that civil convulsion, begun at the throne, must be felt in the remotest parts of its dependence.

The following account is taken from the manuscripts of Thomas Park, of Millwood, high constable of Furness . . .

September 28, 1643. Colonel Rigby continuing his siege at Thurland castle (which continued six weeks before agreement was made) was let know that Mr Kirkby, Mr Rigby, and colonel Hudleston [i.e. Sir William Huddleston of Millom Castle], were in commotion in Furness, and that they had gotten together 1500 horse and foot, many of them out of Cumberland, young Mr Pennington being there with a company, and the rest of Furness: they were about 200 firemen, and the rest clubmen; and they kept their rendezvous at Dalton.

Whereupon Colonel Rigby, at the earnest desire of divers of Furness who fled thither, marched with seven or eight companies of foot, and three troops of horse, all firemen, except about 20, who had pikes; they were all complete, and very stout fellows. I being prisoner at Hornby castle at that time, and three weeks before, was appointed to go with the colonel; and the last of September they came to Ulverston, and rested there that night; and early the 1st of October, 1643, being Sunday, they set forward and had prayers on Swartmoor; which being ended, they marched forward till they came to Lyndal [Lindal]; and there the foot halted; but the horse went on to Lyndal cotte, and drew up in a valley facing, and shouting at Mr Hudleston's horse, who were drawn up on the top of Lindale close, who did shout also in return; which lasted about an hour, while the foot were receiving powder, shot, and match; which being ended, the foot marched up to the horse: then the king's horse fled; whereupon they raised a great shout, and did pursue them very hotly, and took Colonel Hudleston prisoner, Mr Stanley and Mr Latus, Mr Earton with 300 common soldiers, or thereabouts: they took most part of their arms, six colours, two drums, and all the money and apparel the common soldiers had on, with a coup laden with magazeen, drawn by six oxen. The common soldiers plundered Dalton and the parish, and returned that night to Cartmel.

Thomas West
The Antiquities of Furness

The Siege of Carlisle – 1644

'In October, 1644, siege was laid to the city of Carlisle by the parliamentary forces commanded by lieutenant general David Lesley, and continued till June following; during which time, notwithstanding the provisions that had been voluntarily sent in by the country, and otherwise provided by the governor, upon the apprehension of a siege, the city was so reduced that horse flesh without bread or salt, hempseed, dogs and rats were eaten; and in the end was surrendered upon honourable terms.' Nicolson and Burn, History of Westmorland and Cumberland.

These extracts are taken from a narrative written by Isaac Tullie, a seventeen-year-old boy who lived in Carlisle throughout the siege.

A good while after, an order was published to every Citizen to bring in their plate to be coyned, which they did chearfully: but this satisfied not the Governors; soe officers were ordered to come sodainly into the houses, as well of Country Gentlemen as of Citizens, and, under pretence of searching for plate, to take from them what moneys they found; which they exactly performed. My brother twice escaped them so narrowly, that I cannot omitt to relate the circumstances: – Once hearing that the officers had been with Sir Thos Wilm Dalston, and for his moneys had used him uncivilly, he went to church with a large bagg of money in either pocket; after service, as he was walking with Chancellor Burwell, these searchers met him, and Capt. Powley came merily towards him telling him his poccéts sweld to much, but Mins withheld him, saying himselfe would search his studdy. Another time, my Mother seeing them come fastly to her house, my brother gave the key of his desk to my sister, bidding her convey the money somewhither; but she had scarce opened the desk till the searcher entred the house; whereupon she was soe amazed, that she left the money with the cover of the desk open. The searchers demanding the key of my mother's desk, straitway went to that room, where the aforesaid desk was; which when they saw open, and by chance covered with some linnen, one of them laying his hands upon it, said 'there's nothing in there I'll warrant, else thou hadst not been open;' soe they departed with some small moneys of my mother's.

About this time, Dr Basire [Prebendary of Durham Cathedral and

Archdeacon of Northumberland, who took shelter in Carlisle during the Civil War], in his sermon, seasonably reproving the Garrison's excessive drinking, called drisling, prevailed so, that the Governours forthwith appointed a few brewers in every street, to furnish each family sparingly and proportionably; for before, such were their hopes of speady releif, and such their manners, that fifty bushells of Carlisle measure were spent every week, for tenn weeks together.

April 3. Provision for horse was now exhausted in the Towne, such as but the Thatch of houses offered them; shortly after, they were Guarded to grasse.

May 1st. Captaine Robert Philipson commanded the guard, who grassed the cattell in Weary holme; and being alarm'd by the towling of the great bell, was pointed by the flagg to some of the enemies foot, who from a hedge, were fireing at the cattell: these he beat from the hedge, killed two, and dispersed the rest.

May 3d. The cattell grased in Denton holme, from whome 6 horse went towards Newleaths, where they killed the skout; and riding further through Blackall wood, they aspied a troupe of the enemies horse grasing, which they attempted to bring in; but being pursued by another troupe, were forced to quit them.

May 30th. Capt. Blenkinshop came in with newes that the king was come into Westmerland, and that Leslie had warned the Countries carts to fetch away his badgige; which caused the ioyfull garrison to eat that day Three days provision, and repent with a cup of cold water for three dayes after. At this time three shillings peeces were coined out of the Cyttysens plate . . .

June 5th. Major Backstor guld [i.e. gulled, deceived] the City with a gross lye; that the king had taken Manchester and would be with them presently; *facile credimus quod volumus*: and no wonder, considering their small quantity of hors flesh without bread or salt . . . hempseed, dogs, and rats were eaten. [*This last sentence is incomplete –* Ed.]

June 23. The towns men humbly petitioned Sir Thos Glenham that their horse flesh might not be taken from them as formerly; and informed him that they were not able to endure the famine any longer; to which he gave no answer, nor redresse, in 4 dayes space; at which time, a few woomen of the scolds and scum of the citty, mett at the cross, braling against Sir Henry Stradling there present, who first threatned to fire upon them; and when they replyed they would take it as a favor, he left them with tears in his eyes, but could not mend their Commons. Dr Burwell was the only man who at this time had preserved a little Barrel of strong ale, unknowne to any but Sir Tho. Glenham. The first commander sent to treat with Sir Tho. was made so drunk with this ale, that, at his return to Lesly, he could give him no account of his errand, nor utter a wise word.

The next day Lesly sent in a graver person; who, being assured by Sir Tho. that the towne should be surrendered, offered to take his leave with great satisfaction; but was, in civility, conducted by him to the Scots ports [i.e. the North Gate] . . .

But the next day, being 25th of June, the Articles were agreed upon, and the citty of Carlyle, little in circuite, but great and memorable for Loyalty, received a Scots garrison upon the 28 of June, upon these noble articles, which by David Lesleys strict command and personall conduct were punctually performed, both to those that marched out, and to the Cittysons that staid at Home.

Isaac Tullie (seventeenth century)
A Narrative of the Siege of Carlisle (first published 1840)

George Fox in Carlisle Jail – 1653

The next day, after the judges were gone out of town, an order was sent to the jailer to put me down into the dungeon among the moss-troopers, thieves, and murderers, which accordingly he did. A filthy nasty place it was, where men and women were put together in a very uncivil manner, and not even a house of convenience to it; and the prisoners so lousy that one woman was almost eaten to death with lice. Yet, as bad as the place was, the prisoners were all made very loving and subject to me; and some of them were convinced of the truth, as the publicans and harlots were of old; so that they were able to confound any priest, that might come to the grates to dispute. But the jailer was very cruel, and the under-jailer very abusive to me and to Friends that came to see me; for he would beat Friends with a great cudgel, that did but come to the window to look in upon me. I could get up to the grate, where sometimes I took in my meat; at which the jailer was often offended. One time he came in a great rage, and beat me with a great cudgel, though I was not at the grate at that time; and as he beat me, he cried, 'Come out of the window,' though I was then far enough from it. While he struck me, I was made to sing in the Lord's power; and that made him rage the more. Then he fetched a fiddler, and brought him in where I was, and set him to play, thinking to vex me thereby; but while he played, I was moved in the everlasting power of the Lord to sing; and my voice drowned the noise of the fiddle, and struck and confounded them, and made them give over fiddling and go their way.

George Fox (1624–1691)
Journal

The Gibbet on Penrith Beacon – c. 1775

This incident recalls the murder, in 1766, at Cowrake Quarry on the slopes of Penrith Beacon, of Thomas Parker, a butcher from Langwathby. The letters cut in the turf, however, were 'T.P.M.', standing, it would seem, for 'Thomas Parker Murdered' – not, as Wordsworth supposed, the name of the murderer. The latter, who had been hanged at Carlisle, and suspended in chains near the scene of his crime, was, in fact, called Thomas Nicholson, and may well have been a distant relative of the editor.

     I remember well,
That once, while yet my inexperienced hand
Could scarcely hold a bridle, with proud hopes

I mounted, and we journeyed towards the hills:
An ancient servant of my father's house
Was with me, my encourager and guide:
We had not travelled long, ere some mischance
Disjoined me from my comrade; and, through fear
Dismounting, down the rough and stony moor
I led my horse, and, stumbling on, at length
Came to a bottom, where in former times
A murderer had been hung in iron chains.
The gibbet-mast had mouldered down, the bones
And iron case were gone; but on the turf,
Hard by, soon after that fell deed was wrought,
Some unknown hand had carved the murderer's name.
The monumental letters were inscribed
In times long past; but still, from year to year,
By superstition of the neighbourhood,
The grass is cleared away, and to this hour
The characters are fresh and visible:
A casual glance had shown them, and I fled,
Faltering and faint, and ignorant of the road:
Then, reascending the bare common, saw
A naked pool that lay beneath the hills,
The beacon on the summit, and, more near,
A girl who bore a pitcher on her head,
And seemed with difficult steps to force her way
Against the blowing wind. It was, in truth,
An ordinary sight: but I should need
Colours and words that are unknown to man,
To paint the visionary dreariness
Which, while I looked all round for my lost guide,
Invested moorland waste, and naked pool,
The beacon crowning the lone eminence,
The female and her garments vexed and tossed
By the strong wind.

William Wordsworth
From *The Prelude*, Book 12

The Death of Robespierre – 1794

The Levens Estuary, where Wordsworth heard the news of the death of Robespierre, is usually referred to by other travellers as the Ulverston Sands. In a passage omitted from this quotation, Wordsworth tells how, on the same day, he visited Cartmel Churchyard to see the grave of William Taylor, his former teacher at Hawkshead.

O Friend! few happier moments have been mine
Than that which told the downfall of this Tribe
So dreaded, so abhorred. The day deserves
A separate record. Over the smooth sands
Of Leven's ample estuary lay
My journey, and beneath a genial sun,
With distant prospect among gleams of sky
And clouds, and intermingling mountain-tops,
In one inseparable glory clad,
Creatures of one ethereal substance met
In consistory, like a diadem
Or crown of burning seraphs as they sit
In the empyrean . . .

As I advanced, all that I saw or felt
Was gentleness and peace. Upon a small
And rocky island near, a fragment stood
(Itself like a sea rock) the low remains
(With shells encrusted, dark with briny weeds)
Of a dilapidated structure, once
A Romish chapel, where the vested priest
Said matins at the hour that suited those
Who crossed the sands with ebb of morning tide.
Not far from that still ruin all the plain
Lay spotted with a variegated crowd
Of vehicles and travellers, horse and foot,
Wading beneath the conduct of their guide
In loose procession through the shallow stream
Of inland waters; the great sea meanwhile

Heaved at safe distance, far retired. I paused,
Longing for skill to paint a scene so bright
And cheerful, but the foremost of the band
As he approached, no salutation given
In the familiar language of the day,
Cried, 'Robespierre is dead!' – nor was a doubt,
After strict question, left within my mind
That he and his supporters all were fallen.

Great was my transport, deep my gratitude
To everlasting Justice, by this fiat
Made manifest . . .
        I pursued my way
Along that very shore which I had skimmed
In former days, when – spurring from the Vale
Of Nightshade, and St Mary's mouldering fane,
And the stone abbot, after circuit made
In wantonness of heart, a joyous band
Of schoolboys hastening to their distant home
Along the margin of the moonlight sea –
We beat with thundering hoofs the level sand.

William Wordsworth
From *The Prelude*, Book 10

Waterloo Celebrated – 1815

[Keswick, August 23, 1815.]

Monday, the 21st of August, was not a more remarkable day in your
life than it was in that of my neighbour Skiddaw, who is a much
older personage. The weather served for our bonfire, and never, I
believe, was such an assemblage upon such a spot. To my utter
astonishment, Lord Sunderlin rode up, and Lady S., who had en-
deavoured to dissuade *me* from going as a thing too dangerous,

joined the walking party. Wordsworth with his wife, sister, and eldest boy, came over on purpose. James Boswell arrived that morning at the Sunderlins. Edith, the Senhora, Edith May, and Herbert were my convoy, with our three maid-servants, some of our neighbours, some adventurous lakers, and Messrs. Rag, Tag, and Bobtail, made up the rest of the assembly. We roasted beef and boiled plum-puddings there; sung 'God save the King' round the most furious body of flaming tar-barrels that I ever saw; drank a huge wooden bowl of punch; fired cannon at every health with three times three, and rolled large blazing balls of tow and turpentine down the steep side of the mountain. The effect was grand beyond imagination. We formed a huge circle round the most intense light, and behind us was an immense arch of the most intense darkness, for our bonfire fairly put out the moon.

The only mishap which occurred will make a famous anecdote in the life of a great poet, if James Boswell, after the example of his father, keepeth a diary of the sayings of remarkable men. When we were craving for the punch, a cry went forth that the kettle had been knocked over, with all the boiling water. Colonel Barker, as Boswell named the Senhora, from her having had the command on this occasion, immediately instituted a strict inquiry to discover the culprit, from a suspicion that it might have been done in mischief, water, as you know, being a commodity not easily replaced on the summit of Skiddaw. The persons about the fire declared that it was one of the gentlemen; they did not know his name, but he had a red cloak on; they pointed him out in the circle. The red cloak (a maroon one of Edith's) identified him; Wordsworth had got hold of it, and was equipped like a Spanish Don – by no means the worst figure in the company. He had committed this fatal *faux pas*, and thought to slink off undiscovered. But, as soon as, in my inquiries concerning the punch, I learnt his guilt from the Senhora, I went round to all our party, and communicated the discovery, and getting them about him, I punished him by singing a prody, which they all joined in: ''Twas *you* that kicked the kettle down! 'Twas you, Sir, you!'.

The consequences were, that we took all the cold water upon the summit to supply our loss. Our myrmidons and Messrs Rag and Co. had, therefore, none for their grog; they necessarily drank the rum pure; and you, who are physician to the Middlesex Hospital, are doubtless acquainted with the manner in which alcohol acts upon the nervous system. All our torches were lit at once by this mad company, and our way down the hill was marked by a track of fire, from flambeaux dropping the pitch, tarred ropes, etc. One fellow was so drunk that his companions placed him upon a horse, with his face to the tail, to bring him down, themselves being just sober enough to guide and hold him on.

Robert Southey
Letter to his Brother

The Lake Poets

De Quincey's First Meeting with Wordsworth

May 31, 1803

Sir,

I suppose that most men would think that what I am going to say – strange at least or rude; but I am bold enough to imagine that, as you are not yourself 'in the role of common men,' you may be willing to excuse anything uncommon in the liberty I am now taking.

My object in troubling you, Sir, is that hereafter I may have the satisfaction of recollecting that I made one effort at least for obtaining your notice – and that I did not, through any want of exertion on my own part, miss that without which what good can my life do me? I have no other motive for soliciting your friendship than what (I should think) every man, who has read and felt the *Lyrical Ballads*, must have in common with me. There is no need that I should express my admiration and love for those delightful poems; nor is it possible that I should do so. Besides, I am persuaded that the dignity of your moral character sets you as far above the littleness of any vanity which could be soothed by applause feeble and insignificant as mine – as the transcendency of your genius makes all applause fall beneath it. But may I say in general, without the smallest exaggeration, that the whole aggregate of pleasure I have received from some eight or nine other poets that I have been able to find since the world began – falls infinitely short of what those two enchanting volumes have singly afforded me; – that your name is with me forever linked to the lovely scenes of nature; – and that not yourself only but that each place and object you have mentioned – and all the souls in that delightful community of your's – to me

'Are dearer than the sun'

With such opinions, it is not surprising that I should so earnestly and humbly sue for your friendship; – it is not surprising that the hope of that friendship should have sustained me through two years of a life passed partially in the world – and therefore not passed in happiness; – that I should have breathed forth my morning and my evening orisons for the accomplishment of that hope; – that I should now consider it as the only object worthy of my nature or capable of rewarding my pains. Sometimes indeed, in the sad and dreary vacuity of worldly intercourse, this hope will touch those chords that have power to rouse me from the lethargy of despair; and sometimes, from many painful circumstances – many bitter recollections, it is my only refuge . . .

I cannot say anything more than that, though you may find many minds more congenial with your own – and therefore proportionately more worthy of your regard, you will never find any one more zealously attached to you – more full of admiration of your mental excellence and of reverential love for your moral character – more ready (I speak from my heart!) to sacrifice even his life – whenever it could have a chance of promoting your interest and happiness – than he who now bends the knee before you. And I will add that, to no man on earth except yourself and *one* other (a friend of yours), would I thus lowly and suppliantly prostrate myself.

Thomas De Quincey
Letter to William Wordsworth

Wordsworth replied in a kindly, though cautious manner, adding a post-script saying: 'I shall indeed be very happy to see you at Grasmere, if you ever find it convenient to visit this delightful country.' De Quincey did not avail himself of this invitation until 1807: he explains the delay in Re-collections of the Lake Poets.

So far from neglecting Wordsworth, it is a fact that twice I had undertaken a long journey expressly for the purpose of paying my respects to Wordsworth; twice I came so far as the little rustic inn (then the sole inn of the neighbourhood) at Church Coniston; and on neither occasion could I summon confidence enough to present myself before him. It was not that I had any want of proper boldness for facing the most numerous company of a mixed or ordinary character: reserved, indeed, I was, perhaps even shy – from the character of my mind, so profoundly meditative, and the character of my life, so profoundly sequestered – but still, from counteracting causes, I was not deficient in a reasonable self-confidence towards the world generally. But the very image of Wordsworth, as I prefigured it to my own planet-struck eye, crushed my faculties as before Elijah or St Paul. Twice, as I have said, did I advance as far as the Lake of Coniston; which is about eight miles from the church of Grasmere, and once I absolutely went forwards from Coniston to the very gorge of Hammerscar, from which the whole Vale of Grasmere suddenly breaks upon the view in a style of almost theatrical surprise, with its lovely valley stretching before the eye in the distance, the lake lying immediately below, with its solemn ark-like island of four and a half acres in size seemingly floating on its surface, and its exquisite outline on the opposite shore, revealing all its little bays and wide sylvan margin, feathered to the edge with wild flowers and fern. In one quarter, a little wood, stretching for about half a mile towards the outlet of the lake; more directly in opposition to the spectator, a few green fields; and beyond them, just two bowshots from the water, a little white cottage gleaming from the midst of trees, with a vast and seemingly never-ending series of ascents rising above it to the height of more than three thousand feet. That little cottage was Words-worth's from the time of his marriage, and earlier; in fact, from the beginning of the century to the year 1808. Afterwards, for many a year, it was mine. Catching one hasty glimpse of this loveliest of landscapes, I retreated like a guilty thing, for fear I might be surprised by Wordsworth, and then returned faintheartedly to Coniston, and so to Oxford, *re infectâ*.

The following year, De Quincey learned that Coleridge's wife and their three children wished to travel from Bristol to Keswick to join the Southeys, whereupon he offered 'to escort them in a post-chaise'. The offer was made partly to be of service to Coleridge, but chiefly to give him the opportunity of meeting Wordsworth. There is a special poignancy in the journey in that, though De Quincey was not aware of it, Mrs Coleridge was, in fact, separating from her husband.

Leaving Liverpool, after about a week's delay, we pursued our journey northwards. We had slept on the first day at Lancaster. Consequently, at the rate of motion which then prevailed throughout England – which, however, was rarely equalled on that western road, where all things were in arrear by comparison with the eastern and southern roads of the kingdom – we found ourselves, about three o'clock in the afternoon, at Ambleside, fourteen miles to the north-west of Kendal, and thirty-six from Lancaster. There, for the last time, we stopped to change horses, (a ceremony which then took half an hour); and about four o'clock we found ourselves on the summit of the White Moss, a hill which rises between the second and third milestones on the stage from Ambleside to Keswick, and which then retarded the traveller's advance by a full fifteen minutes, but is now evaded by a lower line of road. In ascending this hill, from weariness of moving so slowly, I, with the two Coleridges, had alighted; and, as we all chose to refresh ourselves by running down the hill into Grasmere, we had left the chaise behind us, and had even lost the sound of the wheels at times, when all at once we came, at an abrupt turn of the road, in sight of a white cottage, with two yew-trees breaking the glare of its white walls. A sudden shock seized me on recognizing this cottage, of which, in the previous year, I had gained a momentary glimpse from Hammerscar, on the opposite side of the lake. I paused, and felt my old panic returning upon me; but just then, as if to take away all doubt upon the subject, I saw Hartley Coleridge, who had gained upon me considerably, suddenly turn in at a garden gate; this motion to the right at once confirmed me in my belief that here at last we had reached our port; that this little cottage was tenanted by that man whom, of all the men from the beginning of time, I most fervently desired to see; that in less than a minute I should meet Wordsworth face to face. Coleridge was of opinion that, if a man were really and *consciously* to see an apparition, in such circumstances death would be the inevitable result; and, if so, the wish which we hear so commonly expressed for such experience is as thoughtless as that of Semele in the Grecian Mythology, so natural in a female, that her lover should visit her *en grand costume* – presumptuous ambition, that unexpectedly wrought its own ruinous chastisement! Judged by Coleridge's test, my situation could not have been so terrific as *his* who anticipates a ghost; for, certainly, I survived this meeting; but at that instant it seemed pretty much the same to my own feelings.

Never before or since can I reproach myself with having trembled at the approaching presence of any creature that is born of woman, excepting only, for once or twice in my life, woman herself. Now, however, I *did* tremble; and I forgot, what in no other circumstances I could have forgotten, to stop for the coming up of the chaise, that I might be ready to hand Mrs Coleridge out. Had Charlemagne and all his peerage been behind me, or Caesar and his equipage, or Death on his pale horse, I should have forgotten them at that moment of intense expectation, and of eyes fascinated to what lay before me, or what might in a moment appear. Through the little gate I pressed forward; ten steps beyond it lay the principal door of the house. To this, no longer clearly conscious of my own feelings, I passed on rapidly; I heard a step, a voice, and, like flash of lightning, I saw the figure emerge of a tallish man, who held out his hand, and saluted me with most cordial expressions of welcome.

Thomas De Quincey
Recollections of the Lake Poets

The Daily Round at Grasmere

Friday, 10th October. – In the morning when I arose the mists were hanging over the opposite hills, and the tops of the highest hills were covered with snow. There was a most lovely combination at the head of the vale of the yellow autumnal hills wrapped in sunshine, and overhung with partial mists, the green and yellow trees, and the distant snow-topped mountains. It was a most heavenly morning. The Cockermouth traveller came with thread, hardware, mustard, etc. She is very healthy; has travelled over the mountains these thirty years. She does not mind the storms, if she can keep her goods dry. Her husband will not travel with an ass, because it is the tramper's badge; she would have one to relieve her from the weary load. She was going to Ulverston, and was to return to Ambleside Fair . . . The fern among the rocks exquisitely beautiful . . . Sent off *The Beggars*, etc., by Thomas Ashburner . . . William sat up after me, writing *Point Rash Judgment*.

Saturday, 11th. – A fine October morning. Sat in the house working all the morning. William composing . . . After dinner we walked up Greenhead Gill in search of a sheepfold. We went by Mr Olliff's, and through his woods. It was a delightful day, and the views looked excessively cheerful and beautiful, chiefly that from Mr Olliff's field, where our own house is to be built. The colours of the mountains soft, and rich with orange fern; the cattle pasturing on the hilltops; kites sailing in the sky above our heads; sheep bleating and in lines and chains and patterns scattered over the mountains. They come down and feed, on the little green islands in the beds of the torrents, and so may be swept away. The sheepfold is falling away. It is built nearly in the form of a heart unequally divided. Looked down the brook, and saw the drops rise upwards and sparkle in the air at the little falls. The higher sparkled the tallest. We walked along the turf of the mountain till we came to a track, made by the cattle which come upon the hills . . .

Sunday, October 12th. – Sate in the house writing in the morning while Wm went into the woods to compose. Wrote to John on the morning; copied poems for the L.B. In the evening wrote to Mrs Rawson. Mary Jameson and Sally Ashburner dined. We pulled apples after dinner, a large basket full. We walked before tea by Bainriggs to observe the many-coloured foliage. The oaks dark green with yellow leaves, the birches generally still green, some near the water yellowish, the sycamore crimson and crimson-tufted, the mountain ash a deep orange, the common ash lemon-colour, but many ashes still fresh in their summer green. Those that were discoloured chiefly near the water. Wm composing in the evening. Went to bed at twelve o'clock.

Saturday. – A very fine October morning. William worked all the morning at the sheepfold [i.e. Michael] but in vain. He lay down in the afternoon till 7 o'clock, but could not sleep . . . We did not walk all day . . .

Sunday Morning. – We rose late, and walked directly after breakfast. The tops of Grasmere mountains cut off. Rydale very beautiful. The surface of the water quite still, like a dim mirror. The colours of the large island exquisitely beautiful, and the trees, still fresh and green, were magnified by the mists. The prospects on the west side of the Lake were very beautiful. We sate at the 'two Points' [Mary Point and Sarah Point] looking up to Park's. The lowing of the cattle was echoed by a hollow voice in Knab Scar. We returned home over the stepping-stones Wm got to work . . .

Monday, 20th. – William worked in the morning at the sheepfold. After dinner we walked to Rydale, crossed the stepping stones, and while we were walking under the tall oak trees the Lloyds called out to us. They went with us on the western side of Rydale. The lights were very grand upon the woody Rydale hills. Those behind dark and topped with clouds. The two lakes were divinely beautiful. Grasmere excessively solemn, the whole lake calm, and dappled with soft grey ripples. The Lloyds staid with us till 8 o'clock. We then walked to the top of the hill at Rydale. Very mild and warm. About six glowworms shining faintly. We went up as far as the grove. When we came home the fire was out. We ate our supper in the dark, and went to bed immediately. William was disturbed in the night by the rain coming into his room, for it was a very rainy night. The ash leaves lay across the road.

Tuesday, 21st. – . . . Wm had been unsuccessful in the morning at the sheepfold. The reflections of the ash scattered, and the tree stripped.

Wednesday Morning. – . . . Wm composed without much success at the sheepfold. Coleridge came in to dinner. He had done nothing. We were very merry. C. and I went to look at the prospect from his seat . . . Wm read *Ruth*, etc., after supper. Coleridge *Christabel*.

Dorothy Wordsworth
Grasmere Journal

'Laal Hartley' Puts His Tongue Out

He lived amidst th'untrodden ways
   To Rydal Lake that lead: –
A bard whom there were none to praise,
   And very few to read.

Behind a cloud his mystic sense,
   Deep-hidden, who can spy?
Bright as the night, when not a star
   Is shining in the sky.

Unread his works – his 'Milk-white Doe'
   With dust is dark and dim;
It's still in Longman's shop, and Oh!
   The difference to him!

Hartley Coleridge

Wordsworth in Old Age

In 1845 Harriet Martineau bought a tract of land at Ambleside to build the house where she was to live for the rest of her life, and, when the building was completed, a number of friends, including Wordsworth, were invited to plant a tree in the grounds. The house itself is now part of the Charlotte Mason College of Education.

The planting scene was characteristic. Wordsworth had taken a kindly interest in the whole affair; and where my study now is, he had thrown himself down, among the hazel bushes, and talked of the meadows, and of the right aspect and disposition of a house, one summer day when he and his wife and daughter had come to view the site, and give me the benefit of their experience; and long after, when I had begun to farm my two acres, he came to see my first calf.

On occasion of the planting of his pine, he dug and planted in a most experienced manner, – then washed his hands in the watering-pot, took my hand in both his, and wished me many happy years in my new abode, – and then proceeded to give me a piece of friendly advice. He told me I should find visitors a great expense, and that I must promise him, – (and he laid his hand on my arm to enforce what he said) I must promise him to do as he and his sister had done, when, in their early days, they had lived at Grasmere.

'When you have a visitor,' said he, 'you must do as we did; – you must say "if you like to have a cup of tea with us, you are very welcome: but if you want any meat – you must pay for your board." Now, promise me that you will do this.' Of course, I could promise nothing of the sort. I told him I had rather not invite my friends unless I could make them comfortable. He insisted: I declined promising; and changed the subject ... He was kind enough to be very anxious lest I should overwalk myself. Both he and Mrs Wordsworth repeatedly bade me take warning by his sister, who had lost first her strength, and then her sanity by extreme imprudence in that way, and its consequences. Mrs Wordsworth told me what I could not have believed on any less trustworthy authority, – that Miss Wordsworth had – not once, but frequently, – walked forty miles in a day. In vain I assured them that I did not meditate or perpetrate any such imprudence, and that I valued my recovered health too much to hazard it for any self-indulgence whatsoever. It was a fixed idea with them that I walked all day long. One afternoon Mr Atkinson and I met them on the Rydal road. They asked where we had been; and we told them. I think it was over Loughrigg terrace to Grasmere; which was no immoderate walk. 'There, there!' said Wordsworth, laying his hand on my companion's arm. 'Take care! take care! Don't let *her* carry you about. She is killing off half the gentlemen in the country!' I could not then, nor can I now, remember any Westmoreland gentleman, except my host on Windermere, having taken a walk with me at all ... But, while writing these recollections, the spring sunshine and air which are streaming in through my open window remind me of the advent of the 'tourist season', and of the large allowance to be made for a 'lake poet', subject to the perpetual incursions of flatterers of the coarsest order. The modest and well-bred pass by the gates of celebrated people who live in the country for quiet, while the coarse and selfish intrude, – as hundreds of strangers intruded every year on Wordsworth. When I came into the district, I was told that the average of utter strangers who visited Rydal Mount in the season was five hundred!

For my part, I refused, from the first, to introduce any of my visitors at Rydal Mount, because there were far too many already. Mrs Wordsworth repeatedly acknowledged my scrupulosity about this: but in time I found that she rather wished that I would bear my share in what had become a kind of resource to her husband. I never liked seeing him go the round of his garden and terraces, relating to persons whose very names he had not attended to, particulars about his writing and other affairs which each stranger flattered himself was a confidential communication to himself. One anecdote will show how the process went forward, and how persons fared who deserved something better than this invariable treatment. In the first autumn of my residence, – while I was in lodgings, – Mr Seymour Tremenheere and his comrade in his Educational Commissionership, Mr Tufnell, asked me to obtain lodgings for them, as they wished to repose from their labours beside Windermere. When they came I told them that I could not take them to Rydal Mount. They acquiesced, though much wishing to obtain some testimony from the old poet on behalf of popular education. In a week or two, however, I had to call on Mrs Wordsworth, and I invited the gentlemen to take their chance by going with me. We met Mr and Mrs Wordsworth just coming out of their door into the garden. I twice distinctly named both gentlemen; but I saw that he did not attend, and that he received them precisely after his usual manner with strangers. He marched them off to his terraces; and Mrs Wordsworth and I sat down on a garden seat. I told her the state of the case; and she said she would take great care that, when they returned, Mr Wordsworth should understand who his guests were. This was more easily promised than done, however. When they appeared, Mr Wordsworth uncovered his grey head as usual, wished the gentlemen improved health and much enjoyment of the lake scenery, and bowed us out. My friends told me (what I could have told them) that Mr Wordsworth had related many interesting things about his poems, but that they doubted whether he had any idea who they were; and they had no opportunity of introducing the subject of popular education. That evening, when a party of friends and I were at tea, an urgent message came, through three families, from Rydal Mount, to the effect that Mr Wordsworth understood that Mr Seymour Tremenheere was in the neighbourhood; and that he was anxious to obtain an interview with Mr Tremenheere for conversation about popular education! – Mr Tremenheere called at the Mount the next day. He told me on his return that he had, he hoped, gained his point. He hoped for a sonnet at least. He observed, 'Mr Wordsworth discoursed to me about Education, trying to impress upon me whatever I have most insisted on in my Reports for seven years past: but I do not expect him to read Reports, and I was very happy to hear what he had to say.' The next time I fell in with Mr Wordsworth, he said, 'I have to thank you for procuring for me a call from that intelligent gentleman, Mr Tremenheere. I was glad to have some conversation with him. To be sure, he was bent on enlightening me on principles of popular education which have been published in my poems these forty years: but that is of little consequence. I am very happy to have seen him.'

Harriet Martineau (1802–1876)
Autobiography

Old Wudsworth o' Rydal

And here is the impression that Wordsworth made upon the yeoman and peasants in the dales. 'Nivver a man of many words ye kna, but quite monstrable wi' his own barns at times; I darsay he wud tak em out in a string and nivver say nowt to nin on em at others, but then he was quite an "object man," quite a "kenspeckled" an as we saay ratherly rough feaced an aw girt big faace wi' out much plesser i' it and vara plaainly drest at best o' times. Nivver a man as laughed not to saay laugh right owt, but a decent quiet man, well spokken on by his sarvants at t'Mount, terble kind to fowks as was badly and very highly thowt on, paid his way reglar, vara particler an aw about his accounts, and that was Mrs Wordsworth's doing ye kna, for she was a reglar manasher. Turble fond o' study on t'rwoads, specially at night time, and wi' a girt voice bumming awaay fit to flayte aw the childer to death ameaast, not but what Miss Dorothy did best part o' pitting his potry togidder. He let it fa' and she cam efter and gethered it oop fur him ye kna. Quite yan o' us ye kna, not a bit o' pride in him for o quality thowte ot warld on 'im. But he wasn't a man as was thowte a deal o' for his potry when he was hereabout. It hed no laugh in it same as Lile Hartley's [i.e. Hartley Coleridge], bided a deal o makkin I darsay. It was kept oer long in his head mappen. But then for aw that, he had best eye to mountains and trees, and buildings in the daale, notished ivvry stean o' the fellside, and we nin on us durst bang a bowder stean a bit or cut a bit coppy or raase an old wa' doon when *he* was astir.'

It was 'Mr Wudswuth the stamp-maister, him o'Rydal,' not Wordsworth Poet-Laureate, they knew. Indeed one yeoman who went some miles out of his way to attend a political meeting at Appleby, attracted by the announcement that the Poet-Laureate would address the meeting, was heard to say. 'Schaff on it, its nobbut old Wudswuth o'Rydal efter aw.' and left the meeting in high dudgeon.

As for his poetry, it was 'aw reet eneuf but queer stuff, varra,' and they hardly believed that when the fit of making it was on, Wordsworth was in his right mind. They heard him 'bumming away,' they saw his 'jaws agaain t'whoale time' and thought of him as possessed, and would say, 'Aw yes, I darsay he's quite sensible, whiles, if ya nobbut catch him reet he'll talk as plaain as oyder you or me,' and they were to be pardoned if they looked on his periodical poetry-making on the public highway as periodical fits of mania. Thus it came to pass, as Dr Gibson has chronicled for us, that when one day Hartley Coleridge made his wonted appearance at an artist friend's studio at Ambleside and was accosted with the ordinary salutation of, 'Well, Mr Coleridge, what's your news this morning?' Hartley replied, 'Your enquiry reminds me of the answer I've just had to the same, as I was walking down, I came upon a poor man from Rydal breaking stones, and like you I said, "Good morning, John, what

news have you this morning?" and John answered, "Why, nowte
varra particler only old Wudswurth's brocken lowce ageaan."'

H. D. Rawnsley
Literary Associations of the English Lakes

The Death of Wordsworth, April 1850

Goethe in Weimar sleeps, and Greece,
Long since, saw Byron's struggle cease.
But one such death remain'd to come;
The last poetic voice is dumb –
We stand to-day by Wordsworth's tomb . . .

  Ah, pale ghosts rejoice!
For never has such soothing voice
Been to your shadowy world convey'd,
Since erst, at morn, some wandering shade
Heard the clear song of Orpheus come
Through Hades, and the mournful gloom.
Wordsworth has gone from us – and ye,
Ah, may ye feel his voice as we!
He too upon a wintry clime
Had fallen – on this iron time
Of doubts, disputes, distractions, fears.
He found us when the age had bound
Our souls in its benumbing round;
He spoke, and loosed our heart in tears.
He laid us as we lay at birth
On the cool flowery lap of earth,
Smiles broke from us and we had ease;
The hills were round us, and the breeze
Went o'er the sun-lit fields again;
Our foreheads felt the wind and rain.

Our youth return'd; for there was shed
On spirits that had long been dead,
Spirits dried up and closely furl'd,
The freshness of the early world.

Ah! since dark days still bring to light
Man's prudence and man's fiery might,
Time may restore us in his course,
Goethe's sage mind and Byron's force;
But where will Europe's latter hour
Again find Wordsworth's healing power?
Others will teach us how to dare,
And against fear our breast to steel;
Others will strengthen us to bear –
But who, ah! who, will make us feel?
The cloud of mortal destiny,
Others will front it fearlessly –
But who, like him, will put it by?
Keep fresh the grass upon his grave,
O Rotha, with thy living wave!
Sing him thy best! for few or none
Hears thy voice right, now he is gone.

Matthew Arnold (1822–1888)
From *Memorial Verses*

Dorothy Wordsworth at Dove Cottage

Immediately behind her [i.e. Mrs Wordsworth, the poet's wife]
moved a lady, shorter, slighter, and perhaps, in all other respects, as
different from her in personal characteristics as could have been
wished for the most effective contrast. 'Her face was of Egyptian
brown'; rarely, in a woman of English birth, had I seen a more
determinate gipsy tan. Her eyes were not soft, as Mrs Wordsworth's,

nor were they fierce or bold; but they were wild and startling, and hurried in their motion. Her manner was warm and even ardent; her sensibility seemed constitutionally deep; and some subtle fire of impassioned intellect apparently burned within her, which, being alternately pushed forward into a conspicuous expression by the irrepressible instincts of her temperament, and then immediately checked, in obedience to the decorum of her sex and age, and her maidenly condition, gave to her whole demeanour, and to her con-versation, an air of embarrassment, and even of self-conflict, that was almost distressing to witness. Even her very utterance and enunciation often suffered, in point of clearness and steadiness, from the agitation of her excessive organic sensibility. At times, the self-counteraction and self-baffling of her feelings caused her even to stammer, and so determinately to stammer that a stranger who should have seen her and quitted her in that state of feeling would have certainly set her down for one plagued with that infirmity of speech as distressingly as Charles Lamb himself. This was Miss Wordsworth, the only sister of the poet – his 'Dorothy'; who naturally owed so much to the life-long intercourse with her great brother in his most solitary and sequestered years; but, on the other hand, to whom he has acknow-ledged obligations of the profoundest nature; and, in particular, this mighty one, through which we also, the admirers and worshippers of this great poet, are become equally her debtors – that, whereas the intellect of Wordsworth was, by its original tendency, too stern, too austere, too much enamoured of an ascetic harsh sublimity, she it was – the lady who paced by his side continually through sylvan and mountain tracks, in Highland glens, and in the dim recesses of German charcoal-burners – that first *couched* his eye to the sense of beauty, humanized him by the gentler charities, and engrafted, with her delicate female touch, those graces upon the ruder growths of his nature which have since clothed the forest of his genius with a foliage corresponding in loveliness and beauty to the strength of its boughs and the massiness of its trunks. The greatest deductions from Miss Wordsworth's attractions, and from the exceeding interest which surrounded her in right of her character, of her history, and of the relation which she fulfilled towards her brother, were the glancing quickness of her motions, and other circumstances of her deportment (such as her stooping attitude when walking), which gave an ungraceful, and even an unsexual character to her appearance when out-of-doors. She did not cultivate the graces which preside over the person and its carriage. But, on the other hand, she was a person of very remarkable endowments intellectually; and, in addition to the other great services which she rendered to her brother, this I may mention, as greater than all the rest, and it was one which equally operated to the benefit of every casual companion in a walk – viz. the exceeding sympathy, always ready and always profound, by which she made all that one could tell her, all that one could describe, all that one could quote from a foreign author, reverberate, as it were, *à plusieurs reprises*, to one's own feelings, by the manifest impression it made upon *hers*. The pulses of light are not more quick or more inevitable in their flow and undulation, than were the answering and echoing movements of her sympathizing attention. Her knowledge of literature was irregular, and thoroughly unsystematic. She was content to be ignorant of many things; but what she knew and had really mastered lay where it could not be disturbed – in the temple of her own most fervid heart.

Thomas De Quincey
Recollections of the Lake Poets

Wordsworth to His Sister

. . . Nor perchance,
If I were not thus taught, should I the more
Suffer my genial spirits to decay:
For thou art with me here upon the banks
Of this fair river; though my dearest Friend,
My dear, dear Friend; and in thy voice I catch
The language of my former heart, and read
My former pleasures in the shooting lights
Of thy wild eyes. Oh! yet a little while

May I behold in thee what I was once,
My dear, dear Sister! and this prayer I make,
Knowing that Nature never did betray
The heart that loved her; 'tis her privilege,
Through all the years of this our life, to lead
From joy to joy; for she can so inform
The mind that is within us, so impress
With quietness and beauty, and so feed
With lofty thoughts, that neither evil tongues,
Rash judgments, nor the sneers of selfish men,
Nor greetings where no kindness is, nor all
The dreary intercourse of daily life,
Shall e'er prevail against us, or disturb
Our cheerful faith, that all which we behold
Is full of blessings. Therefore let the moon
Shine on thee in thy solitary walk;
And let the misty mountain-winds be free
To blow against thee; and, in after years,
When these wild ecstasies shall be matured
Into a sober pleasure; when thy mind
Shall be a mansion for all lovely forms,
Thy memory be as a dwelling-place
For all sweet sounds and harmonies; oh! then,
If solitude, or fear, or pain, or grief,
Should be thy portion, with what healing thoughts
Of tender joy wilt thou remember me,
And these my exhortations! Nor, perchance –
If I should be where I no more can hear
Thy voice, nor catch from thy wild eyes these gleams
Of past existence – wilt thou then forget
That on the banks of this delightful stream
We stood together; and that I, so long
A worshipper of Nature, hither came
Unwearied in that service: rather say
With warmer love – oh! with far deeper zeal
Of holier love. Nor wilt thou then forget
That after many wanderings, many years

Of absence, these steep woods and lofty cliffs,
And this green pastoral landscape, were to me
More dear, both for themselves and for thy sake!

> William Wordsworth
> From *Lines Composed a Few Miles above Tintern Abbey*

Dorothy Wordsworth Wakes at Allan Bank

The Wordsworths lived at Allan Bank, Grasmere, from June 1808 to the spring of 1811. In 1930, when Margaret Cropper wrote this poem, the house was the home of Mrs Rawnsley, widow of Canon H. D. Rawnsley.

So she woke here, even as I wake here,
And saw, as I do, from her quiet bed,
The great mountain's shoulder, the deep cleft,
Where Michael worked at his unfinished fold.
Dorothy woke here in the early morning,
To her world of mountain and stream, which, long familiar,
Yet gave her each new day its cool grave secrets,
Its essential loveliness, as one might lay
In the hand of a tried friend some intimate token.
She woke to hear the patter of running feet,
To watch, with virginal affectionate glamour,
William's wild loving brood of little children.
She woke to her steady certainty of faith
In William's genius. If her heart could question
Whether any days could be like those first days
With him, she quietly reassured herself
That he was great, and she had nourished him,
Could nourish him yet, and so fulfil herself,
And bring his thoughts to birth. She woke to share
With shy Mary, a hundred household cares,
Putting out all the rareness of her spirit

Into some simple duty, and interlacing
Plain work with delicate gold of new perceptions,
Gathered within, without, from field or book.
She woke to steady herself against a hurt
So deep she could not longer weep for it;
To see the death in life of the man she loved,
As he had foretold it so sharply and pitifully
In the poems which he would never write any more.
'Tis this that made her womanhood more frail,
That checks the flow of the sap: and yet I see her
Bravely vigorous in spirit and body,
With quick chaste movements, dressing herself demurely,
With half her mind at work out of the window,
Binding the dark curls, now touched with grey:
She who never spoke of the colour or shape
Of any dress she wore, being more concerned
With the birch tree's habit, or the mountain's cloak.
William's genius, unfaltering here, was sure
When he saw her kin to the natural wild things,
The lover and beloved of the sheltered valley,
And high enfolding hills.

Margaret Cropper (1886–   )

Dorothy Wordsworth in Old Age

It is not certain that this poem refers to Dorothy Wordsworth, since the poet gave it no title, but its content and the date of its composition strongly suggest that this is so.

Time was when I could weep; but now all care
Is gone – yet have I gaz'd 'till sense deceived
Almost assures me that her bosom heav'd;
And o'er those features – as the lightest air

The Lake District

On summer sea – Life play'd, did they but bear
One trace of Mind, faintly in sleep perceiv'd,
Wand'ring, from earthly impulse unreliev'd –
Through regions of Emotion, wild or fair.
Her mind is gone! and now, while over all
A ghastly dreaming quiet seems to lie,
All Sounds subdued to mournful harmony,
My heart is tranquil; sunk beyond the Call
Of Hope or Fear; and still must deeper fall,
Down – down with Time, till e'en remembrance die.

Hartley Coleridge

Coleridge Invites Southey to Greta Hall

Our house stands on a low hill, the whole front of which is one field
and an enormous garden, nine-tenths of which is a nursery garden.
Behind the house is an orchard, and a small wood on a steep slope, at
the foot of which flows the river Greta, which winds round and cat-
ches the evening lights in the front of our house. In front we have a
giant's camp – an encamped army of tent-like mountains, which, by
an inverted arch, gives a view of another vale. On our right the
lovely vale and the wedge-shaped lake of Bassenthwaite; and on our
left Derwentwater and Lodore full in view, and the fantastic moun-
tains of Borrowdale. Behind us the massy Skiddaw, smooth, green,
high, with two chasms and a tent-like ridge in the larger. A fairer
scene you have not seen in all your wanderings. Without going from
our own grounds we have all that can please a human being. As to
books, my landlord, who dwells next door, has a very respectable
library, which he has put with mine – histories, encyclopaedias, and
all the modern gentry. But then I can have, when I choose, free access
to the princely library of Sir Gilfrid Lawson, which contains the
noblest collection of travels and natural history of, perhaps, any
private library in England; besides this, there is the Cathedral library

of Carlisle, from whence I can have any books sent to me that I wish; in short, I may truly say that I command all the libraries in the county . . .

The house is full twice as large as we want; it hath more rooms in it than Alfoxden: you might have a bed-room, parlour, study, &c., &c.; and there would always be rooms to spare for your or my visitors. In short, for situation and convenience – and when I mention the name of Wordsworth, for society of men of intellect – I know no place in which you and Edith would find yourselves so well suited.

S. T. Coleridge
Letter to Robert Southey

Southey Sees for Himself

'Twas at that sober hour when the light of day is receding,
And from surrounding things the hues wherewith day has adorn'd
  them
Fade, like the hopes of youth, till the beauty of earth is departed:
Pensive, though not in thought, I stood at the window, beholding
Mountain and lake and vale; the valley disrobed of its verdure;
Derwent retaining yet from eve a glassy reflection
Where his expanded breast, then still and smooth as a mirror,
Under the woods reposed; the hills that, calm and majestic,
Lifted their heads in the silent sky, from far Glaramara
Bleacrag, and Maidenmawr, to Grizdal and westermost Withop.
Dark and distinct they rose. The clouds hath gather'd above them
High in the middle air, huge, purple, pillowy masses,
While in the west beyond was the last pale tint of the twilight:
Green as a stream in the glen whose pure and chrysolite waters
Flow o'er a schistous bed, and serene as the age of the righteous.
Earth was hush'd and still; all motion and sound were suspended:
Neither man was heard, bird, beast, nor humming of insect,
Only the voice of the Greta, heard only when all is in stillness.

Pensive I stood and alone, the hour and the scene had subdued me,
And as I gazed in the west, where Infinity seem'd to be open,
Yearn'd to be free from time, and felt that this life is a thraldom.

Robert Southey
From *A Vision of Judgement*

A Boy's-Eye View of Southey

The church was St Kentigern's, Crosthwaite, on the outskirts of Keswick.

Now hurried we home, and while taking our tea,
We thought – Mr Southey at church we might see.
And then unto sleep we our bodies resigned,
And sunk in oblivion and silence our mind.
Next morning the church, how we wished for the reaching!
I'm afraid 'twas as much for the poet as preaching!
And, oh what a shame! – were shown into a seat
With everything, save what was wanted, replete;
And so dirty, and greasy, though many times dusted,
The ladies all thought it could never be trusted . . .
Howe'er I forgave, – 'deed, I scarcely did know it, –
For really we were 'cheek-by-jowl' with the poet!
His hair was no colour at all by the way,
But half of't was black, slightly scattered with grey;
His eyes were as black as a coal, but in turning
They flashed, – ay, as much as that coal does in burning!
His nose in the midst took a small outward bend,
Rather hooked like an eagle's, and sharp at the end;
But his dark lightning-eye made him seem half-inspired,
Or like his own Thalaba, vengefully fired.
We looked, and we gazed, and we stared in his face;
Marched out at a slow, stopping, lingering pace;
And as towards Keswick delighted we walked,

Of his face, and his form, and his features we talked,
With various chatter beguiling the day
Till the sun disappeared and the light fled away.

> John Ruskin
> From *Iteriad or Three Weeks Among The Lakes*
> (written at the age of eleven)

John Wilson – 'Christopher North'

It is probable that no stranger ever sees that pier at Storrs [i.e. on the shores of Windermere, south of Bowness] without thinking of Professor Wilson; and, indeed, there is no spot in the neighbourhood with which his memory, and the gratitude of his readers, is not associated. Any where such a presence is rarely seen; and it was especially impressive in the places he best loved to haunt. More than one person has said that Wilson reminded them of the first man, Adam; so full was his large frame of vitality, force, and sentience. His tread seemed to shake the ground, and his glance to pierce through stone walls; and, as for his voice, there was no heart that could stand before it. In his hour of emotion, he swept away all hearts, whithersoever he would. No less striking was it to see him in a mood of repose, as he was seen when steering the packet-boat that used to pass between Bowness and Ambleside, before the steamers were put upon the lake. Sitting motionless, with his hand upon the rudder, in the presence of journey-men and market-women, and his eye apparently looking beyond everything into nothing, and his mouth closed above his beard, as if he meant never to speak again, he was quite as impressive and immortal an image as he could have been to the students of his moral philosophy class, or the comrades of his jovial hours. He was known, and with reverence and affection, beside the trout stream and the mountain tarn, and amidst the damp gloom of Elleray, where he could not bring himself to let a tree or a sprig be lopped that his wife had loved. Every old boatman and young angler, every hoary shepherd and primitive dame among the hills of the district, knew him and enjoyed his presence. He made others happy by being so intensely happy himself, when his brighter moods were on him; and when he was mournful, no one desired to be gay. He is gone with his joy and his grief; and the region is so much the darker in a thousand eyes.

Harriet Martineau
Complete Guide to the English Lakes (1855)

Will Ritson Remembers John Wilson

Will Ritson, landlord of The Wastwater Hotel in the nineteenth century, was famous throughout the district as Cumberland's 'biggest liar'.

'T'furst time 'at Professor Wilson cam to Was'dle Head,' said Ritson, 'he hed a tent set up in a field, an' he gat it weel stock'd wi' bread, an' beef, an' cheese, an' rum, an' ale, an' sic like. Then he gedder't up my granfadder, an' Thomas Tyson, an' Isaac Fletcher an' Joseph Stable, an' aad Robert Grave, an' some mair, an' theer was gay deed amang 'em. Then, nowt was sarra [nothing would serve], but he mun hev a bwoat, an' they mun hev a sail. Well, when they gat into t'bwoat, he tell'd 'em to be particlar careful, for he was liable to git giddy in t'head, an' if yan ov his giddy fits sud chance to cum on, he mud happen tummle in t'watter. Well, it pleased 'em all gaily weel, an' they said they'd take varra girt care on him. Then he leaned back an' called oot that they mun pull quicker. So they did, and what does Wilson du then, but toppled ower eb'm ov his back i't'watter wid a splash. Then theer was a girt cry – "Eh, Mr Wilson's i't'watter". An'yan click't, an' anudder click't, but nean o' them cud git hod on him, an' there was sic a scrow as nivver. At last, yan o' them gat him round t'neck as he popped up at teal o't'bwoat, an' Wilson taad him to kep a gud hod, for he mud happen slip him agean. But what, it was nowt but yan of his bits o' pranks he was smirkin' an' laughin' all t'time. Wilson was a fine gay, girt-hearted fellow, as strang as a lion, an' as lish [lithe] as a trout, an' he hed sic antics as nivver man hed. Whativver ye sed tull him ye'd get your change back for it gaily seun . . .

Aa remember, theer was a "murry neet" at Wastd'le Head that varra time, an' Wilson an' t'aad parson was theer amang t'rest. When they'd gitten a bit on, Wilson mead a sang aboot t'parson. He mead it reet off o't'stick end. He began wi' t'parson furst, then he gat to t'Pope, an' then he turn'd it to t'devil, an' sic like, till he hed 'em fallin' off their cheers wi' fun. T'parson was quite stunn'd an' rayder vex't an' all, but, at last he burst oot laughin' wi' t'rest. He was like. Naabody could stand it. It was a' life an' murth amang us, as lang as Professor Wilson was at Wastd'le Head.'

Edwin Waugh
Quoted from *Literary Associations of the English Lakes*
by H. D. Rawnsley

Charlotte Brontë Visits Harriet Martineau

I can write to you now, dear E—, for I am away from home, and relieved, temporarily, at least, by change of air and scene, from the heavy depression which, I confess, has for nearly three months been sinking me to the earth. I never shall forget last autumn! Some days and nights have been cruel; but now, having once told you this, I need say no more on the subject. My loathing of solitude grew extreme; my recollection of my sisters intolerably poignant. I am better now. I am at Miss Martineau's for a week. Her house is very pleasant, both within and without; arranged at all points with admirable neatness and comfort. Her visitors enjoy the most perfect liberty; what she claims for herself she allows them. I rise at my own hour, breakfast alone (she is up at five, takes a cold bath, and a walk by starlight, and has finished breakfast and got to her work by seven o'clock). I pass the morning in the drawing-room – she in her study. At two o'clock we meet – work, talk, and walk together, till five, her dinner-hour, spend the evening together, when she converses fluently and abundantly, and with the most complete frankness. I go to my own room soon after ten, – she sits up writing letters till twelve. She appears exhaustless in strength and spirits, and indefatigable in the faculty of labour. She is a great and good woman; of course not without peculiarities, but I have seen none as yet that annoy me. She is both hard and warm-hearted, abrupt and affectionate, liberal and despotic. I believe she is not at all conscious of her own absolutism. When I tell her of it, she denies the charge warmly; then I laugh at her. I believe she almost rules Ambleside. Some of the gentry dislike her, but the lower orders have a great regard for her . . . I have truly enjoyed my visit here. I have seen a good many people, and all have been so marvellously kind; not the least so, the family of Dr Arnold. Miss Martineau I relish inexpressibly.

> Charlotte Brontë (1816–1855)
> *Letter to Ellen Nussey*
> Quoted from Elizabeth Gaskell's *Life of Charlotte Brontë*

Death of a Literary Lady

Miss Elizabeth Smith – 1776–1806 – came, in 1800, with her parents to live in the Lake District. She was extremely well-read and had taught herself eight to ten languages and published translations from German and Hebrew, yet she does not seem to have shown the least interest in Wordsworth, who was living only a few miles away. The house, which stands on the site where she pitched her tent, is still known as Tent Lodge.

About four years had been delightfully passed in Coniston. In the summer of 1805 Miss Smith laid the foundation of her fatal illness in the following way, according to her own account of the case of an old servant, a very short time before she died: – 'One very hot evening, in July, I took a book, and walked about two miles from home,

when I seated myself on a stone beside the lake. Being much engaged
by a poem I was reading, I did not perceive that the sun was gone
down, and was succeeded by a very heavy dew, till, in a moment, I
felt struck on the chest as if with a very sharp knife. I returned home,
but said nothing of the pain. The next day being also very hot, and
every one busy in the hay-field, I thought I would take a rake, and
work very hard to produce perspiration, in the hope that it might
remove the pain; but it did not.' From that time, a bad cough, with
occasional loss of voice, gave reason to suspect some organic injury
of the lungs. Late in the autumn of this year (1805) Miss Smith
accompanied her mother and her two younger sisters to Bristol,
Bath, and other places in the south, on visits to various friends. Her
health went through various fluctuations until May of the following
year, when she was advised to try Matlock. Here, after spending
three weeks, she grew worse; and, as there was no place which she
liked so well as the Lakes, it was resolved to turn homewards. About
the beginning of June, she and her mother returned alone to Coniston:
one of her sisters was now married; her three brothers were in the
army or navy; and her father almost constantly with his regiment.
Through the next two months she faded quietly away, sitting always
in a tent, that had been pitched upon the lawn, and which remained
open continually to receive the fanning of the intermitting airs upon
the lake, as well as to admit the bold mountain scenery to the north.
She lived nearly through the first week of August, dying on the
morning of August 7; and the circumstances of her last night are thus
recorded by her mother: – 'At nine she went to bed. I resolved to quit
her no more, and went to prepare for the night. Turpin (Miss Smith's
maid) came to say that Elizabeth entreated that I would not stay in
her room. I replied – "On that one subject I am resolved; no power
on earth shall keep me from her; so, go to bed yourself." Accordingly,
I returned to her room; and, at ten, gave her the usual dose of lauda-
num. After a little time, she fell into a doze, and, I thought, slept till
one. She was uneasy and restless, but never complained; and, on my
wiping the cold sweat off her face, and bathing it with camphorated
vinegar, which I did very often in the course of the night, she thanked
me, smiled, and said – "That is the greatest comfort I have." She slept
again for a short time; and, at half past four, asked for some chicken

broth, which she took perfectly well. On being told the hour, she said, "*How long this night is!*" She continued very uneasy; and, in half an hour after, on my enquiring if I could move the pillow, or do anything to relieve her, she replied, "There is nothing for it but quiet." At six, she said, "I must get up and have some mint tea." I then called for Turpin, and felt my angel's pulse: it was fluttering; and by that I knew I should soon lose her. She took the tea well. Turpin began to put on her clothes, and was proceeding to dress her, when she laid her head upon the faithful creature's shoulder, became convulsed in the face, spoke not, looked not, and in ten minutes expired.'

Thomas De Quincey
Recollections of the Lake Poets

Distinguished Visitors

George Fox Preaches on a Hill

George Fox had many sympathizers and followers in the Lake Counties, especially in the neighbourhood of Kendal, Ulverston and Wigton. At Swarthmoor Hall, near Ulverston, he met Judge Fell, whose widow, Margaret, he later married. Firbank is on the western side of the River Lune, a few miles above Sedbergh and not far from Kendal. Both Howgill and Audland became famous Quaker preachers.

The next First-day I came to FIRBANK CHAPEL, in Westmorland, where Francis Howgill, before named, and John Audland, had been preaching in the morning. The chapel was full of people, so that many could not get in. Francis Howgill said, he thought I looked into the chapel, and his spirit was ready to fail, the Lord's power did so surprise him; but I did not look in. They made haste, and had quickly gone, and they and some of the people went to dinner, but abundance stayed till they came again . . . While the others were gone to dinner, I went to a brook and got a little water; and then came and sat down on the top of a rock hard by the chapel. In the afternoon the people gathered about me, with several of their preachers. It was judged there were above a thousand people; amongst whom I declared God's everlasting truth and word of life freely and largely, for about the space of three hours, directing all to the Spirit of God *in* themselves, that they might be turned from darkness to the light, and believe in it, that they might become children of it . . .

Now there were many old people, who went into the chapel and looked out at the windows, thinking it a strange thing to see a man preach on a hill, and not in their church, as they called it; whereupon I was moved to open to the people, that the steeple-house and the ground whereon it stood, were no more holy than that mountain: and that those temples, which they called the dreadful houses of God, were not set up by the command of God and of Christ; nor their priests called, as Aaron's priesthood was; nor their tithes appointed by God, as those amongst the Jews were; but that Christ was come, who ended both the temple and its worship, and the priests and their tithes; and that all should now hearken unto him; for he said, 'Learn of me;' and God said of him, 'This is my beloved Son, in whom I am well pleased, hear ye him.' I declared unto them that the Lord God had sent me to preach the everlasting gospel and word of life amongst them, and to bring them off from all these temples, tithes, priests, and rudiments of the world, which had been instituted since the apostles' days and had been set up by such as had erred from the Spirit and power the apostles were in. Very largely was I opened at this meeting, and the Lord's convincing power accompanied my ministry, and reached the hearts of the people, whereby many were convinced; and all the teachers of that congregation (who were many), were convinced of God's everlasting truth.

George Fox
Journal

John Wesley Finds God in West Cumberland

This was not John Wesley's first visit to Cumberland; indeed, it was at Whitehaven, ten years earlier, that he was overtaken by Charles Wesley, who had rushed north to dissuade his brother from marrying Grace Murray. The 'sand road', of which he speaks, is, of course, the West Coast route over the sands of Morecambe Bay; and the 'four sands' are those of the estuaries of the Kent, the Leven, the Duddon, and the joint estuary of the Esk and the Irt at Ravenglass. – It should be noted that when Wesley says that God is 'no where more present than in the mountains of Cumberland', he is not anticipating Wordsworth. On the contrary, he is implying that these mountains were the last place where anyone would expect to find God!

Sat. 12 [*May, 1759*]. Setting out early [i.e. from Flookborough, a village on the Cartmel peninsula, midway along the Morecambe Bay route], we came to Bottle [Bootle], about twenty-four measured miles from Fluckborough [Flookborough], soon after eight, having crossed the Millam Sand [Millom – i.e. the Duddon Sands], without either guide or difficulty. Here we were informed that we could not pass at Ravenglass before one or two o'clock; whereas, had we gone on, (as we afterwards found) we might have passed immediately. About eleven we were directed to a Ford, near Manchester-Hall [Muncaster], which they said we might cross at noon. When we came thither, they told us we could not cross; so we sat still till about one: We then found we could have crossed at noon. However, we reached Whitehaven before night. But I have taken my leave of the sand road. I believe it is ten measured miles shorter than the other [i.e. overland, by Kendal and Dunmail Raise]: but there are four sands to pass, so far from each other, that it is scarce possible to pass them all in a day: Especially as you have all the way to do with a generation of liars, who detain all strangers as long as they can, either for their own gain or their neighbours'. I can advise no stranger to go this way: He may go round by Kendal and Keswick, often in less time, always with less expense, and far less trial of his patience.

Tues. 15. I rode over to Lorton, a little village at the foot of a high mountain. Many came from a considerable distance, and I believe did not repent of their labour; for they found God to be a God both of the hills and valleys, and no where more present than in the mountains of Cumberland.

Thurs. 17. I inquired into a single instance of Providence. When a coal-pit runs far under the ground, it is customary here to build a partition-wall, nearly from the shaft to within three or four yards of the end, in order to make the air circulate, which then moves down one side of the wall, turns at the end, and then moves briskly up on the other side. In a pit two miles from the town, which ran full four hundred yards under the ground, and had been long neglected, several parts of this wall were fallen down. Four men were sent down to repair it. They were about three hundred yards from the shaft, when the foul air took fire. In a moment it tore down the wall from end to end; and, burning on till it came to the shaft, it then burst and went off like a large cannon. The men instantly fell on their faces, or they would have been burned to death in a few moments. One of them, who once knew the love of God (Andrew English), began crying aloud for mercy. But in a very short time his breath was stopped. The other three crept on their hands and knees, till two got to the shaft and were drawn up; but one of them died in a few minutes. John M'Combe was drawn up next, burned from head to foot, but rejoicing and praising God. They then went down for Andrew, whom they found senseless: The very circumstance which saved his life. For, losing his senses, he lay flat on the ground, and the greatest part of the fire went over him; whereas, had he gone forward on his hands and knees, he would undoubtedly have been burned to death. But life or death was welcome; for God had restored the light of his countenance.

Sun. 20. I preached at eight in an open place at the Gins, a village on one side of the town. Many were there, who never did and never would come to the Room. O what a victory would Satan gain, if he could put an end to field-preaching! But that, I trust, he never will: At least not till my head is laid.

After preaching again at two, I took my leave of Whitehaven, and rode to Cockermouth. At six I preached at the end of the market-house. High and low, rich and poor, attended; and by far the greater part of the audience seemed to be conscious that God was there.

John Wesley (1703–1791)
Journal

Thomas Gray Ventures into Borrowdale

Gray spent ten days in the Lakes in the autumn of 1769, and his Journal, *written in the form of a series of letters to his friend, Dr Warton, was published after his death in William Mason's Memoir of the poet (1775). Five years later it was printed as an appendix to the second edition of Thomas West's* Guide To The Lakes, *in which form it became known to a great many travellers in the district. Quotations from the* Journal *included in this book are taken from the* Guide. *The 'glass' to which Gray alludes was a 'Claude-glass' or convex mirror in which the traveller could view the landscape reduced to about the size of a postcard.*

Oct 3 [1769]. A heavenly day; rose at seven, and walked out under the conduct of my landlord to Borrowdale; the grass was covered with a hoar-frost, which soon melted and exhaled in a thin bluish smoke; crossed the meadows, obliquely catching a diversity of views among the hills, over the lake and islands, and changing prospect at every ten paces . . . Our path here tends to the left, and the ground gently rising, and covered with a glade of scattered trees and bushes on the very margin of the water, opens both ways the most delicious view that my eyes ever beheld. Opposite, are the thick woods of Lord Egremont, and Newland valley, with green and smiling fields embosomed in the dark cliffs; to the left, the jaws of Borrowdale, with that turbulent chaos of mountain behind mountain, rolled in confusion; beneath you and stretching far away to the right, the shining purity of the lake reflecting rocks, woods, fields, and inverted tops of hills, just ruffled by the breeze, enough to shew it is alive, with the white buildings of Keswick, Crosthwaite church, and Skiddaw for a background at a distance. Behind you the magnificent heights of Wallowcrag: here the glass played its part divinely . . . This scene continues to Barrowgate, and a little farther, passing a brook called Barrowbeck, we entered Borrowdale; the crags named Lowdore-banks begin now to impend terribly over the way, and more terribly when you hear that three years since an immense mass of rock tumbled at once from the brow, barred all access to the dale (for this is the only road) till they could work their way through it. Luckily no one was passing by at the time of this fall; but down the side of the mountain, and far into the lake, lie dispersed the huge fragments of this ruin, in all shapes and in all directions: something farther we turned aside into a coppice, ascending a little in front of Lowdore water-fall; the height appeared to be about 200 feet, the quantity of water not great, though (these three days excepted) it had rained daily in the hills for near two months before: but then the stream was nobly broken, leaping from rock to rock, and foaming with fury. On one side a towering crag, that spired up to equal, if not overtop the neighbouring cliffs (this lay all in shade and darkness); on the other hand a rounder, broader, projecting hill, shagged with wood, and illuminated by the sun, which glanced sideways on the upper part of the cataract. The force of the water wearing a deep channel in the ground, hurries away to join the lake. We descended again, and passed the stream over a rude

bridge. Soon after we came under Gowdar-crag, a hill more for-
midable to the eye, and to the apprehension, than that of Lowdore;
the rocks at top deep-cloven perpendicularly by the rains, hanging
loose and nodding forwards, seen just starting from their base in
shivers. The whole way down, and the road on both sides is strewed
with piles of the fragments, strangely thrown across each other, and
of a dreadful bulk; the place reminds me of those passes in the Alps,
where the guides tell you to move with speed, and say nothing, less
the agitation of the air should loosen the snows above, and bring
down a mass that would overwhelm a caravan. I took their counsel
here, and hastened on in silence.

> *Non ragioniam di lor, ma guarda, e passa.*
> ['Let us not discuss them, but take a look and pass by.' Dante:
> *Inferno*, Canto 3]

Thomas Gray (1716–1771)
Journal in the Lakes

Charles Lamb Climbs Skiddaw

(24th September, 1802)
I set out with Mary to Keswick without giving Coleridge any notice,
for, my time being precious, did not admit of it. He received us with
all the hospitality in the world, and gave up his time to show us all
the wonders of the country. He dwells upon a small hill by the side
of Keswick, in a comfortable house, quite enveloped on all sides by a
net of mountains, great floundering bears and monsters they seemed,
all couchant and asleep. We got in in the evening, travelling in a post-
chaise from Penrith, in the midst of a gorgeous sunshine, which
transmuted all the mountains into colours, purple, etc. We thought
we had got into fairy-land. But that went off (and it never came again;
while we stayed we had no more fine sunsets), and we entered Cole-
ridge's comfortable study just in the dusk, when the mountains were
all dark with clouds upon their heads. Such an impression I never
received from objects of sight before, nor do I suppose that I can ever

again. Glorious creatures, fine old fellows, Skiddaw, etc, I never shall forget ye, how ye lay about that night like an intrenchment; gone to bed as it seemed for the night, but promising that ye were to be seen in the morning. Coleridge had got a blazing fire in his study; which is a large, antique, ill-shaped room, with an old-fashioned organ, never played upon, big enough for a church, shelves of scattered folios, an Eolian harp, and an old sofa, half bed, etc. And all looking out upon the fading view of Skiddaw and his broad-breasted brethren. What a night! Here we stayed three full weeks, in which time I visited Wordsworth's cottage, where we stayed a day or two with the Clarksons (good people, and most hospitable, at whose house we tarried one day and night), and saw Lloyd. The Wordsworths were gone to Calais. They have since been in London, and past much time with us; he is now gone into Yorkshire to be married. So we have seen Keswick, Grasmere, Ambleside, Ulswater (where the Clarksons live), and a place at the other end of Ulswater, I forget the name, to which we travelled on a very sultry day over the middle of Helvellyn. We have clambered up to the top of Skiddaw, and I have waded up the bed of Lodore. In fine, I have satisfied myself that there is such a thing as that which tourists call *romantic*, which I very much suspected before; they make such a spluttering about it, and toss their splendid epithets around them, till they give as dim a light as at four o'clock next morning the lamps do after an illumination. Mary was excessively tired when she got about half-way up Skiddaw, but we came to a cold rill (than which nothing can be imagined more cold, running over cold stones), and with the reinforcement of a draught of cold water she surmounted it most manfully. Oh, its fine black head, and the bleak air atop of it, with a prospect of mountains all about and about, making you giddy; and then Scotland afar off, and the Border countries, so famous in song and ballad! It was a day that will stand out like a mountain, I am sure, in my life. But I am returned (I have now been home near three weeks, I was a month out), and you cannot conceive the degradation I felt at first, from being accustomed to wander free as air among mountains, and bathe in rivers without being controuled by any one to come home and *work*. I felt very *little*. I had been dreaming I was a very great man. But that is going off, and I find I shall conform in time to that state of life to which it has pleased God to call me. Besides, after all, Fleet Street and the Strand are better places to live in for good and all than amidst Skiddaw. Still I turn back to those great places where I wandered about, participating in their greatness. After all I could not *live* in Skiddaw. I could spend a year, two, three years among them, but I must have a prospect of seeing Fleet Street at the end of that time, or I should mope and pine away, I know. Still Skiddaw is a fine creature.

Charles Lamb (1775–1834)
Letter to Thomas Manning

John Keats Calls at Rydal Mount

The agreeable diversion to his somewhat monotonous life by a walking-tour through the Lakes and Highlands with his friend Mr Brown was now put into execution . . . From Lancaster they started on foot, and Mr Brown has recorded the rapture of Keats when he became sensible for the first time, of the full effect of mountain scenery. At the turn of the road above Bowness, where the Lake of Windermere first bursts on the view, he stopped as if stupified with beauty. That evening he read aloud the poem of the *Pot of Basil*, which he had just completed. His disappointment at missing Wordsworth was very great, and he hardly concealed his vexation when he found that he owed the privation to the interest which the elder poet was taking in the General Election. This annoyance would perhaps have been diminished if the two poets had happened to be on the same side in politics; but, as it was, no views and objects could be more opposed.

A portion of a rambling journal of this tour remains in various letters.

KESWICK
29 June [1818]

My Dear Tom,

I cannot make my journal as distinct and actual as I could wish, from having been engaged in writing to George, and therefore I must tell you, without circumstance, that we proceeded from Ambleside to Rydal, saw the waterfalls there, and called on Wordsworth, who was not at home, nor was anyone of his family. I wrote a note and left it on the mantelpiece. Thence, on we came to the foot of Helvellyn, where we slept, but could not ascend it for the mist. I must mention that from Rydal we passed Thirlswater [Thirlmere], and a fine pass in the mountains. From Helvellyn we came to Keswick on Derwent Water. The approach to Derwent Water surpassed Windermere: it is richly wooded, and shut in with rich-toned mountains. From Helvellyn to Keswick was eight miles to breakfast, after which we took a complete circuit of the lake, going about ten miles, and seeing on our way the fall of Lodore. I had an easy climb among the streams, about the fragments of rocks, and should have got I think, to the summit, but unfortunately I was damped by slipping one leg into a squashy hole. There is no great body of water, but the accompaniment is delightful; for it oozes out from a cleft in perpendicular rocks, all fledged with ash and other beautiful trees. It is a strange thing how they got there. At the south end of the lake, the mountains of Borrowdale are perhaps as fine as anything we have seen. On our return from this circuit, we ordered dinner, and set forth about a mile and a half on the Penrith road, to see the Druid temple [i.e. Castlerigg]. We had a fag up hill, rather too near dinner-time, which was rendered void by the gratification of seeing those aged stones on a gentle rise in the midst of the mountains, which at that time darkened all round, except at the fresh opening of the Vale of St John. We went to bed rather fatigued, but not so much as to hinder us getting up this morning to Mount Skiddaw. It promised all along to be fair, and we had fagged and tugged nearly to the top, when, at half-past six, there came a mist upon us, and shut out the view. We did not, however, lose anything by it; we were high enough without mist to see the coast of Scotland, the Irish Sea, the hills beyond Lancaster, and nearly all the large ones of Cumberland and Westmoreland, particularly Helvellyn and Scawfell. It grew colder and colder as we ascended, and we were glad, at about three parts of the way, to taste a little rum which the guide brought with him, mixed, mind ye, with mountain water. I took two glasses going and one returning. It is about six miles from where I am writing to the top; so we have walked ten miles before breakfast today. We went up with two others, very good sort of fellows. All felt, on arising into the cold air, that same elevation which a cold bath gives one. I felt as if I were going to a tournament.

Richard Monckton Milnes, Lord Houghton (1809–1885)
The Life and Letters of John Keats

The Lakers Honour Sir Walter Scott

*In the summer of 1825, Scott accompanied by his son-in-law, John Gibson
Lockhart, visited Ireland, returning via North Wales and the Lake District,
where George Canning had invited them to join him at Storrs on Winder-
mere, the house of his friend, Mr Bolton.*

On reaching that lake, we spent a pleasant day with Professor Wilson
at Elleray, and he then conducted us to Storrs. A large company had
been assembled there in honour of the Minister – among others was
Mr Wordsworth. It has not, I suppose, often happened, to a plain
English merchant, wholly the architect of his own fortunes, to enter-
tain at one time a party embracing so many illustrious names. He was
proud of his guests; they respected him, and honoured and loved each
other; and it would have been difficult to say which star in the con-
stellation shone with the brightest or the softest light. There was
'high discourse', intermingled with as gay flashings of courtly wit as
ever Canning displayed; and a plentiful allowance, on all sides, of
those airy transient pleasantries, in which the fancy of poets, however
wise and grave, delights to run riot when they are sure not to be mis-
understood. There were beautiful and accomplished women to adorn
and enjoy this circle. The weather was as Elysian as the scenery. There
were brilliant cavalcades through the woods in the mornings, and
delicious boatings on the lake by moonlight; and the last day, 'the
Admiral of the Lake' [i.e. Professor Wilson] presided over one of the
most splendid regattas that ever enlivened Windermere. Perhaps
there were not fewer than fifty barges following in the Professor's
radiant procession, when it paused at the point of Storrs to admit into
the place of honour the vessel that carried kind and happy Mr Bolton
and his guests. The bards of the Lakes led the cheers that hailed Scott
and Canning; and music and sunshine, flags, streamers, and gay
dresses, the merry hum of voices, and the rapid splashing of innumer-
able oars, made up a dazzling mixture of sensations as the flotilla
wound its way among the richly-foliaged islands, and along bays and
promontories peopled with enthusiastic spectators.

J. G. Lockhart (1794–1854)
The Life of Sir Walter Scott

A Boy's-Eye View of Coniston

In 1830, when Ruskin was eleven, he spent three weeks at the Lakes, with his father and mother, his cousin, Mary, and his nurse. They stayed part of the time at Low Wood on Windermere, and part at the Royal Oak, Keswick. On Tuesday, 6 July, they crossed Windermere by the ferry, drove through Hawkshead to the head of Coniston Lake, dined at the old Waterhead Inn, and returned to Low Wood by Skelwith and Ambleside. From Waterhead he would have been able to look down the lake to the spot where he was to spend his old age.

When dinner was over, as still it did rain,
We thought that we scarcely need longer remain:
So, ordered the carriage, and with no good will,
We ordered that pest of all travels – the bill.
May the money bear witness how quickly they made it.
– Much quicker than we were inclined to have paid it!
Though, without further grumbling, the silver we gave,
And gallopped away from old Coniston's wave.
Yet, ere we should leave it in tempest and rain,
We, turning, looked back on its waters again.
With its deep-bosomed billows in front lay the lake,
Whose waters divided by mountain and cape,
All open and bare they, full lonely did lie,
Exposing their breast to the shadowy sky:
Retiring in distance they mistily lay;
And fainter each inlet, and softer each bay;
Till, appearing no more, by the wild tempest tost,
'Mid mountains and clouds in the distance were lost.
Those mountains all mistily softened away,
Appeared like thin clouds at the dawn of a day;
Still darker and deeper, in bolder relief,
As, nearer approaching, and rising the chief,
The mighty Old Man, with his dark summit reft
Nearer and sterner arose on our left.
Oh, such was the view, sir, and we very well did

The Lake District

Look over each spot as we amply beheld it,
Then turned and rode off . . .

> John Ruskin
> From *Iteriad or Three Weeks Among The Lakes*
> (written at the age of eleven)

Mrs Gaskell Meets Miss Brontë

Fox How was the home of Dr Arnold of Rugby.

It was during this visit at the Briery – Lady Kay Shuttleworth having
kindly invited me to meet her there – that I first made acquaintance
with Miss Brontë. If I copy out part of a letter, which I wrote soon
after this to a friend, who was deeply interested in her writings, I shall
probably convey my first impressions more truly and freshly than by
amplifying what I then said into a longer description.

'Dark when I got to Windermere station; a drive along the level
road to Low-wood; then a stoppage at a pretty house, and then a
pretty drawing-room, in which were Sir James and Lady Kay
Shuttleworth, and a little lady in a black-silk gown, whom I could
not see at first for the dazzle in the room; she came up and shook
hands with me at once. I went up to unbonnet, etc.; came down to
tea; the little lady worked away and hardly spoke, but I had time for
a good look at her. She is (as she calls herself) *undeveloped*, thin, and
more than half a head shorter than I am; soft brown hair, not very
dark; eyes (very good and expressive, looking straight and open at
you) of the same colour as her hair; a large mouth; the forehead
square, broad, and rather over-hanging. She has a very sweet voice;
rather hesitates in choosing her expressions, but when chosen they
seem without an effort admirable, and just befitting the occasion;
there is nothing overstrained, but perfectly simple . . .

'We were only three days together; the greater part of which was
spent in driving about, in order to show Miss Brontë the Westmor-

land scenery, as she had never been there before. We were both included in an invitation to drink tea quietly at Fox How; and I then saw how severely her nerves were taxed by the effort of going amongst strangers. We knew beforehand that the number of the party would not exceed twelve; but she suffered the whole day from an acute headache brought on by apprehension of the evening.

'Briery Close was situated high above Low-wood, and of course commanded an extensive view and wide horizon. I was struck by Miss Brontë's careful examination of the shape of the clouds and the signs of the heavens, in which she read, as from a book, what the coming weather would be. I told her that I saw she must have a view equal in extent at her own home. She said that I was right, but that the character of the prospect from Haworth was very different; that I had no idea what a companion the sky became to any one living in solitude, – more than any inanimate object on earth, – more than the moors themselves.'

The following extracts convey some of her own impressions and feelings respecting this visit: –

You said I should stay longer than a week in Westmoreland; you ought by this time to know me better. Is it my habit to keep dawdling at a place long after the time I first fixed on for departing? I have got home, and I am thankful to say Papa seems, – to say the least, – no worse than when I left him, yet I wish he were stronger. My visit passed off very well; I am glad I went. The scenery is, of course, grand; could I have wandered about amongst those hills *alone*, I could have drank in all their beauty; even in a carriage with company, it was very well. Sir James was all the while as kind and friendly as he could be: he is in much better health . . . Miss Martineau was from home; she always leaves her house at Amble-side during the Lake season, to avoid the influx of visitors to which she would otherwise be subject.

If I could only have dropped unseen out of the carriage, and gone away by myself in amongst those grand hills and sweet dales, I should have drank in the full power of this glorious scenery. In company this can hardly be.

To these extracts I must add one other from a letter referring to this time. It is addressed to Miss Wooler, the kind friend of both her girl-hood and womanhood, who had invited her to spend a fortnight with her at her cottage lodgings.

Haworth, Sept. 27th, 1850

When I tell you that I have already been to the Lakes this season, and that it is scarcely more than a month since I returned, you will understand that it is no longer within my option to accept your kind invitation. I wish I could have gone to you. I have already had my excursion, and there is an end of it. Sir James Kay Shuttleworth is residing near Windermere, at a house called the 'Briery', and it was there I was staying for a little time this August. He very kindly showed me the neighbourhood, *as it can be seen from a carriage*, and I discerned that the Lake country is a glorious region, of which I had only seen the similitude in dreams, waking or sleeping. Decidedly I find it does not agree with me to prosecute the search of the picturesque in a carriage. A waggon, a spring-cart, even a post-chaise might do; but the carriage upsets everything. I longed to slip out unseen, and to run away by myself in amongst the hills and dales. Erratic and vagrant instincts tormented me, and these I was obliged to control, or rather suppress, for fear of growing in any degree enthusiastic, and thus drawing attention to the 'lioness' – the authoress.

Elizabeth Gaskell (1810–1865)
The Life of Charlotte Brontë

Charles Dickens at Windermere Sports

'Nay, you're over weight, John, by two pounds,' says the clerk of the ring to some candidate seated in the weighing scale, who smiles good naturedly, and takes off nearly everything, but still is not quite qualified; he puts, therefore, a couple of great coats on, and takes a run in the road by the lake's side, whereby his too solid flesh being swelled and dissolved into a dew, he comes to scale a light weight after all. There are a great many 'lay-downs' in the first round, so that the wrestling gets select, and very much improves as it proceeds. The third round comprehends, therefore (unless in the case of some accidental defeat) a score of the best men. They strip to their drawers and flannel waistcoats, exhibiting such studies for the painter and the sculptor as are rarely seen else where. They shake hands before commencing, in token of amity; nor indeed in the thick and strain of the struggle, while the face of each is over the shoulder of the other, and every muscle is exerted to the utmost, do these fine fellows exhibit any trace of savageness or personal animosity.

Two umpires, nestors of the wrestling ring, walk round the combatants, and observe them narrowly; nor is their decision ever impugned by the losing man. While the pair are taking hold, gratuitous advice is offered to them freely by their friends, who sit or stand around the ring, but when they grapple each other a perfect torrent of Bonnie Carels, or Bonnie Kendals, as the case may be, cleaves the air. Then they strive, then they strain shoulder to shoulder, neck to neck, and at last touch ground perhaps, so nearly at the same instant as to require the most practised eye to award the fall; or, whirling circularly as in Fakir-dance, are cast violently to earth apart, or one, across the victor's thigh, comes heels over head, and measures all his inches upon the green sward with a thud. This last fall is the only dangerous one, and that only in the case of very heavy weights, and of very indifferent performers. Good wrestlers very rarely hurt one another.

This quiet looking giant by our side, who has been champion often and often, and will be so again this day, although he is nearly forty, and more than twelve years past the wrestler's prime, has never, in his twenty years' experience ever been hurt. He won his first man's belt when a lad of sixteen years old, and in his house, across the lake yonder – a clean, neat little inn, set in a wilderness of flowers – has no less than one hundred and seventy-four of these wrestling zones; of all colours they are, and of all descriptions, from the broad, plain, Manchester-looking belt, won at the matter of fact and unornamental town, to the splendid award of Newcastle, embossed with the silver towers. Besides the merit (although there is nothing like it), there is of course a very considerable prize in money, averaging, perhaps, twenty pounds. Lesser pecuniary rewards are proportionately distributed among the less successful combatants, and besides these, a subscription prize is commonly made up by the stewards or spectators for which the sixteen last standers wrestle over again. Between the light and heavy weight matches (which are generally on following days), there are all sorts of other amusements, running matches, for a mile or so, dog trails, jumping matches, for which not only the aborigines enter, but usually several visitors, University men, and the like, who reckoning upon the iron shod boots and rough appearance of the natives are surprised to find them, when stripped, as lithe and active as themselves, and indeed a trifle more so ! . . .

The heavy weight wrestlers generally close these amusements. If others were Apollos, each of these is surely a Hercules; their grip is like the hug of a bear. The champion here, who was so good as to show us how to 'take hold', the other day, in his garden, has left his mark indelibly in our back, besides having compressed our ribs so that we cannot breathe right yet. It has come to the last round, and our giant friend has but one foe to deal with – a true son of Anak, as tall if not so big as himself – he has got his work cut out for him, say the old hands; but success has made him somewhat over bold. How quietly he suffers these mighty arms to be placed around him, and those strong fingers to feel like one in the dark for a certain hold. Now they have gripped at an advantage, and the foe is only waiting for him to have hold likewise. He has hold! He has hold! see how they grapple and strain. 'Bonnie Robson', 'Bonnie Longmire', so interested this time in the individuals as to call them by their own names instead of the localities from which they come. Three to two on Longmire; two to one, five to – Longmire's down! Robson's felled him! Bonnie Robson! And indeed it was so; very quiet, but very grim our giant looked. 'It is the best of three for the last round,' quoth he as he took up earth in his hands to prevent them slipping, reminding us of the preparatory horn practice which the bull indulges himself in before he charges. This time it is two to one on Robson, who is indeed a very good man, but he is felled nevertheless, and the third time he is felled likewise, after a struggle such as the old Greek gods were wont to delight in sitting above the thunder on Olympus' top, or the Roman Caesars, little less divine, in that great wrestler's ring by the Eternal City. So our giant friend has won his one hundred and seventy-fifth girdle, and is champion after all.

Charles Dickens (1812–1870)
Household Words
Quoted from *Wrestliana: or the History of the Cumberland
and Westmorland Wrestling Society in London* (1870)

Nathaniel Hawthorne Finds All in Excellent Taste

[*July 13th, 1855. Newby Bridge*]. The day after we came, we climbed a high and pretty steep hill, through a path shadowed with trees and shrubbery, up to a tower, from the summit of which we had a wide view of mountain scenery and the greater part of Windermere. The lake is a lovely little pool among the hills, long and narrow, beautifully indented with tiny bays and headlands; and when we saw it, it was one smile (as broad a smile as its narrowness allowed) with really brilliant sunshine. All the scenery we have yet met with is in excellent taste, and keeps itself within very proper bounds, – never getting too wild and rugged to shock the sensitivities of cultivated people, as American scenery is apt to do. On the rudest surface of English earth, there is seen the effect of centuries of civilization, so that you do not quite get at naked Nature anywhere. And then every point of beauty is so well known, and has been described so much, that one must needs look through other people's eyes, and feel as if he were seeing a picture rather than a reality. Man has, in short, entire possession of Nature here, and I should think young men might sometimes yearn for a fresher draught. But an American likes it.

July 16th. On Saturday, we left Newby Bridge, and came by steamboat up Windermere Lake to Lowwood Hotel, where we now are . . . The banks are everywhere beautiful, and the water, in one portion, is strewn with islands; few of which are large enough to be inhabitable, but they all seem to be appropriated, and kept in the neatest order. As yet, I have seen no wildness, everything is perfectly subdued and polished and imbued with human taste, except, indeed, the outlines of the hills, which continue very much the same as God made them. As we approached the head of the lake, the congregation of great hills in the distance became very striking. The shapes of these English mountains are certainly far more picturesque than those which I have seen in Eastern America, where their summits are almost invariably rounded, as I remember them. They are great hillocks, great bunches of earth, similar to one another in their developments. Here they have variety of shape, rising into peaks, falling in abrupt precipices, stretching along in zigzag outlines, and thus making the most of their not very gigantic masses, and producing a remarkable effect.

July 19th. After leaving Ambleside, the road winds in and out among the hills, and soon brings us to a sheet (or napkin, rather, than a sheet) of water, which the driver tells us is Rydal Lake! We had already heard that it was but three quarters of a mile long and one quarter broad; still, it being an idea of considerable size in our minds, we had inevitably drawn its ideal, physical proportions on a somewhat corresponding scale. It certainly did look small; and I said, in my American scorn, that I could carry it away easily in a porringer; for it is nothing more than a grassy-bordered pool among the surrounding hills which ascend directly from its margin; so that one might fancy it, not a permanent body of water, but a rather extensive accumulation of recent rain. Moreover, it was rippled with a breeze, and so, as I remember it, though the sun shone, it looked dull and sulky, like a child out of humor. Now, the best thing these small ponds can do is to keep perfectly calm and smooth, and not attempt to show off any airs of their own, but content themselves with serving as a mirror for whatever of beautiful or picturesque there may be in the scenery around them.

July 21st. I question whether any part of the world looks so beautiful as England – this part of England, at least – on a fine summer morning. It makes one think the more cheerfully of human life to see such a bright universal verdure; such sweet, rural, peaceful, flower-bordered cottages, – not cottages of gentility, but dwellings of the labouring poor; and such nice villas along the roadside, so tastefully contrived for comfort and beauty, and adorned more and more, year after year, with the care and after-thought of people who mean to live in them a great while, and feel as if their children might live in them also, – and so they plant trees to overshadow their walks, and train ivy and all beautiful vines up against their walls, and thus live for the future in another sense than we Americans do. And the climate helps them out, and makes everything moist, and green, and full of tender life, instead of dry and arid, as human life and vegetable life is so apt to be with us. Certainly, England can present a more attractive face, than we can; even in its humbler modes of life, to say nothing of the beautiful lives that might be led, one would think, by the higher classes, whose gateways, with broad, smooth gravelled drives leading through them, one sees every mile or two along the road, winding into some proud seclusion. All this is passing away, and society must assume new relations; but there is no harm in believing that there has been something very good in English life, – good for all classes while the world was in a state out of which these forms naturally grew.

Nathaniel Hawthorne
English Note-Books

The Inhabitants

The Men of Borrowdale

The dale opens about four miles higher, till you come to Seathwaite (where lies the way, mounting to the right, that leads to the wad-mines); all farther access is here barred to prying mortals, only there is a little path winding over the fells, and for some weeks of the year passable to the dalesmen; but the mountains know well that these innocent people will not reveal the mysteries of their ancient kingdom, 'the reign of *Chaos* and *Old Night*'.

Thomas Gray
Journal in the Lakes

Mountain Liberty

Wordsworth must here be referring to his school-days at Hawkshead. Of Cockermouth, where he was born, and where his father was agent to the domineering and avaricious Sir James Lowther, he could not possibly say that no one was respected 'through claims of wealth or blood'.

For, born in a poor district, and which yet
Retaineth more of ancient homeliness,
Than any other nook of English ground,
It was my fortune scarcely to have seen,
Through the whole tenour of my school-day time,
The face of one, who, whether boy or man,
Was vested with attention or respect
Through claims of wealth or blood; nor was it least
Of many benefits, in later years
Derived from academic institutes
And rules, that they held something up to view
Of a Republic, where all stood thus far
Upon equal ground; that we were brothers all
In honour, as in one community,

Scholars and gentlemen; where, furthermore,
Distinction open lay to all that came,
And wealth and titles were in less esteem
Than talents, worth, and prosperous industry.
Add unto this, subservience from the first
To presences of God's mysterious power
Made manifest in Nature's sovereignty,
And fellowship with venerable books,
To sanction the proud workings of the soul,
And mountain liberty. It could not be
But that one tutored thus should look with awe
Upon the highest faculties of man, receive
Gladly the highest promises, and hail,
As best, the government of equal rights
And individual worth.

William Wordsworth
From *The Prelude*, Book 9

The Statesman

The term 'statesman', a corruption of 'estatesman', was applied to a small farmer who held his land by one of the various systems of hereditary tenure which prevailed in the Lake District until the end of the eighteenth century.

Towards the head of these Dales was found a perfect Republic of Shepherds and Agriculturists, among whom the plough of each man was confined to the maintenance of his own family, or to the occasional accommodation of his neighbour. Two or three cows furnished each family with milk and cheese. The chapel was the only edifice that presided over these dwellings, the supreme head of this pure Commonwealth; the members of which existed in the midst of a powerful empire like an ideal society or an organized community, whose constitution had been imposed and regulated by the mountains which protected it. Neither high-born nobleman, knight, nor esquire was here; but many of these humble sons of the hills had a consciousness that the land, which they walked over and tilled, had for more than five hundred years been possessed by men of their name and blood; and venerable was the transition, when a curious traveller, descending from the heart of the mountains, had come to some ancient manorial residence in the more open parts of the Vales, which, through the rights attached to its proprietor, connected the almost visionary mountain republic he had been contemplating with the substantial frame of society as existing in the laws and constitution of a mighty empire.

William Wordsworth
Guide to the Lakes

The Decline of the Statesman

Formerly, every household had nearly all that it wanted within itself. The people thought so little of wheaten bread, that wheat was hardly to be bought in the towns. Within the last few years, an old man of eighty-five was fond of telling how, when a boy, he wanted to spend his penny on wheaten bread; and he searched through Carlisle from morning to evening before he could find a penny-roll. The cultivator among the hills divided his field into plots where he grew barley, oats, flax, and other produce to meet the needs of the household. His pigs, fed partly on acorns or beech-mast, yielded good bacon and hams; and his sheep furnished wool for clothing. Of course he kept cows. The women spun and wove the wool and flax, and the lads made the wooden utensils, baskets, fishing tackle, &c. Whatever else was needed was obtained from the pedlars who came their rounds two or three times a year, dropping in among the little farms from over the hills. The first great change was from the opening of carriage-roads. There was a temptation then to carry stock and grain to fairs and markets. More grain was grown than the household needed, and offered for sale. In a little while the mountain-farmers were sure to fail in competition in the markets with dwellers in agricultural districts. The mountaineer had no agricultural science and little skill; and the decline of the fortunes of the 'statesmen', as they are locally called, has been regular, and mournful to witness. They haunt the fairs and markets, losing in proportion to the advance of improvement elsewhere. On their first losses, they began to mortgage their lands. After bearing the burden of these mortgages till they could bear it no longer, their children have sold the lands: and among the shop-boys, domestic servants, and labourers of the towns, we find the names of the former yeomanry of the district, who have parted with their lands to strangers. Much misery intervened during the process of transition. The farmer was tempted to lose the remembrance of his losses in drink when he attended the fairs and markets. The capacity of the dalesmen in this respect, – in the quantity of strong liquor that they can carry – is remarkable; and they have only too good a training. Spirits are introduced on all occasions. At sales – of which there are many, every spring and autumn, in the dales, and which are attended by all the inhabitants who can go, for miles round – glasses of spirits are handed round among the purchasers, all day long. The settling of accounts at Candlemas is attended by the same curs, – every debtor expecting his creditor to offer him the compliment of a glass of strong liquor. On that day it is unpleasant for ladies to be abroad, near settlements where the Candlemas payments are making, – so many are the drunken people whom they meet. It is common to swallow the strong liquor undiluted, in considerable quantity. An old dalesman, welcome in Ambleside for his shrewdness, simplicity, and originality, appeared one day at a house where the gentleman was absent but the lady at home. The lady asked the visitor to sit down and await her husband's return, proposing to offer him some spirit and water meantime. He replied, – He wonnot be nice about t'first part e't'offer; but as tot' watter, it could be gitten at ony gate [way] side.

To return to the former condition of the 'statesman'. The domestic manufactures he carried to town with him, – the linen and woollen webs woven by his wife and daughters, – would not sell, except at a loss, in the presence of the Yorkshire and Lancashire woollens and cottons made by machinery. He became unable to keep his children at home; and they went off to the manufacturing towns, leaving home yet more cheerless – with fewer busy hands and cheerful faces – less social spirit in the dales – greater certainty of continued loss, and more temptation to drink. Such is the process still going on.

Harriet Martineau
A Complete Guide to the English Lakes

Mooning

De Quincey moved in to Dove Cottage after the Wordsworths had left it.

Two, or, it may be, three years after this time, I was walking to Keswick, from my own cottage in Grasmere. The distance was thirteen miles; the time just nine o'clock; the night a cloudy moonlight, and intensely cold. I took the very greatest delight in these nocturnal walks through the silent valleys of Cumberland and Westmoreland; and often at hours far later than the present. What I liked in this solitary rambling was, to trace the course of the evening through its household hieroglyphics from the windows which I passed or saw: to see the blazing fires shining through the windows of houses, lurking in nooks far apart from neighbours; sometimes, in solitudes that seemed abandoned to the owl, to catch the sounds of household mirth; then, some miles further, to perceive the time of going to bed; then the gradual sinking to silence of the house; then the drowsy reign of the cricket; at intervals, to hear church-clocks or a little solitary chapel-bell, under the brows of mighty hills, proclaiming the hours of night, and flinging out their sullen knells over the graves where 'the rude forefathers of the hamlet slept' – where the strength and the loveliness of Elizabeth's time, or Cromwell's, and through so many fleeting generations that have succeeded, had long ago sunk to rest. Such was the sort of pleasure which I reaped in my nightly walks – of which, however, considering the suspicions of lunacy which it has sometimes awoke, the less I say, perhaps, the better. Nine o'clock it was – and deadly cold as ever March night was made by the keenest of black frosts, and by the bitterest of north winds – when I drew towards the gate of our huge and hospitable friend. [A farmer who had given hospitality to De Quincey and Wordsworth some years earlier.] A little garden there was before the house; and in the centre of this garden was placed an arm-chair, upon which arm-chair was sitting composedly – but I rubbed my eyes, doubting the very evidence of my own eyesight – *a* or *the* huge man in his shirt-sleeves; yes, positively not sunning but *mooning* himself – apricating himself in the occasional moonbeams; and, as if simple star-gazing from a sedentary station were not sufficient on such a night, absolutely pursuing his astrological studies, I repeat, in his shirt-sleeves!

Thomas De Quincey
Recollections of the Lake Poets

The King of Patterdale

'*Mr Mounsey and his forefathers, from time immemorial, have been called Kings of Patterdale, living as it were in another World, having no one near them greater than themselves.*' Nicolson and Burn, Westmorland and Cumberland.

I feel myself at a loss to give a character of his Majesty. I have every possible respect for his advanced age; but the meanness of the miser hinders me from paying it.

He is now in his 93d year, and had a paternal estate of from 150*l.* to 200*l.* a year, which has always given the (imaginary) title of *King of Patterdale* to its possessor: it is said from being formerly exonerated from some particular tax, which might be owing to its very *remote* situation, and not worth gathering.

By his niggardly parsimoniousness he has realized his fortune, according to some, to 600*l.* by many to 800*l.* a year; and I have even heard him said to be worth 40,000*l.* – A strong constitution gave him an opportunity of being laborious, and his industry kept pace with *his desire of gain*. He knew to omit getting one shilling was a certain loss of one penny a year for ever, besides compound interest, that accumulating consideration to THE MISERS of the day.

He had many ponies that he kept upon the common land, which he was entitled to from his landed property in the parish: upon these *lean* beasts he carried his own charcoal over the mountains to the different forges; he used to throw his hat in their faces, to see if they were able to perform the journey; those that did not mind the hat were lucky enough to remain at home, and those which ran aside were thought of sufficient strength . . .

He was reckoned the best boatman between Patterdale and Dunmallart Head [Dunmallet, near Pooley Bridge]; and he used to convey his own slate and wood; or, when other people wanted him, for a trifling sum *per* load. He was once driven by a violent gale of wind upon the largest island. In this situation he remained with his assistant two days. The poor fellow, expecting a short passage, had made no provision; his Majesty always carried bread and cheese in his pocket, to avoid going to ale-houses, although he was never known to refuse when he was offered *to be treated*. When he wanted to eat, he told the man he would go to the other side of the island to see if the wind was likely to change; he then *gormandized* away, and made the man believe he had only been to look after the weather.

I must now mention a custom he has long practised which saves him the expense of providing meals at home: – to use his own words he calls them 'ENTERTAINMENTS.' He lets some fields and small houses, as expressed in the agreement, for so many dinners and suppers, taking care that what to him are dainties are provided for each separate day.

In his tea-drinkings, he takes from ten to fourteen cups, using an immoderate quantity of sugar, of which he is so fond, he generally carries some loose in his pocket; if he omits a day, which was once rarely the case, it is looked upon as fulfilled. – I am told it was a hard bargain to his tenants, but his great age has rather turned in their favour . . .

Perhaps this man is [to be] held up as a *beacon*, to those who might otherwise be misers, for I never saw people that appear less inclined to be so than those around him; and his son is a conspicuous example of the contrary. Brought up in a peculiar manner, his benevolent character shines a just contrast; and the inhabitants say, when he gets possession of the fortune, charity to the poor will be as diffusive in the richest man in Patterdale as sordidness is now. The King allows he never got any thing by the poor; why then should he give them any thing? He sometimes has been heard to complain that a man should be cut off in the prime of his life, at eighty or ninety years – if he could live to the age of Methusalem, he might save a little money.

Joseph Budworth
A Fortnight's Ramble to the Lakes

A Curate of Patterdale

The following extraordinary passages in the life of the Rev. Mr Mattinson, a former curate of Patterdale, are deserving of notice. He buried his mother; he married and buried his father; he christened his wife, and published his own banns of marriage in the church; and he christened and married all his four children, a son and three daughters. He died January 31, 1766, at the age of ninety-six years, sixty of which he had been curate of Patterdale. Till the last years of his life his stipend did not exceed 12*l.* and never reached 20*l.* per annum; yet such was his industry and domestic economy, that on this small pittance he contrived to live comfortably and to save a thousand pounds.

John Robinson, Rector of Clifton, Westmorland
A Guide to the Lakes (1819)

Richard Nicholson, the Disappointed Shepherd

In 1791, he was 77 years of age: was a natural child, born near Mulcaster [Muncaster] house, and like many others in that unhappy state, was left to depend solely on his own industry for support &c. At the age of twenty-one, there was scarce a man in the county, who durst contend with him at the ordinary rural diversions, of running, leaping, wrestling, and playing at foot-ball. About the age of twenty-five, he engaged to enter into the marriage state, with a young woman of his neighbourhood, who proved unfaithful. His passion for her was so powerful, as to induce him to make a *vow*, that he would never afterwards go to *church* or *market*. In his twenty-sixth year, he became a servant, or rather shepherd, in this parish [i.e. Whitbeck, near Bootle], and lived many years with the late Edmund Gibson, Esq. and afterwards with Mr Parke. He not only proved himself, during those services, a skilful shepherd, but gave uncommon testimonies of fidelity and honesty in his station. Richard has occasionally served other farmers, and yeomen, and during the whole succession of fifty years, has *literally* kept his *vow*; has been so far from frequenting the church, that when a sheep, at any time, was caught in briars in the *church-yard*, (which stands in Mr Parke's estate) he hired some neighbour to fetch it out; he has been equally as tenacious of the other part of his vow.

A pair of leather shoes being prepared against his intended marriage, he thenceforth totally denied himself the use of such; and (though his business has been, chiefly twice a-day, to mount the lofty and craggy tops of the Black Combe) has ever since dragged about a pair of huge clogs (wooden shoes) shod with iron, nearly two pounds weight a-piece. His hat tied close over his ears, is not permitted to be taken off, unless, perhaps, sometimes in private. His beard has never been shaved since his twenty-sixth year; but when it grows to an inconvenient length, is shortened with his sheep sheers.

He was constantly possessed of a cow, a few sheep, a dog, a cat, and a parcel of hens, all which were maintained as his wages, by the person whomsoever he served; and as there are a few uninhabited cottages in the parish, he was always in possession of such of them, as his capricious humour inclined him to inhabit. Milk and bread form his princi-

pal diet; the former of which he takes from his cow, as the equal
repast of his dog, his cat, and himself; the benevolent wife of some
cottager, bakes his bread and washes his shirt. At Christmas he always
has a sheep killed to make sweet pies, part of which he superstitiously
keeps till Candlemas. As he was disappointed of a partner in life, so
he refuses the use of a bed, lying constantly upon straw . . .

As he has had little education, his ideas, of course, are confined; but
upon any subject, within the sphere of his observations, his argument
is strong and rational. He interests himself about nothing so much, as
the subject of courting; when he is informed that any person to whom
he wishes well, has got a sweetheart, his first business is to acquaint
himself with the merits or demerits of the parties, after which he
endeavours, as much as possible, to impede or promote the match
accordingly, by his importunate exhortation or dissuasion. Though
a non-attendance at church be the chief error that his well-wishing
neighbours lay to his charge, yet he has frequently been overheard
repeating portions of the church liturgy, and singing psalms, which,
it is to be hoped, will be an acceptable service.

> John Housman (eighteenth century)
> Notes to William Hutchinson's
> *The History of the County of Cumberland*

Clark's Leap

*Thirlmere was the setting of this sad event. There seems to be no connection
between the suicide himself and the narrator, the sardonic surveyor of Keswick.*

A man of the name of Clark was jealous of his wife to that degree that
he was resolved to put an end to his own existence. He communicated
his resolution to his wife, and told her at the same time, that he was
determined to hang himself: to this she objected for fear that it might
prove too painful: he then said he would shoot himself, but from this
she likewise dissuaded him, for fear he might not kill himself outright,

and so suffer extreme pain to no purpose; he next proposed to drown himself; this pleased her, and they went lovingly together to the water's edge: he then proposed to wade in, but she said the water was so cold, that he would suffer much needless pain; they then walked by the waterside till they came to this rock, which she told him she thought was fit for his purpose, as the water was deep enough at the edge to drown him; He was then going to throw himself directly in, but she told him he might hurt himself against the rock before he reached the water, so that he had better take a run and leap as far as he could: He followed her advice, very calmly put off his coat and took his leap; she staid till she saw him drowned, and then returned, fully satisfied that she had done her duty in giving him the best advice she could.

James Clarke
A Survey of the Lakes (1787–9)

The Shoemaker of Gleaston – c. 1860

Gleaston is a small village in the limestone country lying along the northern shore of Morecambe Bay. Waugh and his friends had been visiting Gleaston Castle.

When we were beginning to despair of finding anything like substantial refreshment, we met with it at the very last house on the western edge of the village, a clean little hostelry, where we got an excellent dinner of eggs and bacon, cheese, ale, pickles, salad fresh from the garden behind the house, and three quarts of buttermilk; in addition to which, I had my shoe mended; and we were treated with more than common civility, all for the low charge of three and six-pence, – which was received with satisfaction. The way of the shoe business was this, – I had burst the seam of it, and was getting squashy with wet, for we had had a delightfully rough tramp o'er moss and fell, and through miry bye-roads, that day. The good wife at the ale-

house offered to get it mended for me whilst dinner was cooking.
The old man lent me a shoe of his own to put on meanwhile. It was
as hard as an iron pot; in fact, it had considerable weight of iron work
about it, and for any rough work, I felt that that one shoe was worth
at least four pair such as mine . . . The shoe came back mended before
dinner was over, and a thrill of returning comfort went through my
frame when I got it on, for I had felt as if walking with a wet dish-
cloth round my foot a while before. As we returned through the
village, one of my friends proposed that we should just look in upon
a relation of his, an old shoemaker, and a quaint man, well versed in
the folk lore of the district. He then led us up to one of the most com-
fortable-looking cottages I ever saw. The floor was as clean as a plate
just laid down for dinner, the place smelt as sweet as an herb-stall, and
all the polishable metal things shone like pools of water in moonlight.
The cheerful old wife, whose ruddy face was bedded in a snowy old-
fashioned cap, and whose eyes, in spite of age and spectacles, looked
as bright as the stars on a frosty night, rose from her arm-chair, and
hobbled about with her crutch, smiling and talking, and talking and
smiling, as if she didn't know exactly what to do to show that she was
very fain. At last, opening the door of an inner room, where the
hearty old fellow and his son sat at work, she said, 'What, dinnet ye
see wha's here?' Dropping his hammer, and brushing the dirt from
his leather apron, the old man rose above six feet into the air, pushed
up his spectacles, and shouted, 'Why, it never is, sewer! It cannot be
reightly, can it! It's now i'th warld else, aw declare! Well, this is a
capper, hooivvir! What ye're reight good stuff for sore e'en, mon!
Whatever quarter's th'wind in, at ye're blawn this gate on? Well,
cum, cum; sit ye daan, an' let's mak use on ye while ye are here.' 'Ye
hevn't hed ye're teea, aw warnd,' [warrant] said the good wife. But
we were already primely filled with good things, and no other feast
could have been so delightful as the genial welcome which the old
couple gave us. The day, too, was waning, with an uncertain sky, and
we had several miles to go. As we sat talking with the old man, a fine
pair of new double-soled shooting boots stood at my elbow. I took
them up, and asked what such a pair would cost. He said they couldn't
be done like them under a pound. 'But,' said he, 'ye sud ha' sin a shoe
that I stitched abaat an haar sin, for some poor tramp. I nivver see a

warse made shoe i' my life, I think. An' he couldn't hev hed 'em lang, nawther – t'leather wur so fresh.' As he went on talking, I slowly lifted my foot till it came fairly into his sight. 'Hello!' said he, with a confused gaze. 'What, wor it yaar shoe?' It was. 'Well then,' replied he, 'All at I can say is, at yer wit's a deeal better nor yer understandin'!' We had a good deal of gleeful talk with the old folk; after which six miles' walk in a high wind through the vale of Urswick brought us to Ulverstone, at the edge of dark, well pleased with our day's ramble.

Edwin Waugh
Over Sands to the Lakes

The Terrible Knitters of Dent

This famous and moving story was taken down from the mouth of Betty Yewdale herself by Sarah Hutchinson, Wordsworth's sister-in-law, and Edith May Southey, Southey's daughter, and published in Vol. vii of Southey's long rambling prose work The Doctor. *This seventh volume did not appear until 1847, four years after the poet's death, and was edited by the Rev. John Wood Warter, Southey's son-in-law, who was married to Edith May, so that it is not possible to tell to what extent either Southey or Warter was responsible for the final form and text of the tale. It would seem, however, that the two transcribers, and perhaps the editor, were not well acquainted with the conventions of spelling and the like established by such early dialect writers as Relph and Anderson, and they seem to write, as it were, entirely by ear. The result, especially in the use of such phoneticisms as 'e' for 'in', can look odd at times, but if the reader will rid himself of any preconceived idea of what Westmorland dialect ought to look like, he will find, I think, that the language rings true.*

'It was about six an' fifty year sen, in June, when a woman cam fra' Dent at see a Nebbor of ours e'Langdon [Langdale]. They er terrible knitters e' Dent – sea my Fadder an' Mudder sent me an' my lile Sister, Sally, back we' her at larn at knit. I was between sebben an' eight year auld, an' Sally twea year younger – T'Woman reade on ya Horse, we Sally afore her – an' I on anudder, we a man walking beside me – whiles he gat up behint an' reade – Ee' them Days Fwoak dudu'nt gang e' Carts – but Carts er t'best – I'd rader ride e' yan than e' onny Carriage – I us't at think if I was t'Leady, here at t'Ho [at the Hall], how I wad tear about int' rwoads – but sen I hae ridden in a Chaise I hate t'nwotion ont' warst of ought – for t'Trees gang fleeing by o' ya side, an' t'Wa's on tudder, an' gars yan be as seek as a peeate.

'Weel, we dud'nt like Dent at a' – nut that they were bad tull us – but ther way o' leeving – it was round Meal – an' they *stoult* in int' frying pan, e'keaeks as thick as my fing-er. – Then we wer *stawed* [fed-up with] we' sae mickle knitting – We went to a *Skeul* about a mile off – there was a Maister an' Mistress – they larnt us our Lessons, yan a piece – an' then we o' knit as hard as we cud drive striving whilk cud knit t'hardest yan again anudder – we hed our Darracks [i.e. Day's-work, the name is often given to fields] set afore we com fra' Heam int'mworning; an' if we dudn't git them duun we warrant to gang to our dinners – They hed o' macks o'contrivances to larn us to knit swift – T'Maister wad wind 3 or 4 clues togedder, for 3 or 4 Bairns to knit off – *that* at knit slawest raffled tudders yarn, an' than she gat weel thumpt (but ther was baith Lasses an' Lads at learnt at knit) – Than we ust at sing a mack of a sang, whilk we wer at git at t'end on at every needle, ca'ing ower t'Neams of o' t' fwoak in t'Deaal – but Sally an me wad never ca' *Dent* Fwoak – sea we ca'ed Langdon Fwoak – T'Sang was –

> Sally an' I, Sally an' I,
> For a good pudding pye,
> Taa hoaf wheat, an' tudder hoaf rye,
> Sally an' I, for a good pudding pye.

We sang this (altering t'neams) at every needle: and when we com at t'end cried "off" an' began again, an' sea we strave on o' t'day through.

'We were *stawed*, as I telt yea – o' t'pleser we hed was when we went out a bit to beat t'fire for a nebbor 'at was baking – that was a grand day for us! – At Kursmas teea, ther was t'Maskers – an' on

Kursmas day at mworn they gav us sum reed stuff to t'Breakfast – I think it maun ha' been Jocklat – but we dud'nt like 't at a', 't ommost puzzened us – an' we cared for nought but how we were to git back to Langdon – Neet an' Day ther was nought but *this* knitting. T'nebbors ust at gang about fra' house to house, we' ther wark, – than yan fire dud, ye knaw, an' they cud hev a better – they hed girt lang black peeats – an' set them up an hed in a girt round we' a whole at top – an a't'Fwoak sat about it. When ony o' them gat into a hubble we' ther wark, they shouted out '*turn a Peeat*' – an' *them* 'at sat naarest t'fire turnt yan, an' meaad a *low* [flame] – for they nivver hed onny cannal [candle]. – We knat quorse wosset stockings – some gloves – an' some neet caps, an' wastecwoat breests, an' petticwoats. I yance knat a stocking, for mysell, e' six hours – Sally yan e'sebben – an' t'woman's Doughter, 'at was aulder than us e'eight – an' they sent a nwote to our Fwoak e'Langdon at tell them.

'Sally an' me, when we wer by our sells, wer always contrivin' how we wer at git away, when we sleept by oursells we talk't of nought else – but when t'woman's Doughter sleept we' us we were *qwhite* mum – summat or udder always happent at hinder us, till yan day, between Kursmas an' Cannalmas, when t'woman's Doughter stait at heaam, we teuk off. Our house was four mile on 'todder side o'Dent's Town – whor, efter we hed pass t'Skeul, we axed t'way to Kendal – It hed been a hard frost, an' ther was snaw on t'grund – but it was beginning to thow, an' was varra sloshy an' cauld – but we *poted* alang leaving out lile footings behint us – we hed our cloggs on – for we durst'nt change them for our shoon for fear o' being fund out – an' we had nought on but our hats, an' bits o' blue bedgowns, an' brats – see ye may think we cuddent be verra heeat – I hed a sixpence e' my pocket, an' we hed three or four shillings mare in our box, 'at our Fwoak hed ge'en us to keep our pocket we' – but, lile mafflings [bewildered little things] as we were, we thought it wad be misst an' durst'nt tak ony mare.

'Afore we gat to Sebber [Sedburgh] we fell hungry; an' ther was a fine, girt, reed house nut far off t'rwoad, whar we went an' begged for a bit o' breead – but they wadd'nt give us ought – sea we trampt on, an com to a lile theakt [thatched] house, an' I said – "Sally, thou sall beg t'neesht – thou's less than me, an' mappen they'll sarra us" –

an' they dud – an' gav us a girt shive [slice] of breead – at last we gat
to Scotch Jins, as they ca't'public House about three mile fra Sebber
(o' this side) – a Scotch woman keept it. – It was amaist dark, sea we
axt her at let us stay o'neet – she teuk us in, an' gave us sum boilt milk
and breead – an' suun put us to bed – we telt her our taael; an' she sed
we wer int' reet at run away.

'Neesht mwornin she gav us sum mare milk an' breead, an' we
gave her our sixpence – an' then went off-sledding away amangt'snaw,
ower that cauld moor (ye ken't weel enough) naarly starved to death,
an' maisled – sea we gat on varra slawly, as ye may think – an't'rain'd
tua. We begged again at anudder lile theakt house, on t'Hay Fell –
there was a woman an' a heap of raggelty Bairns stannin round a
Teable – an' she gave us a few of their poddish, an' put a lock of
sugar into a sup of cauld tea tull them.

'Then we trailed on again till we com t'Peeat Lane Turnpike Yat –
they teuk us in there, an' let us warm oursells, an' gav us a bit o'
breead. They sed had duun reet to com away; for Dent was t' poorest
plaace in t'warld, and we wer seafe to ha' been hungert – an' at last we
gat to Kendal, when 't was naar dark – as we went up t'streat we met
a woman, an' axt t'way to Tom Posts – (*that* was t'man at ust te bring
t'Letters fra' Kendal to Ammelsid [Ambleside] an' Hawksheead
yance a week – an' baited at his house when we com fra' Langdon) –
she telt us t'way an' we creept on, but we leaked back at her twea or
three times – an' she was still stanning, leuking at us – then she com
back an *quiesed* us a deal, an'sed we sud gang heam with her – We telt
her whor we hed cum fra' an' o' about our Tramp 'at we hed hed. –
She teuk us to her house – it was a varra poor yan – down beside
t'brig at we had cum ower into t'Town – There was nea fire on – but
she went out, an' brought in sam *eilding* [fuel] (for they can buy a
pennerth, or sea, o' quols or Peeats at onny time there) an' she set on
a good fire – an' put on t'kettle – then laited [searched] up sum of her
awn cleas, an' tiet them on us as weel as she cud, an' dried ours – for
they wer as wet as thack – it hed rained a't'way – Then she meead us
sum tea – an' as she hedden't a bed for us in her awn house she teuk
us to a nebbors – There was an auld woman in a Bed naar us that flaed
us sadly – for she teuk a fit int'neet an' her feace turnt as black as a
cwol – we laid trimmiling, an' hutched oursells ower heead e'bed –

Fwoks com an' steud round her – an' we heeard them say 'at we wer asleep – sae we meade as if we were asleep, because we thought if we wer asleep they waddn't kill us – an' we wisht oursells e't'streets again, or onny whor – an'wad ha' been fain to ha' been ligging under a Dyke.

'Neesht mwornin we hed our Brekfast, an't'woman gav us baith a hopenny Keack beside (that was as big as a penny 'an now) to eat as we went – an' she set us to t'top o't'House o'Correction Hill – It was freezing again, an' t'rwoad was terrible slape; sae we gat on varra badly – an' afore we s com to Staavley (an' that was but a lile bit o't'rwoad) we fell hung'ry an' began on our keacks – then we sed we wad walk sea far, an' then tak a bite – an' then on again an' tak anudder – and afore we gat to t'Ings Chapel they wer o' gane. – Every now an' than we stopped at reest – an' sat down, an' grat [wept], under a hedge or wa' crudled up togedder, taking haud o' yan anudder's hands at try at warm them, for we were fairly maizled wi' t'cauld – an' when we saw onny body cumming we gat up an' walked away – but we dudn't meet many Fwoak – I dunnat think Fwoak warr sea mickle in t'rwoads e' them Days.

'We scraffled [struggled] on t'this fashion – an' it was quite dark afore we gat to Ammelsid Yat – our feet warr sare an' we warr naarly dune for – an' when we turnt round Windermer Watter heead, t'waves blasht sea dowly that we warr fairly heart-brossen – we sat down on a cauld steane an' grat sare – but when we hed hed our belly-full o' greeting we gat up, and feelt better fort' an' sea dreed on again – slaw enough ye may be sure – but we warr e' *kent* rwoads – an' now when I gang that gait I can nwote o't'spots whor we reested – for them lile bye lwoans erent sea mickle altert, as t'girt rwoads, fra what they warr. At Clappersgate t'Fwoak wad ha'knawn us, if it heddent been dark, an' o'ther duirs steeked, an geen us a relief, if we hed begged there – but we began at be flate [frightened] 'at my Fadder an' Mudder wad be angert as us for running away.

'It was twea o'clock int'mworning when we gat to our awn Duir – I ca'ed out "Fadder. Fadder. – Mudder. Mudder." ower an' ower again – She hard us, an' sed – "That's our Betty's voice" – "Thus's nought but fancies, lig still," said my Fadder – but she waddent; an sea gat up, an' opent' Duir and there warr we stanning doddering –

and daized we'cauld, as neer deead as macks nea matter – When she so us she was mare flate than we – She brast out a crying – an' we grat – an' my Fadder grat an'a' – an' they duddent flight [scold], nor said nought tull us, for cumming away, – they warrant a bit angert – an' my Fadder sed we sud nivver gang back again.

'T'Fwoaks e'Dent nivver mist us, tilt' Neet – because they thought 'at we hed been keept at dinner time 'at finish our tasks – but when neet com, an' we duddent cum heam, they set off efter us to Kendal – an' mun ha' gane by Scotch Jins when we warr there – how they satisfied thersells, I knan't, but they suppwosed we hed gane heam – and sea they went back. – My Fadder wasn't lang, ye may be seur, o' finding out t'Woman at Kendal 'at was sea good tull us – an' my Mudder put her down a pot o' Butter, an' meead her a lile cheese an' sent her.'

Sarah Hutchinson (1775–1835)
and Edith May Southey (1804–1871)
Quoted from Robert Southey's *The Doctor*

Betty Yewdale in Old Age

The Yewdales lived at Hackett, in Little Langdale.

'Much was I pleased,' the grey-haired Wanderer said,
'When to those shining fields our notice first
You turned; and yet more pleased have from your lips
Gathered this fair report of them who dwell
In that retirement; whither, by such course
Of evil hap and good as oft awaits
A tired way-faring man, once *I* was brought
While traversing alone yon mountain-pass.
Dark on my road the autumnal evening fell,
And night succeeded with unusual gloom,
So hazardous that feet and hands became

Guides better than mine eyes – until a light
High in the gloom appeared, too high, methought,
For human habitation; but I longed
To reach it, destitute of other hope.
I looked with steadiness as sailors look
On the north star, or watch-tower's distant lamp,
And saw the light – now fixed – and shifting now –
Not like a dancing meteor, but in line
Of never-varying motion, to and fro.
It is no night-fire of the naked hills,
Thought I – some friendly covert must be near.
With this persuasion thitherward my steps
I turn, and reach at last the guiding light;
Joy to myself! but to the heart of her
Who there was standing on the open hill,
(The same kind Matron whom your tongue hath praised)
Alarm and disappointment! The alarm
Ceased, when she learned through what mishap I came,
And by what help had gained those distant fields.
Drawn from her cottage, on that aery height,
Bearing a lantern in her hand she stood,
Or paced the ground – to guide her Husband home,
By that unwearied signal, kenned afar;
An anxious duty! which the lofty site,
Traversed but by a few irregular paths,
Imposes, whensoe'er untoward chance
Detains him after his accustomed hour
Till night lies black upon the ground. "But come,
Come," said the Matron, "to our poor abode;
Those dark rocks hide it!" Entering, I beheld
A blazing fire – beside a cleanly hearth
Sate down; and to her office, with leave asked,
The Dame returned.

　　　　Or ere that glowing pile
Of mountain turf required the builder's hand
Its wasted splendour to repair, the door

Opened, and she re-entered with glad looks,
Her Helpmate following. Hospitable fare,
Frank conversation, made the evening's treat;
Need a bewildered traveller wish for more?
But more was given; I studied as we sate
By the bright fire, the good Man's form, and face
Not less than beautiful; an open brow
Of undisturbed humanity; a cheek
Suffused with something of a feminine hue;
Eyes beaming courtesy and mild regard;
But, in the quicker turns of the discourse,
Expression slowly varying, that evinced
A tardy apprehension . . .

'Roused by the crowing cock at dawn of day,
I yet had risen too late to interchange
A morning salutation with my Host,
Gone forth already to the far-off seat
Of his day's work. "Three dark mid-winter months
Pass," said the Matron, "and I never see,
Save when the sabbath brings its kind release,
My helpmate's face by light of day. He quits
His door in darkness, nor till dusk returns.
And, through Heaven's blessing, thus we gain the bread
For which we pray; and for the wants provide
Of sickness, accident, and helpless age.
Companions have I many; many friends,
Dependants, comforters – my wheel, my fire,
All day the house-clock ticking in mine ear,
The cackling hen, the tender chicken brood,
And the wild birds that gather round my porch.
This honest sheep-dog's countenance I read;
With him can talk; nor blush to waste a word
On creatures less intelligent and shrewd.
And if the blustering wind that drives the clouds,
Care not for me, he lingers round my door,
And makes me pastime when our tempers suit . . ."

The Matron ended – not could I forbear
To exclaim – "O happy! yielding to the law
Of these privations . . .
For you the hours of labour do not flag;
For you each evening hath its shining star,
And every sabbath-day its golden sun".'

William Wordsworth
From *The Excursion*, Book 5

A Second Opinion on Betty Yewdale

This story is supposed to be given in the words of a widow from Oxenfell, above Little Langdale, but its authenticity is in doubt because of Dr Gibson's marked prejudice against Wordsworth. It is, nevertheless, a good example of the dialect of High Furness.

'Ther' hed been a funeral fray about t'Ho'garth, an' varry nar o' t'men fooak about hed geean wi't' till Cunniston [Coniston]. Nixt fooarneeun, Betty Yewdale com' through fray Hackett, an' says she till me, "Hes yower meeaster gitten back fray t'funeral?" "Nay," says I, "he hesn't!" "An'irrn't ye gan ut lait him?" says Betty. "Lait him!" says I, "I wodn't lait him if he didn't cu heeam for a week." "Why, why!" says she, "yee ma' due as ye like, but I mun bring mine heeam, an' I *will*!" An' off she set i' t' rooad till Cunniston. On i't'efterneeun, she co' back, driving Jonathan afooer her wi' a lang hezle stick – an'he sart'ly was a sairy object. His Sunda' cleeas leeuk't as if he'd been sleepi' i' them on t'top of a durty fluer. T'tye of his neckcloth hed wurk't round till bela t'ya lug, an' t'lang ends on't hung ooer ahint his shou'der. His hat hed gitten bulged in at t'side, an' t'flipe on't was cock't up beeath back an frunt. O'togidder, it wod ha' been a queerly woman body 'at wod ha' teean a fancy till Jonathan that day.

'Says I till Betty, "What, ye *hev* fund him than?" "Fund him!"

says she, "ey, I fund him! I kna't what ut lait him! I fund him at t'Black Bull, wi'yower meeaster, an'a lock meear o't'seeam sooart. They wor just gan ut git the'r dinner, wi'a girt pan o' beef-steeaks set on t'middle o't'teeable. I meead t'frying pan an't'beef-steeaks flee gaily murrily oot o't'duer, an' I set on an'geh them o' sike a blackin' as they willn't seeun forgit. Than I hail't Jonathan oot fray amang them; bit when I'd gitten him oot wi'me, I sham't ut be seen on t'rooads wi' him. Dud iver ye see sike a pictur"? "Why, nay! nit sa offen, indeed," says I. "Well," says Betty, "as I wodn't be seen i'rooads wi'him, we had to teeak t'fields for't, an', as it wasn't seeaf ut let him climm t'wo's, I meead him creep t'hog-hooals,"* says Betty, "an' when I gat him wi' his heead in an'his legs out, I dud switch him."'

Dr Alexander Craig Gibson (1813–1874)
The Folk-Speech of Cumberland

The Beauty of Buttermere

At the beginning of the nineteenth century, the story of Mary Robinson of Buttermere became one of the most celebrated popular 'sensations' of the day. It began in 1792, when Capt. J. Budworth, called at the Fish Inn and was struck by the looks of the landlord's young daughter. It is doubtful if he spoke to her, since he does not even get her name right, but, when he published his Fortnight's Ramble to the Lakes, *he indulged in the following sentimental over-praise of the girl's charms:*

SALLY OF BUTTERMERE

Her mother and she were spinning woollen yarn in the back kitchen. On our going into it, the girl flew away as swift as a mountain sheep, and it was not until our return from Scale Force that we could say we first saw her. She brought in part of our dinner, and seemed to be about fifteen. Her hair was thick and long, of a dark

* 'Hog-holes' are small gaps left in the bottom of a dry-stone wall, to allow the sheep to pass through from one field to another.

brown, and, though unadorned with ringlets, did not seem to want them; her face was a fine oval, with full eyes, and lips as red as vermilion; her cheeks had more of the lily than the rose; and although she had never been out of the village (and I hope will have no ambition to wish it), she has a manner about her which seemed better calculated to set off dress, than dress *her*. She was a very Lavinia,

Seeming, when unadorn'd, adorn'd the most!

When we first saw her at her distaff, after she had got the better of her first fears, she looked an angel; and I doubt not but she is the reigning lily of the valley.

Ye travellers of the Lakes, if you visit this obscure spot, such you will find the fair SALLY OF BUTTERMERE.

Budworth's book had considerable success, and, as a result, Mary Robinson found herself the object of much curiosity both from tourists and from the local people. Wordsworth, Southey and De Quincey were among those who made her acquaintance, and the walls of the Fish Inn were scrawled with compliments to her beauty. Budworth now realized the harm his words might have done, and, in 1798, he revisited Buttermere and tried to put matters right by an article, published in The Gentleman's Magazine, *Jan. 1800, from which these extracts are taken.*

I now went downstairs, and had the pleasure to hear my health drunk. Some of [the company], understanding there was not any more tobacco to be procured, came and opened all their little papers in the dish; and they agreed that 'I was yan of the cheeriest strangers they had e'er seen he Buttermere.' . . .

I told them I had somewhere read of a 'Sally of Buttermere,' and asked which was her? A friend [of hers] replied. 'My name is *Sally*; but this Mary here is the Sally the South-countryman wrote about, and I love her above all the world.' . . .

Mary Robinson has really a heavenly countenance, yet is she far from a perfect beauty; and in a few years she may even grow too large ever to have been thought what she now is. She is nineteen, and very tall; her voice is sweetly modulated; and in every point of manners she appeared such as might be fitted,

> Or, to shine in Courts with unaffected ease, &c.

On speaking about her hair, her friend immediately unpinned her cap, and let it afloat; and, at my request, that natural ornament was left to flow . . .

About two, the party went, as they had come, all together. A homely bed served me as well as a bed of down could have done; for the hurry both of body and mind, in so interesting a day, chased away sleep; yet I had sufficiency to be refreshed. In the morning, our heroine was in her working dress; and she exhibited just enough of hair, to convince me that she had taken my hint properly.

The weather was louring; and I did not wish, in case of a downfall, to be entombed in Buttermere; therefore, taking the opportunity of our being alone, I told her I knew the author of 'A Fortnight's Ramble,' and as such had something to say to her. She curtsied respectfully; and taking her by the hand I began:

'Mary, I wrote it; and rejoice in having had such an opportunity of minutely observing the propriety of your behaviour. You may remember, I advised you, in that Book, never to leave your native valley. Your age and situation require the utmost care. Strangers WILL come, and have come, purposely to see you; and some of them with very bad intentions. We hope you will never suffer from them; but never cease to be upon your guard. You really are not so handsome as you promised to be; and I have long wished, by conversation like this, to do away what mischief the flattering character I gave of you may expose you to. Be merry and wise.'

She told me she sincerely thanked me; and said, 'I hope, Sir, I ever have, and trust I always shall take care of myself.'

I then bade her farewell! and, teeming with good wishes towards my fellow-mortals, toiled out of the Valley of Buttermere.

Budworth's hopes of having done away with the mischief were, un-fortunately, unfounded. In July 1802, there arrived in Keswick a seemingly well-to-do tourist calling himself the Hon. Alexander Augustus Hope, who, before long, found his way to Buttermere and went through a form of marriage with Mary Robinson at Lorton, early in October of that year. Since Mary was by now a local celebrity, her wedding was reported in the newspapers and so came to the notice of people who knew that the real Col Hope was, at that time, in Vienna. Mary's 'husband' turned out, in fact, to be an impostor named Hatfield, a forger as well as a bigamist. Hatfield was arrested but escaped over Stye Head Pass to Ravenglass, and thence to South Wales where he was eventually captured. He was taken to Carlisle, tried, and hanged in September 1803. Mary later married a local man.

This sad little story aroused immense interest and excitement throughout England. It was repeated in dozens of magazines and journals; was put into rhyme and sold as a broadsheet; was acted in London as a melodrama; and, as late as 1841, was the subject of a novel.

In the third edition of A Fortnight's Ramble, *published in 1810, Budworth adds the following apologetic note:*

Having brought her into notice, as the reigning Lily of the Valley, when her days were few; and in a re-visit to Buttermere witnessed her unassuming and correct behaviour, under the gaiety of rural festivity; a Rambler will always retain his cordial good wishes; at the same time, takes this opportunity of deploring that he ever wrote in commendation of any young living creature, as vanity, alas, is the most intoxicating of human plants! and too apt to spread, when unfortunately introduced to public approval. Indeed, few minds are proof against it; and happy would it be for many a flower, were they

Born to blush unseen.

Joseph Budworth
A Fortnight's Ramble to the Lakes
(first edition, 1792; second edition, 1795; third edition, 1810)

John Gough, the Blind Botanist

A sincere, if somewhat solemn, tribute to John Gough's remarkable character and capabilities is made by Wordsworth in Book VII of The Excursion. *It was Gough who supplied the 'Botanical Notices' printed in later editions of the poet's* Guide to the Lakes.

John Gough, . . . 'The Blind Philosopher', was born in Kendal, the 17th of January, in the year 1757, . . . Before the completion of his third year, he was attacked with small-pox, which deprived him of his sight. The whole globe of the left eye was destroyed: the damage done to the other was not so extensive: for, though the greater part of the cornea was rendered opaque, there was a minute pellucid speck to the right of the pupil, which permitted a ray of light to fall upon the verge of the retina, and thus he was enabled to distinguish between day and night: but he had no perception of the form or colour of objects around him; so that, for all useful purposes, vision was completely lost . . . Nature was ever the idol of his mind; plants found a place in his early affections. For we learn that, in his eighth year, he was in the habit of visiting an aged couple, who had a few flowering plants, standing at a window. The powerful odour of one of these (a Moldavian balm), attracted his attention: groping his way to the specimen, he examined its stem, leaves, and the whorl in which the flowers were arranged; and as carefully also did he compare these different parts with the corresponding parts of another plant, which stood beside the balm, . . . Hitherto, he had no idea that books were devoted to plants. But this ignorance was presently to be removed. It was in his thirteenth summer that his father carried him and his eldest sister into the fields, and observing his son deeply absorbed in examining a specimen of Henbane, he gathered a handful of wild flowers, telling him, at the same time, that plants had been named and described in books; and that this had been done, in part, by a Kendal man, John Wilson. This intelligence excited his curiosity; and he never rested till he had made himself master of a copy of Wilson's 'Synopsis of British Plants' . . .

His method of examining plants must be briefly told. Systems of classification were but little valued, except so far as they aided him in recognizing individual form. The plant to be examined was held by the root or base in one hand, while the fingers of the other travelled slowly upwards, over the stem, branches, and leaves, till they reached the flower. If the species had been already met with, this procedure was sufficient for its recognition; if it proved to be a novelty, its class was first determined by the insertion of the elongated tip of his tongue within the flower: thus he discovered the number and arrangement of the stamens and the pistils. When the flower was small, he requested his reader to ascertain these points with a lens. The class and order being determined, the genus was next worked out, word by word of the description, so far at least as the state of the specimen would allow. But his perceptive power over form was most conspicuous in the analysis of species. It was truly wonderful to witness the rapidity with which his fingers ran among the leaves, taking cognizance of their divisions, shape, serratures, and of the presence or absence of hairs. The finest down was detected, by a stem or leaf being drawn gently across the border of his lower lip; so fine, indeed, that a young eye often required a lens to verify the truth of the perception. Another peculiarity is worthy of notice. Repeated perusal of descriptions had enabled him to pre-figure in his mind's eye, the form without the presence of specimens; so that, when a species for the first time came within his touch, he at once named it from memory.

Cornelius Nicholson (1804–1889)
Annals of Kendal

Tyson

The old hen house draws Tyson out each dawn.
Before the sun is warm he clanks
with pail and sack
through icy grass
not thinking of the hens or eggs
he grasps in familiar warmth
but gathers in the drinking tins
and fills with dew mechanically.

His pretties, as he calls them, cluck,
part protest, part delight, at sight
of corn and Tyson's sack.
And when he's gone, they scratter on,

robbed, and start again as Tyson,
on the fell, pauses at his laden pail,
cracks the brownest speckled egg
and sucks it down, sweet as any ale.

Irvine Hunt (1930–   )

Carol

There was a Boy bedded in bracken,
Like to a sleeping snake all curled he lay;
On his thin navel turned this spinning sphere,
Each feeble finger fetched seven suns away.
He was not dropped in good-for-lambing weather,
He took no suck when shook buds sing together,
But he is come in cold-as-workhouse weather,
  Poor as a Salford child.

John Short (1911–   )

A Nice Derangement of Epitaphs

I

To the Rev. Ralph Tirer, Vicar of Kendal, died 1627. From a memorial in Kendal Parish Church.

London bredd me, Westminster fedd me,
Cambridge sped me, my sister wed me,*
Study taught me, Living sought me,
* i.e. as a parson he officiated at his sister's wedding.

296

Learning brought me, Kendal caught me,
Labour pressed me, Sickness distressed me,
Death oppressed me, & Grave possessed me,
God first gave me, Christ did save me,
Earth did crave me & Heaven would have me.

2

On a stone beside the road over Irton Pike, between Eskdale and Santon Bridge.

In memory of William Malkinson,
Wesleyan local preacher,
died here suddenly, Sunday, February, 21st, 1886.
'Be ye also ready.'

3

On a grave-stone in the churchyard of St John's, Ulpha. The seeming quotation is adapted from King Lear.

In memory of
JAMES CROSBIE JENKINSON
of Whitehaven
Who perished on Birker Moor
during the 'pelting of the pitiless
storm,' on the 1st of January 1826
aged 17 years.

4

On a tomb in the churchyard of Holy Trinity, Millom. The name of the house is now usually spelt 'Po House', *to the amusement of visitors.*

In Memory of
Miles Postlethwaite late of Powhouse in this Parish,
Gent, who Departed this Life the last Day of March
1742 in the 73rd year of his Age.

Under this Stone lies also the Body of ELIZABETH his only Daughter.

> Her Soul inform'd with ev'ry softer Grace;
> Youth's fairest Honours op'ning in her Face;
> Sweet as the Flow'r that drinks the vernal Dew,
> As glossy bright and ah! as transient too:
> Such was the Maid on whose untimely Herse
> Flows the sad Tribute of this humble Verse:
> Mind, ye fair, ye young, the normal Lay;
> The Form of Youth, of Life, is but a Day.

> She died of the small pox the 16th of October 1758.
> Aged twenty two Years but for one Day.

Customs and Social Conditions

Rush-Bearing at Grasmere

Clarke seems to be mistaken over the date, since, before 1845, the Rush-bearing was held on the Sunday nearest to St Oswald's Day, i.e. 5 August. The custom has been revived in this century and is now a popular tourist attraction.

I happened once to be here at what they call a *Rush-bearing*. This is an ancient annual custom, formerly pretty universal here, but now generally disused, and consisted of the following rural procession. About the latter end of September, a number of young women and girls (generally the whole parish) go together, to the tops of the hills, to gather rushes; these they carry to the church, headed by one of the smartest girls of the company.

She who leads the procession is stiled the Queen, and carries in her hand a large garland, and the rest usually have nosegays. The Queen then goes and places her garland upon the pulpit, where it remains till after the next Sunday; the rest then strew their rushes upon the bottom of the pews, and at the church-door they are met by a fiddler, who plays before them to the public house, where the evening is spent in all kinds of rustic merriment. The origin of this custom seems to be to guard the people from suffering from the damp and cold of the church, which is neither flagged nor boarded.

I now come to a story which of all others I wish to conceal; yet it must be told – must be read – and (by Cumbrians at least) not only read, but *understood*. Yet, after all this, it is no more than a pun, or rather three puns in one – harmless – inoffensive. Yet I would advise those readers who cannot relish a *joke of every colour*, forthwith to take a pair of compasses, and by their help cut out a paper, or papers, 7¼ inches long, and 4 inches broad, *viz*. the exact dimensions of the ensuing paragraph, which I measured for that purpose; lay their paper over it, and then proceed with the book as if no such paragraph had ever been written – *verbum sapienti*.

At one of those rushbearings her Majesty was attended to her own habitation by one of those blades who are called (I know not why) *fine* gentlemen. – (Here I drop a curtain for some months over my story, as I could say nothing consistent with historic modesty of what passed in the interim.) – Some time, however, (within nine months) her Majesty's waist underwent a visible alteration, and as the crime of manufacturing (I mean without a license) an human creature was held almost equal to the demolishing of one, she was hurried before a neighbouring magistrate. The justice, when he had heard the information, put on his spectacles (whether for *inspection* or not is a question which perhaps none but his Worship could answer:) 'Well, wench,' says he, elevating his eye-brows, and throwing himself back in his judicial chair – 'Well wench, where were you got with child?' – 'At the *Nick*, Sur,' replied the unfortunate fair one, with a low curtsey. The justice first surveyed the girl attentively – then looked up – then down – then at the constable – then at the delinquent again. 'Nick!' – says he to himself – 'Nick! why, I believe that is always the case.' – 'What do you say, hussy? – Where is that?' – 'Between the *wike* and *tail-end*, Sur.'*

James Clarke
A Survey of the Lakes (second edition, 1789)

Barring out the Schoolmaster

The custom of 'barring out' the schoolmaster was very prevalent in the Lake Counties in the eighteenth century, and that it was not unduly frowned on can be guessed from the fact that John Richardson, who tells this story, was himself a village schoolmaster in the Vale of St John, only a few miles from his birthplace at Naddle. It seems unlikely, however, that his academic qualifications were very great, since he began life as a waller, and, indeed, built the school in which he later taught.

When I went to t'scheull – oh! man, but theer hes been a deal o' ups an' doons sen that – I's abeun sebbenty noo, an' seeah it'ill be mair ner fifty year sen than. Bit i'them days fwoke use to gang far langer to t'scheull ner they deu noo. They hev to start wark noo-a-days ameast be they're peat-hee [no higher than the thickness of a peat]; while
* *Nick*, *Wike* and *Tail-End* were, of course, farms in the Grasmere area.

fifty year sen they dud nowte bit gang till they war girt lumps o'fellows, gayly nar as big as I is noo.

Well, as I was gaan to tell ye, I went to St Jwohn's scheull, when Preest Wilson was t'maister. He was racken't a varra good maister, teu. Sartenly, he was parlish [rather] sharp on us at times; an' some o't'laal uns war nar aboot freetent to deith on 'im. Bit theer was on tull a scwore o'us girt fellows varra nar up tull men, an' we yan egg'd anudder on into aw maks o'mischieves, till he was fworc't owder to be gayly sharp on us, or else we wad ha' gitten t'maister on 'im awtogidder.

By jing! hedn't we rare barrin's oot i'them days! Theer nowte et mak [nothing of the same sort] noo, for fwok hes gitten sa mickle pride, an' sa menny new-fanglet ways, 'at them auld customs ur aw deun away wi'. It use to be than, when t'time com for brekkin' up for t'Cursmas er Midsummer hellidays, 'at when t'maister went heamm tull his dinner, we use to bar up aw t'dooers an'windows, an'waddent let'im in agean. An' then we wreatt on a bit o'paper, 'at we wantit seeah menny week helliday, an' neah tasks, an'pot it through t'kaywholl. If we could nobbut manish to keep 'im oot, we gat oor helliday, an' neah tasks owder; but if he contrib't enny way to git in, we use to hev to slenk of to oor seats gayly sharply, hingen oor lugs. An' than we gat ivvery yan on us a gay lang task to git'off i't'hellidays, an' a lock o't'warst on us, mebby, a good hiden to be gaan on wi'.

Wy, theer was ya midsummer, – I can think on't as weel as if it hed nobbut been yesterday, – 'at we war varra detarmin't, an' we contriv't aw to hev oor dinners wi'us that day, an' as seun as ivver t'maister hed gean tull his dinner, we began to prepare. We hed three or fower girt tubs riddy, an' we browt them into t'scheull, an' than we fetch't watter oot o't'scheull dem [dam] till they war as full as they cud hod; an'we warrent varra partickler aboot gitten't varra clean nowder. An' than we had swirts [squirts] meade o' kesks to swirt watter at 'im, if he try't to git in at t'windows.

We next bar't t'dooer, an' nail't t'window casements, an' meade aw as secure as we cud, an' than we waitit till he com. As seun as he com an' fand' at he cuddent git in, he shootit varra illnatur't like, 'at we mud oppen't dooer; bit asteed o'that we pot oor bit o' paper through t'kaywholl demanden a month helliday, an' neah tasks. When he saw that, he was madder ner ivver, an' he sed 'at he wad owder be in or know 'at he cuddent git.

Efter that we hard neh mair on'im for a canny bit, an' we began to think 'at he'd gone awtogidder bit we war ower auld to oppen t'dooer, teu. We keep't watchen, an'peepen oot for a while, an'efter a bit whea dud we see bit greet Joe Thompson, at Sykes', an' their sarvant man, Isaac Todd, an' t'maister, aw cummen togidder, an' they had geavlecks an' hammers ower their shooders, to brek t'dooer in wi'. We war gayly flate [frightened] than. This Joe Thompson was a girt fellow, a gay bit abeun two yerds lang, an' he was as strang as a cuddy [donkey], bit as num as a coo; an' a job o' that mak just suitit 'im. He wad ha' gone hofe a duzzen mile for a bit fun, enny time. Poor Joe! he was neah bad fellow, wassent Joe, bit he's deid an' gean abeun twenty year sen.

Bit, awivver, we consultit togidder, an' we thowt 'at as we'd begun, theer was neah way bit feightin't oot; an' seeah as seun as ivver enny o'them com nar t'window we aw let flee wi'oor swirts, an' hofe droon't them wi' durty watter. We dreave them back i' that way a gay lock o'times, bit they all'as come on agean, an' at last they brack t'casement in wid a greet hammer. For aw that they cuddent git in when they'd deun. We ram't furms an' things into t'wholl, an'dash't watter at them, till we fairly dreave them back agean.

Efter that aw was whiet for a while, an' we began to think 'at we'd banish't them awtogidder; bit we fand it oot efter 'at they war nobbut waitin' till Isaac Todd hed gone to late [find] some tin-cans. It wassent lang till they began to throw watter through t'window, ya canful efter anudder, that fast, 'at we war gaan to be fairly droon't oot. We duddent know what to deu than for a laal bit, bit oor mettle was fairly up, an' we detarmin't to mak what t'soldiers caw a sortie. Seeah, we aw rush't oot pell'mell, an'sed we wad put them aw three in t' scheull dem. Two or three o't'biggest gat hoald o'Isaac Todd, an'dud throw 'im in heid fwormost, an' telt 'im to git oot agean t'best way he could.

Theer was aboot a scwore on us buckel't greet Joe, bit he mannish't to git hoald o't'dial post, an' he was that strang 'at we cuddent aw stur 'im. We mud as weel ha' try'd to trail Skiddaw, as Joe an't'dial

post, an' seeah we left 'im, an'aw teuk efter t'Preest, like a pack
o'hoonds i'full cry; bit he was a young lish fellow than, an'cud keep
up a rattlin' pace for menny a lang mile. He teuk reet away on to
t'Lowrigg, an'we seunn lost 'im; an' I dar say if t'treuth was known
we war pleas't enuff 'at we duddent catch 'im.

Bit, awivver, we'd won t'day, an' ye may be seur 'at we meadd
neeah laal noise aboot it, when theer was atween thirty an' forty on us
aw talken togidder, an' tellen what greet feats we'd deun.

It was mid-efterneun than, bit we set to wark an' sidit [tidied]
t'scheull up as weel as we could. An' than we meadd a collection
amang oorsels, an' hed spworts, sek as russelin', an'lowpin [jumping],
an'feut-reacin'; an't'maister an' Joe Thompson com back an'join't us,
an' aw was as reet as could be.

We saw neah mair o'Isaac Todd. We thowt 'at he'd mebby geann
heamm an' to bed till his cleass gat dry.

John Richardson
Cummerland Talk

Buried by the Parish

Wednesday, 3rd September [1800]. – Coleridge, Wm, and John went
from home, to go upon Helvellyn with Mr Simpson. They set out
after breakfast. I accompanied them up near the blacksmith's . . . I then
went to a funeral at John Dawson's. About 10 men and 4 women.
Bread, cheese, and ale. They talked sensibly and cheerfully about
common things. The dead person, 56 years of age, buried by the
parish. The coffin was neatly lettered and painted black, and covered
with a decent cloth. They set the corpse down at the door; and, while
we stood within the threshold, the men with their hats off sang with
decent and solemn countenances a verse of a funeral psalm. The
corpse was then borne down the hill, and they sang till they had passed
the Town-end. I was affected to tears while we stood in the house,
the coffin lying before me. There were no near kindred, no children.
When we got out of the dark house the sun was shining, and the
prospect looked as divinely beautiful as I ever saw it. It seemed more

sacred than I had ever seen it, and yet more allied to human life. The green fields, neighbours of the church yard, were as green as possible; and, with the brightness of the sunshine, looked quite gay. I thought she was going to a quiet spot, and I could not help weeping very much. When we came to the bridge, they began to sing again, and stopped during four lines before they entered the churchyard ... Wm and John came home at 10 o'clock.

Dorothy Wordsworth
Grasmere Journal

Bidden Funerals

In most parts of Westmorland, the **regular ancient system of** conducting funerals was to invite what was called the *bidding*, being a certain extent of houses, considerably less than the township, but which had been called the 'bidding' for ages. In very thinly inhabited places, it was customary to 'bid' two at a house; but where the country is more populous, only one was 'bidden' at each house. On arriving at the 'funeral house', a large table was set out, covered with cheese, wheat bread, and oat cake; ale also, cold or warm, according to the season of the year, was served round to each of the company, and a small wheaten loaf given to carry home. It was also customary for each attendant to touch the corpse. This arose from an old superstition, firmly believed through all the country, that if the murderer touched the person he had murdered, the corpse would begin to bleed; hence all who attended funerals were required to pass this ordeal to prove they were innocent of the deceased's death. A few miles below Lancaster, an entirely different form prevails, even at this day. All who are bidden are expected to present the mistress of the house with a shilling each, towards defraying the expense of the funeral. The provision is what they term *white posset*, made of milk, &c. and currants. The posset is served up in very large bowls, generally borrowed for the purpose. This is placed upon a long narrow table, so that three persons on each side of the table can sit to each bowl, and feed themselves with spoons. After the posset, ale is carried round in flagons to the company. At Dalton-in-Furness, however, the most singular mode of conducting funerals prevails. A full meal of bread and cheese and ale is provided at the 'funeral house', and after the corpse is interred, the parish clerk proclaims, at the grave side, that the company must repair to some appointed public house. Arrived there, they sit down by fours together, and each four is served with two quarts of ale. One half of this is paid for by the conductor of the funeral, and the other half by the company. While they are drinking the ale, a waiter goes round with cakes, serving out one to each guest, which he is expected to carry home. Even the passing-bell and tolling vary considerably in the course of a few miles. At Heversham, on the morning of the funeral, each of the three bells is tolled six times for a child, ten times for a woman, and twelve for a man. This is repeated three times, thus, for a child, the first bell tolls six times, the second bell six times, and the third bell six times; then the first bell six times etc. In the afternoon, the bells toll at intervals till the funeral; tolling six or eight minutes, and resting six or eight minutes, successively. This method of 'crossing the bells' is common, we believe, in several other places. In some places, the largest bell tolls every minute its 'solemn knell'. This has certainly the most solemnity in it.

> John Briggs
> Notes to *Westmorland As It Was* by the Rev. Mr Hodgson

Clap Bread

Here it was I saw the oat Clap bread made: they mix their flour with water so soft as to rowle it in their hands into a ball, and then they have a board made round and something hollow in the middle riseing by degrees all round to the edge a little higher, but so little as one would take it to be only a board warp'd, this is to cast out the cake thinn and so they clap it round and drive it to the edge in a due proportion till drove as thinn as a paper, and still they clap it and drive it round, and then they have a plaite of iron same size with their clap

307

board and so shove off the cake on it and so set it on coales and bake it; when enough on one side they slide it off and put the other side; if their iron plaite is smooth and they take care their coales or embers are not too hot but just to make it looke yellow, it will bake and be as crisp and pleasant to eate as any thing you can imagine; but as we say of all sorts of bread there is a vast deale of difference in what is house-wifely made and what is ill made, so this if its well mixed and rowled up and but a little flour on the outside which will drye on and make it mealy is a very good sort of food; this is the sort of bread they use in all these countrys; . . . they have no other sort of bread unless at mar-ket towns and that is scarce to be had unless the market days, soe they make their cake and eate it presently for its not so good if 2 or 3 dayes old; it made me reflect on the description made in scripture of their kneeding cakes and bakeing them on the hearth when ever they had Company come to their houses, and I cannot but thinke it was after this maner they made their bread in the old tymes especially those Eastern Countreys where their bread might be soone dry'd and spoil'd.

Celia Fiennes
Through England on a Side Saddle

Rum Butter for a Lying-in

Previous to the time [i.e. of the birth], a quantity of sweet butter was prepared; for many of the Dale-landers believed that a lying-in woman would never recover unless she had plenty of sweet butter. It was thus prepared. The butter was melted (not boiled) in a brass pan, till the milk ran to the top, and the salt sunk to the bottom. The milk was then scummed off, and the butter decanted clear from the salt. A quantity of rum and sugar, having been well beat together in a bowl, with a little grated nutmeg, was then mixed with the butter, when all was stirred till the mixture began to cool. Thus prepared, it would keep for any length of time; and few houses were without a pot of sweet butter at all seasons of the year. On this occasion, or at funerals, a certain range of families was called '*the laiting*'; the principal females of which were *laited*. So soon as the child was born, its head was washed over with rum . . . Before the women departed, they sat down to tea, whatever time of day or night it might be. As soon as the good woman could bear to sit up, the neighbouring women were invited to a second tea party, called the '*wiving*', when they all attended with presents – some brought bread, butter, sugar, wine, or any thing deemed necessary at such a time. A great deal of etiquette was observed on these occasions. It was a great insult if one within the *laiting* was forgot in the general invitation. It was also an insult, if one of them was not invited till after the child was born.

> John Briggs
> Notes to *Westmorland As It Was* by the Rev. Mr Hodgson

Dinner at Grasmere

After as good and well-dressed a dinner, at Robert Newton's, as a man could wish, we set out to surmount the steep ascent of Helm Crag; but the dinner was so cheap, I must mention what it consisted of:

Roast pike, stuffed,
A boiled fowl,
Veal-cutlets and ham,
Beans and bacon,
Cabbage,
Pease and potatoes,
Anchovy sauce,
Parsley and butter,
Plain butter,
Butter and cheese,
Wheat bread and oat cake,
Three cups of preserved gooseberries, with a bowl of rich cream in the centre:
For two people, at ten-pence a head.

> Joseph Budworth
> *A Fortnight's Ramble to the Lakes* (third edition, 1810)

An Inn at Kentmere – Early Nineteenth Century

You can form no idea of the comforts and accommodations of a genuine Lake inn of the *old school* . . . The floor was bespread with tubs, pans, chairs, tables, piggins, dishes, tins, and other equipage of a farmer's kitchen. In the dusk of the evening, and the darkness of the house, the things were only just visible; and we felt some hesitation in approaching the fire, lest some accident might befall us in working our way through the innumerable obstacles that intervened between us and the *cozey hearth*. A robust girl, in a short petticoat of *Kendal bump*, however, with more agility than might have been expected from her very unpromising appearance, presently pushed the tubs and pots aside, and by that means formed a tolerable avenue to the fire . . .

My uncle now requested that something might be added to the fire, as we were thoroughly wet and very cold. 'Put some mear peats tet fire,' said the landlord, 'thor folks are varra ill drabbled.' While the maid was reconstructing the fire, we had time to reconnoitre our quarters.

There was no fire-place; but a paved area of about two square yards, raised perhaps six inches from the floor, and attached to the end wall, formed the hearth where the fire burned. Parallel to the end wall, a beam, belonging the room floor above us, crossed the house about two yards from the end wall. The space above this beam was shaped like a pyramid; gradually tapering to the top, where it could not be above a yard square. Up this funnel or chimney the smoke ascended in fine convolving wreaths, very amusing to us, as it gave a dingy hue to the speck of sky which appeared like the lid of the chimney.

Under this huge vacant pyramid, and within what they term the *chimney wing*, we sat, on one side of the hearth. On the other, close to an oven in the wall, sat the ancient landlord, and beside him sat the landlady, a good looking woman with a very young infant on her knee. In the middle was our mountain Venus of a waiting maid, erecting a fire. This seemed to be a feat of skill; for she first collected all the red fragments of the former fire and placed them in a neat heap. Then she surrounded this heap of fire with a circle of half peats, set on end; and again with two rows of whole peats set on end. The hollow in the middle was then filled with small fragments of peats, so as to rise highest in the middle. In about five minutes the fire began to burn brightly . . .

Hitherto we had been sufficiently amused with their rude but well meant endeavours to render us comfortable. But as we began to warm we began to feel faint: and my uncle requested the maid to bring my sister a glass of warm shrub, as he supposed they would keep no wine, and each of us a glass of his favourite rum and new milk. The girl stood and looked '*unutterable things*'. [The quotation is from Thomson's *The Seasons*.] But the landlord replied, 'We hae nae rum.' 'A little gin and warm water then,' said my uncle. 'We niver keep nae spirits,' replied Boniface. 'Let us have something at any rate,' replied my father. 'We hae capital ale,' observed the landlord; 'bring 'em ivery yan a pint.' 'And a pint for your master,' added my uncle. The landlord's face brightened up at this; and all was very pleasant till we tasted the nauseous beverage. However it was all we could procure; and it was our duty to submit to necessity. Beside, whatever our comforts might be, we might rank them among the curiosities of our lake tour.

John Briggs
Letters from the Lakes

How They Lived at Wastdale Head

The green and perfect level, to which the mountains come down with a sheer sweep, is partly divided off into fields; and a few farmhouses are set down among the fields, on the bends of the gushing and gurgling stream. There is a chapel, – the humblest of chapels, – with eight pews, and three windows in three sides, and a skylight over the pulpit. There is also a school. The schoolmaster is entertained on 'whittlegate' terms; that is, he boards at the farmhouses in turn. An old man told us that the plan answers. 'He gets them on very well,' said he; 'and particularly in the spelling. He thinks if they can spell, they can do all the rest.' Such are the original conclusions arrived at in

Wastdale Head. It struck us that the children were dirtier than even in other vales, though the houses are so clean that you might eat your dinner off the board or the floor. But the state of the children's skin and hair is owing to the superstition in all these dales; and the schoolmaster is the one who should cure the evil. A young lady who kindly undertook to wash and dress the infant of a sick woman, but who was not experienced in the process, exclaimed at the end, 'O dear. I forgot its hands and arms. I must wash them.' The mother expressed great horror, and said that 'if the child's arms were washed before it was six months old, it would be a thief;' and, added she, pathetically, 'I would not like that.' The hair and nails must not be cut for a much longer time, for fear of a like result. The Yorkshire people put the alternative of dirty and clean rather strongly in their proverb, 'Better hev a bairn wi a mucky feace than wash its noase off:' but the Cumberland folk view the matter more in a moral way, and refuse to have their children baptized into thievery.

Harriet Martineau
A Complete Guide to the English Lakes

Town-Evils at the Heart of the Mountains

Two large proprietors in the neighbourhood are draining the land extensively, and thus preparing a healthy soil and atmosphere for a generation of residents yet to come. The unhealthiness of many settlements is no less a shame than a curse, for the fault is in Man, not in Nature. Nature has fully done her part in providing rock for foundations, the purest air, and amplest supplies of running water; yet the people live – as we are apt to pity the poor of the metropolis for living – in stench, huddled together in cabins, and almost without water. The wilfulness of this makes the fact almost incredible; but the fact is so. There are several causes for this, all of which are remediable. The great landed proprietors are, in too many cases, utterly careless about the ways of living of their humble neighbours; and those humble neighbours need enlightenment about sanitary matters. They are also too often at the mercy of their rich neighbours, who may interest themselves about the building of handsome houses for opulent persons, but never raise a cottage, or will dispose of their land for sites. The labouring class, therefore, suffer in health and morals as much as the poor of great towns. In places where the fresh mountain winds are always passing hither and thither, and the purest streams are forever heard gushing down from the heights, and the whole area is made up of slopes and natural channels, there are fever nests, as in the dampest levels of low-lying cities. The general absence of poverty makes the way to amendment open and clear. There can hardly be a safer or more profitable investment than cottage building here, for a good dwelling is as convertible a property as a banknote. The railroads, which some have so much feared, will be no small blessing to the district if they bring strangers from a more enlightened region to abolish the town-evils, which harbour in the very heart of the mountains.

Harriet Martineau
A Complete Guide to the English Lakes

Harriet Martineau Welcomes the Railway

We have no fear of injury, moral or economical, from the great recent change, – the introduction of railways. The morals of rural districts are usually such as cannot well be made worse by any change. Drinking and kindred vices abound wherever, in our day, intellectual resources are absent: and nowhere is drunkenness a more prevalent and desperate curse than in the Lake District. Any infusion of the intelligence and varied interests of the towns-people must, it appears, be eminently beneficial: and the order of work-people brought by the railways is of a desirable kind. And, as to the economical effect, – it cannot but be good, considering that mental stimulus and improved education are above every thing wanted ...

In a generation or two, the dale-farms may yield wool that Yorkshire and Lancashire, and perhaps other countries may compete for; the cheese may find a market, and the butter may be in request. And at the same time, the residents may find their health improved by the greater wholesomeness of their food; and, before that, their minds will have become stirred and enlarged by intercourse with strangers who have, from circumstances, more vivacity of faculty and a wider knowledge. The best as well as the last and greatest change in the Lake District is that which is arising from the introduction of the railroad.

Harriet Martineau
A Complete Guide to the English Lakes

But Wordsworth Objects

Proud were ye, Mountains, when, in times of old,
Your patriot sons, to stem invasive war,
Intrenched your brows; ye gloried in each scar:
Now, for your shame, a Power, the Thirst of Gold,
That rules o'er Britain like a baneful star,
Wills that your peace, your beauty, shall be sold,
And clear way made for her triumphal car
Through the beloved retreats your arms enfold!
Hear YE that Whistle? As her long-linked Train
Swept onwards, did the vision cross your view?
Yes, ye were startled; – and, in balance true,
Weighing the mischief with the promised gain,
Mountains, and Vales, and Floods, I call on you
To share the passion of a just disdain.

William Wordsworth
On the Projected Kendal and Windermere Railway (written 1844)

Work

Kendal in 1671

Kendall, or rather Kirkby Kendale (writ antiently Kirkby in Kendale, i.e., the church town in Kendale). It is the chief town for largeness, neatness, buildings and trade in this county, and is most pleasantly seated, for the most part, on the west bank of the river Kent, so called from Kent-meer in this county, where its head is, which river gave name to a fruitful vale called Kent-dale, wherein this town is placed, and to Kent-Sands in Lancashire, this town gave name to the whole Barony. Here was kept the sessions of the peace for this part of the county, as the sessions for the other part is holden at Appleby, which two parts do comprehend the whole county, and do somewhat resemble the Ridings in Yorkshire. This town is seated in a very good air, and its healthfulness is improved partly by the cleanliness of the people, and partly by its situation on a hill side, the river carrying away whatever filthiness the descending rain washeth out of it. It hath two broad and long streets, fairly built, crossing the one over the other, two large stone bridges, and one of wood. It hath also a fair church, which doth contain every Sunday as many people (almost) as any parish church in England . . .

This town is a place of excellent manufacture, and for civility, ingenuity, and industry so surpassing, that in regard thereof it deservedly carrieth a great name. The trade of the town makes it populous, and the people seem to be shaped out for trade, improving themselves not only in their old manufactures of cottons, but of late of making of drugget, serges, hatts, worsted, stockins, etc., whereby many of the poor are daily set on work, and the town much enriched. The inhabitants are generally addicted to sobriety and temperance, and express a thriftiness in their apparrel, the women using a plain tho' decent and handsome dress, above most of their neighbours.

Sir Daniel Fleming of Rydal
Description of the County of Westmoreland (1671)

Penrith in 1698

The town of Penrith is, of course, built largely of red sandstone. In her spelling of the name, Miss Fiennes quite correctly echoes what was then the normal pronunciation.

The stones and slatt about Peroth [Penrith] look'd so red that at my entrance into the town thought its buildings were all of brick, but after found it to be the coullour of the stone which I saw in the Quarrys look very red, their slatt is the same which cover their houses; its a pretty large town a good market for cloth that they spinn in the country, hempe and also woollen; its a great market for all sorts of cattle meate corne etc.

> Celia Fiennes
> *Through England on a Side Saddle*

Cumberland Farming in the Eighteenth Century

Arthur Young, in his tour of the North of England made in 1768, was concerned primarily with agriculture, but his comments on the landscape, like those of Thomas Pennant, were repeatedly quoted in the travel books of the time. He visited only four lakes, including the then little-known Haweswater, and his remarks are mostly unremarkable and conventional. To the subject of farming, however, he brought the trained eye of a specialist, and his report helps to fill those blanks in the scene where Gilpin and Gray saw only the Picturesque.

About *Keswick* the husbandry is as follows:

The soil is both a hazel mould, sand, gravel, and moory; the first but shallow: The inclosed letts from 20s. to 30s. right of commonage included.

Farms, from 10*l*, to 80*l* a year.

Their course,

1. Oats on turf

2. Fallow
3. Barley
4. Wheat
5. Oats and grasses.

They plow twice for wheat, sow two bushels and an half, about *Michaelmas*, and reap thirty-five to forty, upon an average. They also stir twice for barley, sow six bushels in *April* or *May*, and reap forty in return. For oats they stir but once, sow seven bushels, and gain fifty. They have no beans, very few pease, and as little rye. They stir three times for turneps, hoe them once or twice; the average value about 55s. use them for feeding sheep, and stall-fatting oxen. They know but little of clover; one or two farmers have tried it with barley, but found it good for nothing. It must have been upon strange land! ...

Good grass land letts at 30s. an acre; use it mostly for dairying; an acre and a half they reckon sufficient for a cow, and an acre for four sheep. Manuring it is common. Their breed of cattle is the long-horned, and they reckon them best: Fat their oxen to fifty stone; their swine to twenty-four, or thirty.

The product of a cow they reckon at 3*l*. 13s. 6d. and six gallons *per* day a common quantity of milk *per* cow: Do not keep above one hog to ten. The winter food, straw and hay; of the latter they eat about two ton. The summer joist is 35s. In winter they are kept in the house. Their calves suck about two months.

Their flocks rise from an hundred to a thousand; the profit they reckon at 4s. 3d. a head; that is, lamb 3s. and wool 1s. 3d. sometimes 5s. They keep them, in both winter and spring, on the commons. The average weight of the fleeces, 4 lb.

In their tillage, they reckon that twelve horses are necessary for the management of one hundred acres of arable land. They use sometimes four, and sometimes two in a plough, and do an acre a day with them. The annual expense of keeping a horse they reckon at 6*l*. 10s. the summer joist 2*l*. 2s.

The price of plowing, *per* acre, is from 5s. to 6s. and *March* the time of breaking up for a fallow. – Hire of a cart and horse 3s. a day.

In the hiring and stocking of farms, they reckon 360*l*. or 400*l*. necessary for one of 80*l*. a year.

Land sells at from thirty-five to forty years purchase.

Poor rates 9d. in the pound. – The employment of the women and children, spinning, and winding yard.

No small estates.

The following particulars of farms will shew their general economy.

    100 acres in all
     90 arable
     10 grass
    £50 rent
      8 horses
     10 cows
      4 fatting beasts
     20 young cattle
    400 sheep (common right)
      1 man
      1 maid
      1 boy
      1 labourer.

Another,

    220 acres in all
    100 grass
    120 arable
     30 young cattle
      5 fatting beasts
    400 sheep (right of common)
    £80 rent
     12 horses
     22 cows
      1 man
      2 maids
      2 boys
      3 labourers.

LABOUR

In harvest, 1s. and beer.
In hay-time, ditto.
In winter, 6d. and board.
Reaping wheat, 6s.
Mowing grass, 2s.
Ditching, 4d. to 5d. *per* rood.
First man's wages, 10*l.* to 11*l.*
Next ditto, 6*l.*
Boy of ten or twelve years, 3*l.* to 3*l.* 10s.
Dairymaid, 4*l.* 14s. 6d.
Other ditto, 3*l.* 3s.
Women *per* day, in harvest, 1s. and beer.
In hay-time, ditto.
In winter, 6d. and beer.

Arthur Young (1741–1820)
A Six Months Tour Through the North of England

Herdwick Sheep

This passage is full of inaccuracies and misunderstandings, but it was so often quoted by travellers and the writers of guide books that it has become part of the folk lore of the Lakes.

There is a kind of sheep in these mountains called *Herdwicks*, which when fed to the highest growth, seldom exceed nine or ten pounds a quarter; they, contrary to all other sheep I have met with, are seen before a storm, especially of snow, to ascend against the coming blast, and take the stormy side of the mountain, which, fortunately for themselves, saves them from being overblown. This valuable instinct was first discovered by the people of *Wasdalehead*, a small village, whose limits join those of Borrowdale. They, to keep this breed as much as possible in their own village, bound themselves in a bond, that no one of them should sell above five ewe (or female) lambs in one year; means, however, were found to smuggle more, so that all the shepherds now have either the whole or half breed of them; especially where the mountains are very high, as in *Borrowdale*, *Newlands* and *Skiddaw*, where they have not hay for them in winter. These sheep lye upon the very tops of the mountains in that season as well as in summer; and, as I said before, keep to the stormy side, where the wind blows the snow off the surface of the ground . . .

Whence this breed first came I cannot learn; the inhabitants of *Nether Wasdale* say they were taken from on board a stranded ship; however, till within these few years, their number was very small: they grow very little wool; eight or nine of them jointly not producing more than a stone, yet their wool is pretty good.

James Clarke
A Survey of the Lakes (second edition, 1789)

A Crack about Herdwick Sheep

I. HOMING INSTINCT

The most remarkable characteristics of these Herdwick sheep are their homing instinct and their marvellous memories. Of this latter there are many proofs to hand. For example, a flock of sheep, driven down a road which was blocked at the time, had to pass through a gate, and so back again through another opening in the wall to the roadway. This was when they were being driven back to the fells. They did not pass along that road again for many months. The road was no longer blocked, and the wall had been built up, but as soon as they came to the place where the wall had been built up, they all topped the wall and insisted on going back again through the gate. I have myself seen a flock driven along the road, suddenly, when they came to a certain place, spring into the air, and was told that at that particular point in the former year, a pole had been across the road, and the sheep had jumped it when they came to the place. Though no obstruction now existed, they leapt over an imaginary pole.

But the homing instinct is the most remarkable feature of their character. If a lamb, after being suckled on the mountain 'heaf' or place of pasture, is taken away from it after six or seven weeks, and carried miles away, it will never forget the place of its infancy, but will, as soon as the restless feeling of the next springtime calls it to the mountain tops, if it has the opportunity, make its way though fair or foul over miles of country back again to its 'heaf'. I have met solitary sheep in the dales wandering back from their far-off wintering pastures to their fellside 'heafs', and once, late at night, I came upon a ewe passing up the Keswick main street, probably on its way to Helvellyn. I have heard of a flock being sold at the Cockermouth market, and taken right away to Skinburness on the Solway, with the result that the bulk of them went back of their own accord to the mountain heights, miles away to the south of Cockermouth.

2. SMIT AND LUG MARKS

Before the lambs go up to the fells they are ear-marked and 'smit' or 'smitted'. These ear-marks come down from a very ancient past. They are the 'lug'-marks or 'law'-marks of the Norsemen, 'lug' and 'log' being in the Scandinavian tongue the same word for law. Each flockmaster has his own mark. Some ears are 'slit'; others are 'ritted'; others are 'tritted'; others are 'spoon'-marked; others are 'key-bitted', 'fork-bitted', 'under-bitted', 'upper-halved', 'under-halved', or 'half-sheared'. Others again are 'stoved', 'stuffed' or 'cropped', that is, have the whole of the tip of the ear cut off. It is only certain manorial hall farms that have the right to cut off the whole ear. It is considered a very dishonourable thing to tamper with the ear or lug-mark. The word 'cut-lug', as applied to a man, is a term of greatest opprobrium. The first thing that a sheep-stealer would do, of course, is to tamper with the lug-marks, or to cut off the whole ear to prevent recognition.

With regard to the 'smit'-marks, these take the form of bugles, or sword marks or crosses, or simply 'smits' or 'strakes', with 'pops' or dots, and these in black or red or blue are put on different parts of the body, according to the flockmaster's traditional usage.

3. COUNTING SHEEP

It should, perhaps, be said that some students of dialect are doubtful whether this sheep-counting system remained in use as long as Canon Rawnsley and others would have us believe.

These flock-masters and shepherds talk of their sheep in the Norse tongue. They speak of the sheep 'raking', that is going one after another across the fells, as they do in Iceland today. They have their 'out-rakes' and 'intakes' that are found in Norway. 'Gimmer' and 'twinter' or two winters, 'trinter' three winters, are all Icelandic words, and though they have forgotten to count sheep as their fore-fathers did up to the beginning of last [i.e. the nineteenth] century, anyone who will refer to local history of the past, can be assured that the method of counting must have been either found here among the Celts or brought over by the Norsemen themselves. These numerals are spoken of as 'hinyartic'. They certainly are found to have a remarkable likeness to Welsh and Breton numerals, and the North American Indians used apparently similar numerals for sheep scoring...

The following are what were in use in Borrowdale:

1. Yan.	11. Yan-a-dick.
2. Tyan.	12. Tyan-a-dick.
3. Tethera.	13. Tethera-a-dick.
4. Methera.	14. Methera-a-dick.
5. Pimp.	15. Bumfit.
6. Sethera.	16. Yan-a-bumfit.
7. Lethera.	17. Tyan-a-bumfit.
8. Hovera.	18. Tethera-a-bumfit.
9. Dovra.	19. Methera -a-bumfit.
10. Dick.	20. Giggot.

But when we go to Westmoreland, we find 'tedra' and 'meddera' were used instead of 'tethera' and 'methera', and the word 'mimph' was used for fifteen and not 'bumfit'. In Eskdale, sethera, lethera, hovera, dovera, dick, became seckera, leckera, hofa, dofa, dec. In another dale, hovera, dovera were changed to hata, slata.

I have never been able to find that these numerals have been used by shepherds of our own time. The oldest men I have spoken with could only say that their fathers told them that their grandfathers always counted that way. One cannot help hoping that this old traditional way of counting may be held in mind. It is a link with a very ancient past, and we who dwell in the land of the shepherd must view with regret any passing into oblivion of shepherd customs or shepherd speech.

H. D. Rawnsley
By Fell and Dale (1911)

The Sheep-Fold

Greenhead Gill lay only about a mile away from Wordsworth's home at Dove Cottage, but it is interesting to note that he learned the story of the sheep-fold, not from his neighbours at Grasmere, but, years earlier, from Anne Tyson, when he lodged at her cottage as a schoolboy at Hawkshead.

If from the public way you turn your steps
Up the tumultuous brook of Green-head Gill,
You will suppose that with an upright path
Your feet must struggle; in such bold ascent
The pastoral mountains front you, face to face.
But, courage! for around that boisterous brook
The mountains have all opened out themselves,
And made a hidden valley of their own.
No habitation can be seen; but they
Who journey thither find themselves alone
With a few sheep, with rocks and stones and kites
That overhead are sailing in the sky.
It is in truth an utter solitude;
Nor should I have made mention of this Dell

But for one object which you might pass by,
Might see and notice not. Beside the brook
Appears a straggling heap of unhewn stones!
And to that simple object appertains
A story – unenriched with strange events,
Yet not unfit, I deem, for the fireside,
Or for the summer shade. It was the first
Of those domestic tales that spake to me
Of Shepherds, dwellers in the valleys, men
Whom I already loved; – not verily
For their own sakes, but for the fields and hills
Where was their occupation and abode.
And hence this Tale, while I was yet a Boy
Careless of books, yet having felt the power
Of Nature, by the gentle agency
Of natural objects, led me on to feel
For passions that were not my own, and think
(At random and imperfectly indeed)
On man, the heart of man, and human life.
Therefore, although it be a history
Homely and rude, I will relate the same
For the delight of a few natural hearts;
And, with yet fonder feeling, for the sake
Of youthful Poets, who among these hills
Will be my second self when I am gone.

Upon the forest-side in Grasmere Vale
There dwelt a Shepherd, Michael was his name;
An old man, stout of heart, and strong of limb.
His bodily frame had been from youth to age
Of an unusual strength: his mind was keen,
Intense, and frugal, apt for all affairs,
And in his shepherd's calling he was prompt
And watchful more than ordinary men.
Hence had he learned the meaning of all winds,
Of blasts in every tone; and oftentimes,
When others heeded not, he heard the South

Make subterraneous music, like the noise
Of bagpipers on distant Highland hills.
The Shepherd, at such warning, of his flock
Bethought him, and he to himself would say,
'The winds are now devising work for me!'
And, truly, at all times, the storm, that drives
The traveller to a shelter, summoned him
Up to the mountains: he had been alone
Amid the heart of many thousand mists,
That came to him, and left him, on the heights.
So lived he till his eightieth year was past.
And grossly that man errs, who should suppose
That the green valleys, and the streams and rocks,
Were things indifferent to the Shepherd's thoughts.
Fields, where with cheerful spirits he had breathed
The common air; hills, which with vigorous step
He had so often climbed; which had impressed
So many incidents upon his mind
Of hardship, skill or courage, joy or fear;
Which, like a book, preserved the memory
Of the dumb animals, whom he had saved,
Had fed or sheltered, linking to such acts
The certainty of honourable gain;
Those fields, those hills – what could they less? had laid
Strong hold on his affections, were to him
A pleasurable feeling of blind love,
The pleasure which there is in life itself.

Michael was married and had a son, called Luke, and the poem goes on to tell how, when Luke was seventeen, his father was innocently involved in a family misfortune as a result of which he was in danger of losing his land. In this crisis he and his wife decided that the boy should leave home for some years to work for a well-to-do kinsman, and so earn the money to pay off the debts on the farm and redeem the inheritance for his own future.

Near the tumultuous brook of Green-head Gill,
In that deep valley, Michael had designed

To build a Sheep-fold; and, before he heard
The tidings of his melancholy loss,
For this same purpose he had gathered up
A heap of stones, which by the streamlet's edge
Lay thrown together, ready for the work.
With Luke that evening thitherward he walked:
And soon as they had reached the place he stopped,
And thus the old Man spake to him: – 'My son,
Tomorrow thou wilt leave me: with full heart
I look upon thee, for thou art the same
That wert a promise to me ere thy birth,
And all thy life hast been my daily joy . . .'

    At this the old Man paused;
Then, pointing to the stones near which they stood,
Thus, after a short silence, he resumed:
'This was a work for us; and now, my Son,
It is a work for me. But, lay one stone –
Here, lay it for me, Luke, with thine own hands.
Nay, Boy, be of good hope; – we both may live
To see a better day. At eighty-four
I still am strong and hale; – do thou thy part;
I will do mine. – I will begin again
With many tasks that were resigned to thee:
Up to the heights, and in among the storms,
Will I without thee go again, and do
All works which I was wont to do alone,
Before I knew thy face. – Heaven bless thee, Boy!
Thy heart these two weeks has been beating fast
With many hopes; it should be so – yes – yes –
I knew that thou couldst never have a wish
To leave me, Luke: thou hast been bound to me
Only by links of love: when thou art gone,
What will be left to us! – But I forget
My purposes. Lay now the corner-stone,
As I requested; and thereafter, Luke,
When thou art gone away, should evil men

Be thy companions, think of me, my Son,
And of this moment; thither turn thy thoughts,
And God will strengthen thee: amid all fear
And all temptation, Luke, I pray that thou
Mayst bear in mind the life thy Fathers lived,
Who, being innocent, did for that cause
Bestir them in good deeds. Now, fare thee well –
When thou return'st, thou in this place wilt see
A work which is not here: a covenant
'Twill be between us; but, whatever fate
Befall thee, I shall love thee to the last,
And bear thy memory with me to the grave.'

The Shepherd ended here; and Luke stooped down,
And, as his Father had requested, laid
The first stone of the Sheep-fold. At the sight
The old Man's grief broke from him; to his heart
He pressed his Son, he kiss ed him and wept;
And to the house together they returned.
– Hushed was that House in peace, or seeming peace,
Ere the night fell: – with morrow's dawn the Boy
Began his journey, and, when he had reached
The public way, he put on a bold face;
And all the neighbours, as he passed their doors,
Came forth with wishes and with farewell prayers,
That followed him till he was out of sight.

A good report did from their Kinsman come,
Of Luke and his well-doing: and the Boy
Wrote loving letters, full of wondrous news,
Which, as the Housewife phrased it, were throughout
'The prettiest letters that were ever seen.'
Both parents read them with rejoicing hearts.
So, many months passed on: and once again
The Shepherd went about his daily work
With confident and cheerful thoughts: and now
Sometimes when he could find a leisure hour

He to that valley took his way, and there
Wrought at the Sheep-fold. Meantime Luke began
To slacken in his duty; and, at length,
He in the dissolute city gave himself
To evil courses: ignominy and shame
Fell on him, so that he was driven at last
To seek a hiding-place beyond the seas.

There is a comfort in the strength of love;
'Twill make a thing endurable, which else
Would overset the brain, or break the heart:
I have conversed with more than one who well
Remember the old Man, and what he was
Years after he had heard this heavy news.
His bodily frame had been from youth to age
Of an unusual strength. Among the rocks
He went, and still looked up to sun and cloud,
And listened to the wind; and, as before,
Performed all kinds of labour for his sheep,
And for the land, his small inheritance.
And to that hollow dell from time to time
Did he repair, to build the Fold of which
His flock had need. 'Tis not forgotten yet
The pity which was then in every heart
For the old Man – and 'tis believed by all
That many and many a day he thither went
And never lifted up a single stone.

William Wordsworth
From *Michael*

The Charcoal Burners

*Charcoal was manufactured in great quantities in the woods of High Furness
to be used in the smelting of iron ore from the mines of Low Furness.*

Soon after dawn the men and carts arrive
and horses, fresh uncreaked from night's sleep,
stand sorrow-eyed within the wood.
The charcoal pit lies derelict and deep in fern;
the burners' hut a sagging den; and piles of wood,
stacked months before, overgrown in tangled grass,
seeming waste, but by those woodmen known and understood.

It hardly seems a place for toil, yet soon
the rough is cleared, and in among the sapling trees
the burners' axes chop and cut. By ten, the hut is
fresh repaired and on a fire a blackened kettle steams.

The burners toil steadfastly,
setting sapling on the mount until it stands,
a passive lump, the wood entombed within the turf,
and wind among the trees around keening softly
as if it knows that each axe blow meant death for each shorn stump.

At noon next day the waiting mound is fired.
Hot coals stream within its heart
and when the inner crack of singing wood is heard,
the final sealing turf is laid.
And muttering and crackling, the mound takes on a life
that's all its own, reeking smoke and steam
and uttering half-heard thoughts
of bowers where the light runs green
and endless glades of sun
and forests by the sea.

All night and all next day the charcoal men
nurse the smouldering mound,

pouring earth on spurts of flame,
splashing water from the beck,
damping flames and snatching sleep
as best they may, on bracken-beds and turf.

For three long days and nights the smell of burning,
And then the fire seems to die.
The smoke is gone, but all there know
the embers still glow bright within.
And suddenly tired men regain their drive
as in each mind the thought prevails:
Has it worked; had the burn gone well?
Slowly, the cooled mound is turned back.
The tired burners smile. The prize, the charcoal,
glistens satin-black, and rings clear as a bell.

Irvine Hunt

The Lead Mine of Borrowdale

The most remarkable *Mundick Vein* upon these *Mountains* is that we call *Wadd* or *Black-Lead*.

This *Vein* was found upon *Borrowdale* Mountains, near *Keswick*, and there is not any other of the same kind in *England*, nor perhaps in *Europe*, at least that I ever heard of.

Its Composition is a black pinguid, and shining Earth, impregnated with *Lead* and *Antimony*. This *Ore* is of more Value than either *Copper*, *Lead* or *Iron*.

Its natural Uses are both *Medical* and *Mechanical*. It's a present *Remedy* for the *Cholick*; it easeth the Pain of *Gravel*, *Stone*, and *Strangury*; and for these and the like Uses, it's much bought up by *Apothecaries* and *Physicians*, who understand more of its *medicinal* Uses than I am able to give Account of.

The manner of the Country Peoples using it, is thus; First, they beat it small into *Meal*, and then take as much of it in white Wine, or Ale, as will lie upon a *Sixpence*, or more, if the Distemper require it.

It operates by *Urine*, *Sweat*, and *Vomiting*. This Account I had from those who had frequently used it in these Distempers with good Success; besides, those Uses that are *Medicinal*, it hath many other Uses, which increase the Value of it.

At the first discovering of it, the Neighbourhood made no other use of it, but for marking their *Sheep*; but it's now made use of to glazen and harden *Crucibles*, and other Vessels made of *Earth* or *Clay*, that are to endure the hottest *Fire*; and to that end it's wonderfully effectual, which much inhaunceth the Price of such Vessels.

By rubbing it upon *Iron-Arms*, as *Guns*, *Pistols*, and the like, and tinging of them with its Colour, it preserves them from rusting.

It's made use of by Dyers of *Cloath*, making their *Blues* to stand unalterable; for these and other Uses, it's bought up at great Prices by the *Hollanders*, and others.

The *Lords* of this *Vein* are the Lord *Banks*, and one Mr *Hudson*. This *Vein* is but opened once in seven years, but then such quantities of it are got, that are sufficient to serve the Country.

This Mundick *Ore* having little of *Sulphur* in its Composition, will not flow without a violent Heat. It produceth a white *Regulus*, shining like *Silver*. It cannot be made *malleable*.

[*John Postlethwaite, in* Mines and Mining in the Lake District (*1871*), *says: ' The graphite found in this mine is remarkable for its purity, indeed it is unequalled by any other of its kind in the world. It was at one time considered of such importance as to merit a special Act of Parliament for its protection . . . In the year 1800 it was deemed necessary that a house should be built over the mouth of the principle level, and armed men were kept on guard there during the night. The miners were also stripped and carefully searched on leaving their work; and when the graphite was sent to the Company's warehouse in London, an armed escort accompanied it as far as Kendal.*']

Thomas Robinson, Rector of Ousby
An Essay towards a Natural History of Westmorland and Cumberland

Mining in the Early Days

Before the invention of gunpowder, levels were cut through the hard rock by the miners of those days with 'stope and feather', implements consisting of two thin pieces of iron, called feathers, about six inches long and half-an-inch broad, flat on one side and round on the other, and a thin tapering wedge or stope of the same length and width. A hole was bored in the rock and the feathers placed in it, with their flat sides together, and parallel with the cleavage of the rock; the point of the stope was then introduced between them and then driven in with a hammer until the rock was rent. This must have been a very slow and laborious process, because those who made use of it were very careful not to make the aperture larger than was required to admit one man. There are still remains of these primitive works in several of the mines in the Lake Country; levels measuring from five to six feet in height, and eighteen or twenty inches in width, and which only require a very superficial inspection to convince anyone that the old miners must have been very expert in the use of these tools . . .

When the miner has penetrated into the earth a distance of fifteen or twenty fathoms, either vertically or horizontally, the supply of fresh air fails; his candle refuses to burn unless it is placed in a leaning or nearly horizontal position, and he experiences difficulty in breathing, therefore it becomes necessary to create a current of air by artificial means. In some cases this is done by machinery, and in others by means of a waterfall, and the current thus created is conveyed to the workmen through wooden tubes; but the most natural and easy means of ventilation is to have, where practicable, more than one opening into the mine, by which a free circulation of air will be produced spontaneously.

Noxious gases are frequently liberated from cavities in the rock, which have a very injurious effect upon the miner's respiratory organs; and these, combined with the mineral dust which he inhales, produce in him the seeds of disease and premature old age. He becomes an old man at forty-five or fifty, and rarely lives out the allotted term of three score years and ten. But I cannot think that the beneficent God who called into being the agents by which fissures were formed in the earth's crust, and afterwards stored with mineral wealth, intended that the men who opened those store-houses of nature, should have to surrender one-fifth of the ordinary term of life.

John Postlethwaite
Mines and Mining in the Lake District (1877)

A Black Journey

Hard Knott and Wrynose are the names of two mountain passes linking Eskdale, Dunnerdale and Little Langdale.

Visit the collieries [at Whitehaven], entering at the foot of a hill, not distant from the town, attended by the agent: the entrance was a narrow passage, bricked and vaulted, sloping down with an easy descent. Reach the first beds of coal which had been worked about a century ago: the roofs are smooth and spacious, the pillars of sufficient strength to support the great superstructure, being fifteen yards square, or sixty in circumference; not above a third of the coal having been worked in this place; so that to me the very columns seemed left as resources for fuel in future times. The immense caverns that lay between the pillars exhibited a most gloomy appearance. I could not help enquiring here after the imaginary inhabitant, the creation of the labourer's fancy,

The swart fairy of the mine,

and was seriously answered by a black fellow at my elbow, that he really had never met with any; but that his grandfather had found the little implements and tools belonging to this diminutive race of subterraneous spirits.

The beds of coal are nine or ten feet thick, and dip to the west one yard in eight. In various parts are great bars of stone, which cut off the coal: if they bend one way, they influence the coal to rise above one's head; if another, to sink beneath the feet. Operations of nature past my skill to unfold.

335

Reach a place where there is a very deep descent: the colliers call this hardknot, from a mountain of that name: and another wrynose. At about eighty fathoms depth began to see the workings of the rods of the fire-engine, and the present operations of the colliers, who now work in security, for the fire-damps, formerly so dangerous, are almost overcome; at present they are prevented by boarded partitions, placed a foot distance from the sides, which causes a free circulation of air throughout: but as still there are some places not capable of such conveniences, the colliers, who dare not venture with a candle in spots where fire-damps are supposed to lurk, have invented a curious machine to serve the purpose of lights: it is what they call a steel-mill, consisting of a small wheel and a handle; this they turn with vast rapidity against a flint, and the great quantity of sparks emitted not only serves for a candle, but has been found of such a nature as not to set fire to the horrid vapour.

Formerly the damp or fiery vapour was conveyed through pipes to the open air, and formed a terrible illumination during night, like the eruptions of a volcano; and by its heat water could be boiled: the men who worked in it inhaled inflammable air, and if they breathed against a candle, puffed out a fiery stream . . .

Reached the extremity of this black journey to a place near two miles from the entrance, beneath the sea, where probably ships were then sailing over us. Returned up the laborious ascent, and was happy once more to emerge into day-light.

Thomas Pennant
A Tour in Scotland and Voyage to the Hebrides in 1772

The Iron Makers

Graham Sutton's novel Shepherd's Warning *tells of the clash of interest between farming and industry in West Cumberland in the middle eighteenth century.*

The furnace was lit, the pig-bed raked into rows, the vent sealed till the first run-out should be ready. Aloft the fillers shot their charges, barrows of fuel and ore mixed; and each time they unroofed the kiln to do this, flames licked out brighter than day. Mossop watched the work unremittingly.

He had hoped to cast before dinner; but with the furnace standing cold, and the soft weather, there was no hurrying her; by dusk, he reckoned, the first hearthful of iron would run. Yet I found plenty to watch, and to hear too; for now, where all had been still and idle, was a new world full of busy sound. The thrash and mutter of the wheel, the gurgle of sluices, the great groaning bellows, the muffled roar of the fire prisoned in its thick walls, the barrow-men hurrying: above us a fearsome glare, each time the kiln was fed: below, at the back of a deep arch, the starry brightness of the flame which I could see through small peep-holes where the blast snouts went in. From time to time, as the iron neared its maturity, they skimmed the slag from it by a vent over the sealed tapping-hole; and it slid out in liquid fire.

Mossop durst not leave the work, and I would not. So at dinner-hour I shared my bread and cheese with him, as I'd have done with Will at home; but the furnacemen gaped at us two squatting there, and furtively nudged each other, as though they'd seen something odd. Old Mossop seemed to have conceived a fancy for me now, and instructed me: not formally, as on my uncle's order, but from plain pride in his job. 'It's right furnace-weather!' says he, as we sat snug below the kiln with the red earth miring our boots; a moist dull day, I mind it was, and the clouds lowering. 'T'blast thrives, this time o' year; it's t'dry weather bothers us. Ye'd say damp air in t'blast was bad – but I tell thee, it's betterer! Aye, that sounds daft; it's like a lot o' things these modern times is learnin' us – daft but true!'

He showed me how to test ore by licking it – if roasted right, it adhered like clay to the tongue; and a cunning trick to extend the blast, by letting slag form a nose on it: and how to break down the clinker 'scaffolding' which gathered inside the furnace – but he'd let none do this but himself . . . So rapt was I, watching him a little before dusk, I missed my uncle's approach: nor knew that trouble was afoot till I heard his voice sharp behind us.

He had his back to the kiln: his clerk with him, urging some affair which seemed to displease him much, for he said curtly: 'I am here, let them speak!'

'In your office rather, sir?' suggested the clerk. My uncle raised his voice.

'Step forward, one of you! I'll hear what you would say.' Then I saw where a dozen miners stood, not far off, with their caps in their hands. At his word they lurched towards us; and it was now twilight enough for the gleam from the furnace-vents to illumine their sullen faces. One advanced farther than the rest, and began mumbling a confused sort of harangue, half-defiant, half-servile: that elsewhere, in Lancashire, they'd heard, their job fetched higher wages; that they knew times was bad, but the Duke's guns had given Bigrigg a set-up, and now this new cast being made, and a hard bitter winter it had been as Mr Fleming was 'ware, which made their work difficulter; but the guns was grand business any road, for all knew what-like these army contracts were, no-questions-asked and damn-the-cost; so it was right that lads who'd helped to make the guns, in mucky weather and all, shouldn't be losers, and they asked another twopence a day . . .

Mr Fleming refuses the men's request, and the narrator then resumes.

I marvelled at two things. First at his harshness: not so much the words he used, for they were reasonable enough, but the cold finality of his voice; at the great house when Barbara showed such bitter scorn for the men he employed, he'd seemed humaner; but now I caught in his level tones the same arrogance, and perceived that he and she were a pair. And second at the men's meekness: but not so much, when I remembered Whitehaven whence he could have refilled Bigrigg three times over. They trudged away towards the gates; for it was full dusk now, and everyone knocking off except the furnacemen who would continue by shifts, night and day. Old Mossop had seemed to pay no heed to the dispute (likely he was used to them) but I noticed that when my uncle approached the miners, Mossop edged out to where he had their group in view, an iron crow in his hands. Now, Eldon having watched the malcontents out of sight, Mossop informed us that the first cast was fit for running.

Never shall I forget it. At Mossop's hoarse cry, the paddle was stopped, the bellows ceased labouring, the roar of the blast died. Uncanny, the hush seemed, after the din and bustle that had filled our ears hour by hour. At the pig-bed or by the idle wheel, men leaned on their bars, watching; none spoke. No sound but a drip-drip of water from the sluice, and a sort of intestine muttering that the huge kiln still made, whispering to itself. In its dark arch, Mossop was picking at the vent-seal with his long crow, and seemed to make no progress; till suddenly with a fierce blinding gush the iron slid out, burst the remainder of the seal and leapt at us in a flood.

Down the long straight foss leading to the sows it ran; not red-hot, nor white-hot even, but molten light: scorching us, far as we stood back: searing our blind eyes: hissing, stinking . . . at the foss-end it swerved like a live thing and flowed the length of the lowest sow: spilling into each pig. When the litter was complete, a man ran forward into the glare and thrust a long clay spade into the torrent, diverting it, so that it began to fill the next sow: and in turn, the next above that. Not till three rows of pigs were made could we bear to look steadily at their great comb of light, lacing the steamy ground: sluggish now, not moving, but abating gradually to a pale saffron tint, and thence by slow degrees into red. I glanced up, and saw the glare reflected on the undersides of the clouds that sagged over our valley. The kiln, the silent men, the great dripping wheel were tawny with its fierce brightness. And away over Keekle beck, where the ground climbs to Cleator, it lit the faces of a hubble of folk who had gathered to watch our cast made; for in all Cumberland at this time there was hardly a furnace save my uncle's in work, and his not often.

Graham Sutton (1892–1959)
Shepherd's Warning

The Quarrymen of Honister

The green-slate quarries of Honister are working today, and the alpine lady's mantle can still be found growing close to the road over the pass.

A rough and rugged road leads up between the stream – the Seatoller beck – and the mountain; the stream becoming wilder, and the mountain sterner, and the road a harder problem for wheeled things to solve, and the whole scene a grander gathering of natural forces, and a nobler revelation. With its human uses too; which is more than can be said of every mountain pass; for down that scarred and lined and tear-streamed face are the most famous slate quarries in the lake district, and whence was hewn the slate 'that took the prize' in the exhibition of '51. The first you come to are on the right-hand side, in Yew Crag, where was hewn that prize slab, but the second and more important are on the left, in Honister.

This slate quarrying is awful to look at; both in the giddy height at which men work, and in the terrible journies which they make when bringing down the slate in their 'sleds'. It is simply appalling to see that small moving speck on the high crag, passing noiselessly along a narrow grey line that looks like a mere thread, and to know that it is a man with the chances of his life dangling in his hand. As we look the speck moves; he first crosses the straight gallery leading out from the dark cavern where he emerged, and then he sets himself against the perpendicular descent, and comes down the face of the crag, carrying something behind him – at first slowly, and, as it were, cautiously; then with a swifter step, but still evidently holding back; but at the last with a wild haste that seems as if he must be overtaken, and crushed to pieces by the heavy sled grinding behind him. The long swift steps seem almost to fly; the noise of the crashing slate comes nearer; now we see the man's eager face; and now we hear his panting breath; and now he draws up by the road-side – every muscle strained, every nerve alive, and every pulse throbbing with frightful force. It is a terrible trade – and the men employed in it look wan and worn, as if they were all consumptive or had heart disease. The average daily task is seven or eight of these journies, carrying about a quarter of a ton of slate each time; the downward run occupying only a few minutes, the return climb – by another path not quite so perpendicular, where they crawl with their empty sleds on their backs, like some strange sort of beetle or fly – half an hour. Great things used to be done in former times, and the quarrymen still talk of Samuel Trimmer, who once made fifteen journies in one day, for the reward of a small percentage on the hurdle and a bottle of rum; and of Joseph Clark, a Stonethwaite man, who brought down forty-two and a half loads, or ten thousand eight hundred and eighty pounds of slate, in seventeen journies; travelling seventeen miles – eight and a half up the face of the crag, and the same number down, at this murderous pace ... Twelve journies a day rank now as a feat scarcely to be compassed; for no man of modern slate-quarrying powers can do anything near to these giants of the elder time.

The quarrymen have small sleeping huts among the crags, and remain during the week at their work, going home only from the Saturday night to the Monday morning, which leaves scarcely too much time for the building up of a man's domestic life; but they are not a bad race, though rough and uncouth, as are all men whose business leads them to much separation from women and exclusive companionship with each other. About the base of the crag are broad tracts of alpine ladies' mantle (*alchemilla alpina*), while forked spleen-wort (*asplenium septentrionale*), and many a rare plant besides, are to be found among the screes and shelving sides.

E. Lynn Linton
The Lake Country

Play

The Church Does Not Approve of Sunday Football

All scandalous persons hereafter mentioned are to be suspended from
the sacrament of the Lord's Supper, this is to say – any person that
shall upon the Lord's Day use any dancing, playing at dice, or cards,
or any game, masking, wakes, shooting, playing at football, stool
ball, wrestling . . . These Counties of Cumberland and Westmorland
have been hitherto as a Proverb and a by-word in respect of ignorance
and prophaneness: Men were ready to say of them as the Jews of
Nazareth, Can any good thing come out of them?

> *The Agreement of the Associated Ministers and Churches
> of the Counties of Cumberland and Westmorland* (1656)

But an Eighteenth-Century Parson Does

It is much to be regretted, that, in less than a single century, it has been
found impossible, after a very diligent enquiry, to collect any con-
siderable information of a former rector of this parish [i.e. Ousby];
who, in his day, was an useful and valuable man; and whose works
still reflect no ordinary credit on our county. The person here alluded
to, is the Rev. *Thomas Robinson*, who was the author of *The Natural
History of Westmoreland and Cumberland* . . .

Our author is said to have been happily beloved and respected by
his parishioners and neighbours. – One trait of his character is still
remembered in the parish; which shews him to have been, not only of
a cheerful and convivial disposition, but also a man of humour. It was
his constant practice, after Sunday afternoon prayers, to accompany
the leading men of his parish to the adjoining ale-house, where each
man spent a penny, and *only a penny*: that done, he set the younger
sort to play at foot-ball, (of which he was a great promoter) and other
rustical diversions. However much at variance this may be deemed
from modern maxims and manners, it should be recollected, as an
apology for Mr Robinson's indulging in it, that this mode of spending

the sabbath after the services of the church were over, (which there is reason to believe were then far more strictly and constantly attended, than is now the fashion) was actually enjoined by *The Book of Sports*; which it is well known, the established clergy long regarded, in opposition to the puritanical ideas respecting the observance of the sabbath, so different from all the rest of Christendom, which were then but beginning to be countenanced.

> Jonathan Boucher (1738–1804)
> Notes, signed 'Biographia Cumbria'
> in Hutchinson's *History of Cumberland*

The Origin of Wrestling

William Litt, the author of the classic book on Cumberland and Westmorland Style Wrestling from which these extracts are taken, was himself one of the most renowned wrestlers of his time. He was born and brought up in West Cumberland, but his fame as a wrestler brought him little fortune, and he finally emigrated to Canada where he died, a broken and disappointed man.

We find in the 32nd chapter of Genesis, that Jacob having passed his family over the brook Jabbok, was left alone. In its history of events at this early period of the world, with a brevity commensurate with its high importance, the Bible minutely relates only those particular occurrences which refer to some covenant, or promise, then made, renewed, or fulfilled. It narrates facts, without commenting upon them. Therefore, although Jacob's wrestling with the Angel was too remarkable an incident to be omitted, yet we are not told in what manner he came, nor of any preliminary conversation or agreement between them. It however appears very evident that until the Angel manifested his miraculous power, Jacob believed his opponent was a mere mortal like himself; and on whichever side the proposal originated, it was acceded to by the other, either as a circumstance not unusual, or as an amicable amusement, which might be practised without the least infringement on cordiality. If it was not unusual, we are warranted in supposing it a common diversion antecedent to that period, and that Jacob was himself a scientific practiser of the art when he was the father of a large family. Nay, we might even *hint*, his celestial opponent was himself no stranger to that athletic amusement. If it *then* had its origin, no admirer of this athletic science can wish for one more ancient, or more honourable. That the Patriarch's antagonist was a being of a superior order, and sent by Divine authority, no Christian has ever yet disputed. That it was a corporeal struggle, or *bona fide*, a wrestling match between them, is universally admitted. It cannot therefore be denied that it is either of divine origin, or that a Being more than mortal has participated in it. It is true, many of the commentators dwell upon it as a *spiritual*, as well as a *corporeal* struggle; this we are very ready to admit; but we will at the same time contend, that instead of diminishing, it adds considerably to its splendour. An amusement from which so many inferences and conclusions have been drawn to promote the welfare of Christianity cannot be either degrading, or confined in its nature; but on the contrary, noble and scientific.

> William Litt (1785–1847)
> *Wrestliana* (Whitehaven, 1823)

Some Celebrated Wrestlers

Bampton school, on the borders of Westmorland, was perhaps the most celebrated seminary in England for turning out good Wrestlers. It was usual at that period for those designed for the church, or any learned profession, to frequent school when grown up to manhood; and if a young man was known to be a Bampton scholar, it was considered conclusive of his being a good Wrestler. Among those educated at this instructive seminary whose genius led them to acquire a competent knowledge of the bodily powers of man, before they were honoured with the charge of his more important requisites, was the Reverend and celebrated ABRAHAM BROWN. This gentleman was the first of whom we have any authentic records of excelling as a *buttocker*. Having lost no time in perfecting himself in this manly exercise when a *scholar*, he fully maintained the character of a very *first rate*, when acting in the more exalted situations of *usher* and *schoolmaster* in different places; and occasionally after he became a curate. When a very young man he acquired great renown in carrying away a silver cup of considerable value from Eamont Bridge, which divides the counties of Cumberland and Westmorland, and which was consequently in the very centre of the most noted wrestling country in England. After his establishment at Egremont, Mr Brown had no objection, in the spirit of good fellowship, to oblige any man who felt extremely anxious for a trial of skill with him, and in these casual turn ups it is said he was never vanquished. Abraham being a man of considerable humour, and good nature, palmed himself more than once, as a friend of Parson Brown's, on men, who hearing of his celebrity, expressed a strong desire to try a fall with him. On such occasions he pretended to be well acquainted with the Parson, and assured them that if they could throw him easily, they would prove a match for Brown, when they met with him. This of course caused a contest – and Master Abraham, after giving them full satisfaction, would advise them to go home, as he could assure them they were not able to vanquish the Parson. We have heard him assert that when nineteen years of age, he did not weigh more than twelve stones, but a stranger to him in his younger days would have judged of him very differently. He could not be less than six feet high, and when at a proper age for entering the church, must have weighed fifteen stones at least. This well known character died within the last twelve months, and it is but justice to his memory to observe, that though occasionally addicted to the bottle, he preserved through life, both in his public and private character, the regard and esteem, not only of his parishioners in general, but of nearly all who were acquainted with him...

Taking leave for the present of the eastern side of the Derwent, we must go westward as far as Gosforth before we find another Wrestler of such celebrity as to entitle him to notice in these Memoirs. In that place we find one of the most distinguished characters at that period between Derwent and Duddon, in the person of JOHN WOODALL, who was brought up as a husbandman, and succeeded his father as proprietor of a small estate in Gosforth. Woodall though not the tallest, was we believe the strongest man we have yet noticed. His person was symmetry itself; he stood about five feet eleven inches high, weighed upwards of sixteen stones, and all who knew him agree in considering that he was the strongest man in the west of Cumberland. As a Wrestler, Woodall was more indebted to strength, than science; but he possessed the former requisite to such an uncommon degree, that he was considered no unequal opponent for the powerful and scientific curate of Egremont. At the King's Arms, in that place, Woodall exhibited a remarkable, and rather extraordinary specimen of his prodigious strength. Having been thrown for a prize by a shoemaker of the name of Carr, a well-known Wrestler, the latter, flushed with his victory, began to ridicule Woodall on the circumstance; Woodall, though a very peaceable man, yet willing to turn the laugh against Carr, caught him up in his arms as if he had been an infant, and hung him by his breeches waistband upon one of the hooks in the ceiling! . . .

We shall now proceed to notice a transaction which occasioned considerable interest among the admirers of this athletic exercise in this immediate vicinity: – We mean the arrival of the Westmorland militia, which was stationed at Whitehaven towards the close of the seventeenth century. In this regiment were several celebrated Wrestlers, among whom we will particularize the two whose names became 'most familiar in men's mouths', during the time the regiment remained at Whitehaven. These were PHILIP STEPHENSON and THOMAS MADGE . . . The only reverse the military experienced was at Saint Bees Moor during the annual races. Stephenson's officers were somewhat noisy respecting his great capabilities, when a friendly wager was offered them to produce a man on the ground to wrestle him a single fall. The offer was immediately accepted, and Philip eager to be at work soon appeared in the ring fully prepared for action, and anxiously expecting his opponent. After waiting some time, Ponsonby, the man selected for the trial, entered to him, rather the worse, or probably the better, for the 'water of life' which had been plentifully administered to him; but no solicitations could prevail upon him to strip. Fully satisfied that if he won the fall it must be without loss of time, he chose to decide the business with his clothes on. The quickness and impetuosity of Ponsonby's attack carried all before it. Notwithstanding the boasted guard of the soldier, his neck and shoulders instantly exchanged situations with his feet. Philip was up in a moment and anxious for another trial, but Ponsonby was not to be had, his friends had carried him off in triumph, and Philip was obliged to wait for another opportunity of balancing accounts with him.

William Litt
Wrestliana

William Litt

'*A gentleman who, by his writings and conduct in the ring, has conferred greater lustre on, and added greater distinction to the "backhold"wrestling of Cumberland and Westmorland, than any other individual.*' *J. Robinson and S. Gilpin.*

WILLIAM LITT, the author of *Wrestliana*, was born at Bowthorn, near Whitehaven, in November, 1785. His parents held a highly respectable position in society and he received a liberal education, with the object of fitting him for a clergyman in the Church of England. This intention was, however, given up, in consequence of a manifest tendency to out-door sports, and a 'loose' sort of life. The parents seeing that young Litt had rendered himself in some measure unfit for the Church, placed him with a neighbouring farmer to get an insight into practical, as well as theoretical, agricultural pursuits. On arriving at manhood, with a vacillation much regretted in after life, farming was neglected and abandoned.

Christopher North, in old 'Maga', [i.e. *Blackwoods Magazine*] says, 'Mr Litt is a person in a very respectable rank of life, and his character has, we know, been always consistent with his condition. He is in the

best sense of the word a gentleman', was an 'honest, upright, indepen-
dent Englishman. We remember Mr Litt most distinctly: a tall,
straight, handsome, respectable, mild-looking, well dressed man. If
we mistake not, he wrestled in top-boots, a fashion we cannot approve
of.'

In concluding this notice, we should have been glad to state that his
career through the world, in more important respects, had been
attended by gratifying results. The truth, however, is that from the
time he left the paternal roof, his course through a checkered life to
the bitter end, was marked by a series of disastrous failures. Attending
wrestling and race meetings unfits many persons for a steady and
attentive devotion to business. This in marked degree was the case
with Litt. Farming duties became neglected, and then given up. Next
he embarked in a large brewery at Whitehaven. A collapse, and loss
of nearly all the capital employed, followed in little more than twelve
months. He then went to reside at Hensingham, finding part em-
ployment in some triflingly remunerative parochial offices, expecting
daily that he would get an appointment from the ruling powers at
Whitehaven.

Disappointed in this expectation, he resolved on emigrating to
Canada, in 1832, and retrieve his broken fortunes in taking the cutting
of canals, and works of a like description. A break down again
occurred, and he tried to gain a living by writing for the Canadian
journals. This failing, he became a teacher. Suffering, however, from
'home sickness' – a craving often fatal to natives of mountainous
regions – his mental as well as bodily powers began failing before
attaining his sixtieth year . . .

He died at Lachine, near Montreal, in 1847, when sixty-two years
old; regret and sorrow at forced banishment from his native 'hills and
dales', no doubt, hastening decay and the destroyer's final blow.

Jacob Robinson and Sidney Gilpin
Wrestling and Wrestlers (Carlisle, 1893)

A Nineteenth-Century Parson Approves of Grasmere Sports

The Grasmere Sports are to the dalesman of Westmorland and Cumberland what the gathering for the Highland games is to men across the Border. Thanks to the steady persistence of the committee to keep intoxicants from the Sports' field, their endeavours to discountenance betting on the events, and to see that 'buying and selling' is prevented, the Grasmere wrestling-ring has grown steadily in favour, both with wrestlers and with the public. We remember the time when chairs and forms were brought out of the nearest cottages to the field, for the few ladies and gentlemen to sit on and see the sport. Now we have a high-banked gallery of three tiers for the peasants, round a ring an eighth of a mile in circumference; and carriages and coaches in quadruple rank; behind this, a grand stand, a band stand, and all the rest of it.

Everybody goes to 'Girsmer' on Sports' Day, and the fact that everybody has to take some trouble in the going – for Grasmere is eight miles from the nearest railway station – is one of the factors in the success of the games.

The dalesmen, in Sunday best, come bent on sport and not on licence, and very grimly and with obstinate patience does the dark crowd sit through sun and shower from first to last, cracking of nuts and popping of ginger-beer bottles, at times, alone breaking the silence of expectation.

They have come, some of them, twenty miles on foot; they have paid their shilling admission to the field, and they intend to have their shilling's worth undisturbed.

The gentlefolk, with their spanking teams and their gay carriages have come, it is true, more to see their friends than the games; but they are present, and their presence ensures a kind of feeling that all things must be done decently and in order. If it is the 'Lillie Bridge' of the North for some of the athletically minded males, it is the 'Lord's' of the North for their fair companions. And there is that same delightful chance of meeting old friends from the far corners of the earth that makes the gathering day so enjoyable an expectation, so pleasant a memory.

What a parson's pleasure-ground that Grasmere Sports' field has become! Deans, Canons, Bishops, and Archbishops are seen in the happiest and most unprofessional of moods. There is one parson at least on the Sports' Committee, and round the ring they may be counted by scores. One is not sorry that this is so; the more our spiritual shepherds meet and mingle with such simple country shepherds' sport as Grasmere provides, the healthier and happier the tone of English national amusement, the surer the advent of the day when 'joy in wildest commonalty spread'* shall be the keynote of the churches in the land.

H. D. Rawnsley
Life and Nature at the English Lakes (1899)

Regatta on Derwentwater – 6 September 1782

Mr Pocklington was the owner of the island, now called Derwent Island, on which he had built a series of picturesque follies, including a fort and a miniature replica of Stonehenge. His extravagances were much criticized by some of the early visitors.

At eight o'clock in the morning, a vast concourse of ladies and gentlemen appeared on the side of the Derwent lake, where a number of marquees, extending about four hundred yards, were erected for their accommodation. At twelve, such of the company as were invited by Mr Pocklington, passed over in boats to the island which bears his name; and, on their landing, were saluted by a discharge of his artillery. – This might properly be called the opening of the Regatta: for as soon as the echo of this discharge had ceased, a signal gun was fired, and five boats, which lay upon their oars (on that part of the water which runs nearest the town of Keswick), instantly pushed off the shore, and began the race.

* The misquotation of 'widest commonalty spread' from Wordsworth's *The Recluse* is probably merely a misprint, but is retained here in case Canon Rawnsley was intending to make a joke.

A view from any of the attendant boats (of which there were several) presented a scene which beggars all description. The sides of the hoary mountains were clad with spectators, and the glassy surface of the lake was variegated with a number of pleasure barges, which, tricked out in all the gayest colours, and glittering in the rays of a meridian sun, gave a new appearance to the celebrated beauties of this matchless vale.

The contending boats passed Pocklington's-island, and, rounding St Herbert's and Rampsholme, edged down by the outside of Lord's-island, describing in the race almost a perfect circle, and, during the greatest part of it, in full view of the company.

About three o'clock, preparations were made for the sham-attack on Pocklington's-island. The fleet (consisting of several barges, armed with small canon and musquets) retired out of view, behind Friar-crag, to prepare for action; previous to which, a flag of truce was sent to the governor, with a summons to surrender upon honourable terms. A defiance was returned; soon after which, the fleet was seen advancing, with great spirit, before the batteries, and instantly forming in a curved line, a terrible cannonade began on both sides, accompanied with a dreadful discharge of musquetry. This continued for some time, and being echoed from hill to hill, in an amazing variety of sounds, filled the ear with whatever could produce astonishment and awe. All nature seemed to be in an uproar, which impressed on the awakened imagination, the most lively ideas of the 'war of elements' and 'crush of worlds'.

After a severe conflict, the enemies were driven from the attack, in great disorder. A *Feu-de-joye* was then fired in the fort, and oft repeated by the responsive echoes. The fleet, after a little delay, formed again, and, practising a variety of beautiful manoeuvres, renewed the attack. Uproar again sprung up, and the deep-toned echoes of the mountains again joined in the solemn chorus, which was heard to the distance of ten leagues to leeward, through the eastern opening of that vast amphitheatre, as far as Appleby.

The garrison at length capitulated, and the entertainments of the water being finished (towards the evening), the company moved to Keswick; to which place, from the water's edge, a range of lamps was fixed, very happily disposed, and a number of fire-works were played off.

An assembly room (which has been built for the purpose) next received the ladies and gentlemen, and a dance concluded this annual festivity; – a chain of amusements which, we may venture to assert, no other place can possibly furnish, and which wants only to be more universally known, to render it a place of more general resort than any other in the kingdom.

From the *Cumberland Pacquet* (Whitehaven)
Quoted from West's *Guide to the Lakes*

Skating on Esthwaite Water

And in the frosty season, when the sun
Was set, and visible for many a mile
The cottage windows blazed through twilight gloom,
I heeded not their summons: happy time
It was indeed for all of us – for me
It was a time of rapture! Clear and loud
The village clock tolled six, – I wheeled about,
Proud and exulting like an untired horse
That cares not for his home. All shod with steel,
We hissed along the polished ice in games
Confederate, imitative of the chase
And woodland pleasures, – the resounding horn,
The pack loud chiming, and the hunted hare.
So through the darkness and the cold we flew,
And not a voice was idle; with the din
Smitten, the precipices rang aloud;
The leafless trees and every icy crag
Tinkled like iron; while far distant hills
Into the tumult sent an alien sound
Of melancholy not unnoticed, while the stars
Eastward were sparkling clear, and in the west
The orange sky of evening died away.

The Lake District

Not seldom from the uproar I retired
Into a silent bay, or sportively
Glanced sideways, leaving the tumultuous throng,
To cut across the reflex of a star
That fled, and, flying, still before me, gleamed
Upon the glassy plain; and oftentimes,
When we had given our bodies to the wind,
And all the shadowy banks on either side
Came sweeping through the darkness, spinning still
The rapid line of motion, then at once
Have I, reclining back upon my heels,
Stopped short; yet still the solitary cliffs
Wheeled by me – even as if the earth had rolled
With visible motion her diurnal round!
Behind me did they stretch in solemn train,
Feebler and feebler, and I stood and watched
Till all was tranquil as a dreamless sleep.

William Wordsworth
From *The Prelude*, Book I

Keats at a 'Merry Neet'

July 1st [*1818*]. – We are this morning at Carlisle. After Skiddaw, we
walked to Ireby, the oldest market town in Cumberland, where we
were greatly amused by a country dancing-school, holden at the
'Tun'. It was indeed 'no new cotillion fresh from France'. No, they
kickit and jumpit with mettle extraordinary, and whiskit, and friskit,
and toed it, and go'd it, and twirl'd it, and whirl'd it, and stamped it,
and sweated it, tattoing the floor like mad. The difference between
our country dances and these Scottish figures is about the same as
leisurely stirring a cup of tea and beating up a batter-pudding. I was
extremely gratified to think that, if I had pleasures they knew nothing
of, they had also some into which I could not possibly enter. I hope I
shall not return without having got the Highland fling. There was as

fine a row of boys and girls as ever you saw; some beautiful faces, and one exquisite mouth. I never felt so near the glory of patriotism, the glory of making, by any means, a country happier. This is what I like better than scenery. I fear our continued moving from place to place will prevent our becoming learned in village affairs: we are mere creatures of rivers, lakes, and mountains.

John Keats
Quoted from Lord Houghton's *The Life and Letters of John Keats*

Wordsworth at a 'Merry Neet'

The setting of the experience here recounted cannot be located with certainty, but it must be somewhere near Hawkshead. In this district the term 'ground' is usually given to farms which were once part of the estate of Furness Abbey.

The memory of one particular hour
Doth here rise up against me. 'Mid a throng
Of maids and youths, old men, and matrons staid,
A medley of all tempers, I had passed
The night in dancing, gaiety, and mirth,
With din of instruments and shuffling feet,
And glancing forms, and tapers glittering,
And unaimed prattle flying up and down;
Spirits upon the stretch, and here and there
Slight shocks of young love-liking interspersed,
Whose transient pleasure mounted to the head,
And tingled through the veins. Ere we retired,
The cock had crowed, and now the eastern sky
Was kindling, not unseen, from humble copse
And open field, through which the pathway wound,
And homeward led my steps. Magnificent
The morning rose, in memorable pomp,
Glorious as e'er I had beheld – in front,

The sea lay laughing at a distance; near,
The solid mountains shone, bright as the clouds,
Grain-tinctured, drenched in empyrean light;
And in the meadows and the lower grounds
Was all the sweetness of a common dawn –
Dews, vapours, and the melody of birds,
And labourers going forth to till the fields.
Ah! need I say, dear Friend! that to the brim
My heart was full; I made no vows, but vows
Were then made for me; bond unknown to me
Was given, that I should be, else sinning greatly,
A dedicated Spirit. On I walked
In thankful blessedness which yet survives.

William Wordsworth
From *The Prelude*, Book 4

D'Ye Ken John Peel?

It is odd to think that the author of what has practically become the national anthem of Cumberland should have left his home county and emigrated to Tasmania. The song is given here in the original version which differs slightly from that usually sung today.

D'ye ken John Peel with his coat so gray?
D'ye ken John Peel at the break of day?
D'ye ken John Peel when he's far, far away,
With his hounds and his horn in the morning?

'Twas the sound of his horn brought me from my bed,
An' the cry of his hounds has me oft-times led;
For Peel's view holloa would 'waken the dead,
Or a fox from his lair in the morning.

D'ye ken that bitch whose tongue is death?
D'ye ken her sons of peerless faith?

D'ye ken that a fox, with his last breath,
Curs'd them all as he died in the morning?
      'Twas the sound of his horn, etc.

Yes, I ken John Peel and auld Ruby too,
Ranter and Royal and Bellman as true;
From the drag to the chase, from the chase to the view,
From the view to the death in the morning.
      'Twas the sound of his horn, etc.

An' I've follow'd John Peel both often and far,
O'er the rasper-fence, the gate, and the bar,
From Low Denton-holme up to Scratchmere Scar,
Where we vied for the brush in the morning.
      'Twas the sound of his horn, etc.

Then, here's to John Peel with my heart and soul,
Come fill, fill to him another strong bowl;
For we'll follow John Peel thro' fair or thro' foul,
While we're wak'd by his horn in the morning.

'Twas the sound of his horn brought me from my bed,
An' the cry of his hounds has me oft-times led;
For Peel's view holloa would 'waken the dead,
Or a fox from his lair in the morning.

                    John Woodcock Graves (1795–1886)

To the Memory of John Peel

These verses, topographically more accurate and explicit than Woodcock Graves's famous poem, first appeared in the Wigton Advertiser.

The horn of the hunter is silent,
  By the banks of the Ellen no more

Or in Denton is heard its wild echo,
    Clear sounding o'er dark Caldew's roar.

For forty long years have we known him –
    A Cumberland yeoman of old –
But thrice forty years they shall perish
    Ere the fame of his deeds shall be cold.

No broadcloth or scarlet adorn'd him,
    Or buckskins that rival the snow,
But of plain 'Skiddaw gray' was his raiment,
    He wore it for work, not for show.

Now, when darkness at night draws her mantle,
    And cold round the fire bids us steal,
Our children will say, 'Father, tell us
    Some tales about famous John Peel!'

Then we'll tell them of Ranter and Royal,
    And Briton, and Melody, too,
How they rattled their fox around Carrock,
    And pressed him from chase into view.

And often from Brayton to Skiddaw,
    Through Isel, Bewaldeth, Whitefiel,
We have galloped, like madmen, together,
    And followed the horn of John Peel.

And tho' we may hunt with another,
    When the hand of old age we may feel,
We'll mourn for a sportsman and brother.
    And remember the days of John Peel.

                    Jackson Gillbanks (nineteenth century)

*Jackson Gillbanks has also left us a prose note on John Peel, quoted here
from* Foxhunting on the Fells, *by Richard Clapham.*

John Peel was a good specimen of a plain Cumberland yeoman. On less than £400 per annum he hunted at his own expense, and un-assisted, a pack of foxhounds for half a century. John has in his time drawn every covert in the country, and was well known on the Scottish borders. Except on great days he followed the old style of hunting – that is, turning out before daylight, often at five or six o'clock, and hunted his fox by the drag. He was a man of stalwart form, and well built; he generally wore a coat of home-spun Cum-berland wool – a species called 'hoddengray'. John was a very good shot, and used a single-barrel, with flint lock, to the last. Though he sometimes indulged too much, he was always up by four or five in the morning, no matter what had taken place the night before; and, perhaps, to this may be attributed his excellent health, as he was never known to have a day's sickness, until his last and only illness.

A Day with the Mellbreak

The Mellbreak he spoke of was a pack of foxhounds which was followed on foot. No horses could hunt where these dogs travelled – on the fells. And possibly because of the pedestrian effort involved, there was no aristocracy to make the occasion courtly, nor that gentlemanly professionalism of men in love with horses and sport but also conscious of a fine nerve of correctness which gave to hunts such as those described by Siegfried Sassoon the knightly aspect of a personal quest. The Mellbreak hounds were owned by the tenant-farmers and their labourers and kept at home by them through the summer. In the autumn they would go to the kennels for the hunts-man and his whipper-in to work into a pack. The huntsman himself did casual work in the summer and claimed huntsman's pay from September: his wage was met by donations from the various hunt committees in the villages from which he would set out, and the food for the dogs was as often as not provided, in dead carcasses and left-overs, by the men – themselves living on very strict budgets – who owned them.

When the season opened, the huntsman, in red coat, red waistcoat, red tie, hard black bowler, brown jodhpurs and thick nailed boots with black leggings going from ankle half-way up his calf would blow the small horn he kept in one of his pockets – and they were away. He would settle in a village, staying free of charge in the pub, and – as still today – hunt about that locality for about a week before moving on to the next spot. At that time his range was not as wide as it became, and most days he would be out around Loweswater Lake, hunting under the dominating cone of the Mellbreak Fell from which the pack took its name.

All the men involved were mad on the sport. They would set aside good cuts for their dogs, go without a drink themselves if the hounds needed some sherry, look out for the foxes in the summer, note down bolt holes and badger sets, bet on the staying power or speed of their hounds, and talk, talk and talk of nothing but the hunt throughout the winter . . .

The hunt met on this Saturday morning outside Kirkstile Inn. The yard was full of hounds and the forty or so dogs sniffed and scuttered around the outbuildings incessantly. They would be loosed at nine o'clock. Hardisty [i.e. the huntsman] was in the pub taking his nip of whisky with the landlord, and Isaac – greeted by all and besieged by the dogs so that he had to wade through them to the door – went in for 'a bit of the same'. The bar was full, though few of the men were drinking, and John, tingling from the walk across the fells with his brother, sat down delighted to see so many new faces, luxuriating in the knowledge that he would be two days away from the farm, from the cottage. Yes, even from Emily and the baby. As he looked around and grasped the glass of spirits which Isaac put into his hand, he considered himself in rare company.

The men were dressed in their working clothes, patched jackets dangling open, stained waistcoats lacing up their chests with tarnished buttons, boots and leggings and corduroy, hands thick as bricks, caps containing faces shining red from their beating with the weather. One or two had terriers which would be set down the holes, and John saw something he had not often seen – a bitch terrier and her pup chained together by a short length which led from collar to collar; they would run together all day, and every day until the pup had learned how to work with the hounds . . .

They went over to draw Holme Wood, a fox having been noted there on the return from a hunt a few weeks back, and John and Isaac stood outside the wood as the hounds streamed through the trees, their bark echoing the axe-blows which came across the valley from the wood at Mosser. The day was grey but there was nothing to prevent the scent rising strongly and the hounds were as skittish as kittens.

John looked around him. Everywhere the fells rose, their yellow-green winter grass cut across by the dark bracken, the scree grey, a dull glint of mineral which would later glitter under the sun. Even under such canopied cloud, the air seemed to leap at your flesh and bark its shins on your skin. Farms and cottages sat along the valley bottom and on the lower slopes as easily as rock-pools left by the tide; and from the intent face of Isaac to the top of the Mellbreak itself, the day was made for such as this.

Holme Wood yielding nothing, they moved on to a small planting at the foot of Little Dodd. The hounds clamoured – but for no more than a hare, and John laughed at the electric hopping of that animal as its white tail flashed up the fell-side. Hardisty called the dogs back to him and they went up the Mosedale Beck, right into the fells, their sides rising steeply. This was the time for conserving talk and energy and the two or three dozen men tramped steadily through the peaty bottoms, skirted the bouldering outcrops, said little, intent on Hardisty, scarlet at their head. Before them the hounds fanned out until the bare hill sides seemed to breed dogs out of those cavities and clefts which pocked them. Heads to the ground, feet padding ceaselessly, long tails swaying gently, the brown, black-white patched dogs muzzled for the scent. They went the length of that climbing valley without raising more than a crow. Even the sheep seemed unimpressed, merely scattering a few yards distant and then standing to look on the procession, rigidly still.

It was after midday that the fox was raised – down towards Burtless Wood beside Buttermere. It turned immediately and ran back the way the men had come and John had a view – the fox racing across the skyline, clinging to the ground it seemed, tail straight up in the air to leave no scent. But the hounds had the view as well, and they were after it.

It gave them a hard run. Into Mosedale bottom where it crossed the beck three times, around Hen Comb, behind Little Dodd, back the other direction towards Kirkstile. They lost it for a few minutes there until someone halloed they had seen it slipping up the beck – and they were off again.

John seemed to swoop and roll among the fells as he followed the chase. The field spread out, the hounds themselves strung along a quarter of a mile, two or three of them off on a scent of their own – lost to the day's sport: one hound cut its paw so badly on a wall that it dropped out, the terriers scurried along, the tied pair, like a diminutive canine monster. There were halloos every few minutes and the men themselves became hunters, climbing the heights in anticipation of a vantage which would give them a total view and enable them to race down when the kill was near, cutting up the loose screes and perhaps finding that the valley they reached was already clear of the chase, making for the badger sets down at High Nook which the fox itself could be expected to make for (they had been blocked the previous night), suddenly, by the action of that lush red-brown fox, spread out over a full range of hills and valleys.

Isaac's plan was to stay with the whipper-in. A younger and faster man even than Hardisty who could cut off this and hedge that, he held down his job to a great degree by his ability to stay close to the hounds – even when they broke and raced as furiously as they did now. No man could keep right up with them on that ground – but as near as anyone could get, the whipper-in did. With Isaac at his shoulder and John, sometimes gasping in agony, behind. As if to find yet more use for his breath, Isaac yipped and whooped all the way along – his belly shaking with the efforts he made, the hills ricocheting with the barks and shouts, and on his face an unshakeable grin. 'What a day, lad!' He shouted back to John. 'O look at yon stupid hound! What a size – eh? Did you see him lad? Did you see that brush – like a bluddy Christmas tree. Eh! Come on! Come on! My God, they're scalin' those screes. We'll slither down yonder, lad, like fish on slab. Yip! Yip! That big hound'll hold out. My money's on that 'un –

Bellman it is. Go on boy! Look at him lift! Come on, lad! Come away! Eh! What sport!'

They killed him down near Holme Wood where they had started the day and the early winter darkness rapidly fastened over the sky; the tops of the fells were in total darkness as they arrived back at the pub, lamp-lit windows, the men dispersing across the fields to eat before drinking, a few crows settling in the tops of the bare trees, John's legs shaking unsteadily as he made his way down the twisting lane.

Melvyn Bragg (1939–   )
The Hired Man

Canny Cummerlan' or
Oor Mak o' Sang

Canny Cummerlan'

'Twas ae neet last week, wi' our wark efter supper,
  We went owre the geate cousin Isbel to see;
There was Sibby frae Curthet, and lal Betty Byers,
  Deef Debby, forby Bella Bunton and me;
We'd scarce begun spinning, when Sib a sang lilted,
  She'd brong her frae Carel by their sarvent man;
'Twas aw about Cummerlan' fwok and fine pleaces;
  And, if I can think on't ye's hear how it ran.

Yer buik-larn'd wise gentry, that's seen monie countries,
  May preach and palaver, and brag as they will
O' mountains, lakes, valleys, woods, watters and meadows,
  But canny auld Cummerlan' caps them aw still:
It's true we've nea palaces shinin' amang us,
  Not tall marble towers to catch the weak eye;
But we've monie fine castles, whoar fit our brave fadders,
  When Cummerlan' cud any county defy.

Whea that hes clim'd Skiddaw, hes seen sec a prospect,
  Whoar fells frown on fells, and in majesty vie?
Whea that hes seen Keswick, can count hawf its beauties,
  May e'en try to count hawf the stars i' the sky:
There's Ullswater, Bassenthwaite, Wastwater, Derwent,
  That thousands on thousands hae travell'd to view,
The langer they gaze, still the mair they may wonder,
  And aye, as they wonder, may fin'summet new.

We help yen anudder; we welcome the stranger;
  Oursels and our country we'll iver defend;
We pay bit o' taxes as weel as we're yable,
  And pray, like true Britons, the war hed an end;
Then, Cummerlan' lads, and ye lish rwosy lasses.
  If some caw ye clownish, ye needn't think sheame;

Curthat: Curthwaite
Carel: Carlisle

Be merry and wise, enjoy innocent pleasures.
　　And aye seek for health and contentment at heame.

Robert Anderson (1770–1833)

Bonny Smurking Sally

O what a deal of beauties rare
　　Leeve down in Caldew's valley,
Yet theer not yen 'at can compare
　　Wi' bonny smurking Sally.

O' fortunes great my ded oft tells,
　　But I cry shally-wally:
I mind nae fortunes, nor ought else,
　　My heart's sae set o' Sally.

Let others round the teable sit
　　At fairs, and drink and rally;
While to a corner snug I git,
　　And kiss and hark wi' Sally.

Some lads court fearfu' hard, yet still
　　Put off and drive and dally:
The priest, neest Sunday, if she will,
　　May publish me and Sally.

O how my heart wad lowp for joy
　　To lead her up the ally;
And with what courage could I cry,
　　I Simon tak' thee Sally.

And sud not we a bargain strike?
　　I's seer our tempers tally;
For duce a thing can Simon like
　　But just what likes his Sally.

I's seek, and wait nae what to de;
   The Doctor and his galley-
Pots will not signify a flea –
   O send off hand for Sally!

Josiah Relph (1712–1743)

Harvest or *The Bashful Shepherd*

When welcome rain the weary reapers drove
Beneath the shelter of a neighbouring grove;
ROBIN, a love-sick swain, lagg'd far behind,
Nor seem'd the weight of falling showers to mind;
A distant solitary shade he sought,
And thus disclos'd the troubles of his thought: –
   Ay, ay, thur drops may cuil my out-side heat;
Thur callar blasts may wear the boilen sweat; –
But my het bluid, my heart aw in a bruil,
Nor callar blasts can wear, nor drips can cuil.
   Here, here it was (a wae light on the pleace!)
At first I gat a gliff o' BETTY's feace:
Blyth on this trod the smurker tripp'd, and theer,
At the deail-head, unluckily we shear:
Heedless I glim'd, nor could my een command,
Till gash the sickle went into my hand:
Down hell'd the bluid, – the shearers aw brast out
In sweels of laughter, – BETTY luik'd about; –
Reed grew my fingers, reeder far my feace, –
What cou'd I de in seck a dispert kease?
   Away I sleeng'd, to grandy made my mean;
My grandy (God be wud her, now she's geane)
Skilfu', the gushen bluid wi' cockwebs staid,
The on the sair an healen plaister laid:
The healen plaister eas'd the painful sair; –

gliff: glimpse	*glim'd:* looked sideways
trod: path	*grandy:* grandmother

The arr indeed remains – but naething mair.
   Not sae that other wound, that inward smart, –
My grandy cou'd not cure a bleedin heart.
I've bworn the bitter torment three lang year,
And aw my life-time mun be fworc'd to bear,
'Less BETTY will a kind physician pruive;
For nin but she has skill to medcin luive.
   But how should honest BETTY give relief?
BETTY's a perfet stranger to my grief:
Oft I've resolv'd my ailment to explain;
Oft I've resolv'd indeed – but all in vain:
A springin blush spred fast owr aither cheek,
Down ROBIN luik'd, and deuce a word cou'd speak.
   Can I forget that night! – I never can –
When on the clean-sweep'd hearth the spinnels ran:
The lasses drew their line wi' busy speed;
The lads as busy minded every thread;
When, sad! the line sae slender BETTY drew,
Snap went the thread, and down the spinnel flew:
To me it meade – the lads began to glop –
What cou'd I de? I mud, mud take it up;
I tuik it up, and (what gangs pleaguy hard)
E'en reach'd it back without the sweet reward.
   O lastin stain! e'en yet it's eith to treace
A guilty conscience in my blushen feace:
I fain wou'd wesh it oot, but never can;
Still fair it bides, like bluid of sackless man.
   Nought sae was Wully bashfu' – Wully spy'd
A pair of scissars at the lass's side;
Thar lows'd, he sleely dropp'd the spinnel down –
And what said BETTY? – BETTY struive to frown
Up flew her hand to souse the cowren lad,
But, ah! I thought it fell not down owr sad:
What follow'd I think mickle to repeat –
My teeth aw watter'd then – and watter yet.
   E'en weel is he 'at ever he was bworn!

arr: scar   *glop:* open eyes wide

He's free frae aw this bitterment and scworn!
What! mun I still be fash'd wi' straglen sheep,
Wi far-fetch'd sighs, and things I said asleep;
Still shamefully left snafflen by my sell,
And still, still dogg'd wi' the damn'd name o' *mell*!

    Whare's now the pith (this luive! the deuce ga' wi't)
The pith I show'd whene'er we struive to beat;
When a lang lwonin throught the cworn I meade,
And, bustlin far behind, the leave survey'd.

    Dear heart! that pith is geane, and comes nae mair,
Till BETTY's kindness sall the loss repair:
And she's not like (how sud she?) to be kind,
Till I have freely spoken out my mind;
Till I have learn'd to feace the maiden clean,
Oil'd my slow tongue, and edg'd my sheepish een.

    A buik there is – a buik – the neame – shem faw't!
Some thing o' compliments I think they caw't,
'At meakes a clownish lad a clever spark:
O hed I this! this buik wad de my wark;
And I's resolv'd to have't, whatever't cost:
My flute – for what's my flute if BETTY's lost?
And, if sae bonny a lass but be my pride,
I need not any comforts lait beside.

    Farewel my flute, then yet ere Carl fair
I to the stationer's will straight repair,
And boldly for thur compliments enquear:
Care I a fardin, let the 'prentice jeer.
That duine, a handsome letter I'll indite,
Handsome as ever country lad did write;
A letter 'at sall tell her aw I feel,
And aw my wants, without a blush, reveal.

    But now the clouds brek off, and sineways run;
Out frae his shelter lively luiks the sun;
Brave hearty blasts the droopin barley dry,
The lads are gawn to shear – and sae mun I.

Josiah Relph
Carl: Carlisle

mell: the wooden spoon   *pith:* pluck, energy

Barley Broth

If tempers wer' put up to seale.
    Our Jwohn's wad bear a deuced price;
He vow'd 'twas barley i'the broth –
    Upon my word, says I, it's rice.

'I mek nea faut,' our Jwohnny says,
    'The broth is gud an' varra nice;
I nobbet say – it's barley broth.'
    'T'ou says what's wrang,' says I, 'it's rice.'

'Did iver mortal hear the like!
    As if I hadn't sense to tell!
T'ou may think rice the better thing,
    But barley broth dis just as well.'

'An' sae it mud, if it was there;
    The deil a grain is i' the pot;
But t'ou mun ayways threep yen doon –
    I've drawn the deevil of a lot!'

'An' what's the lot 'at I hev drawn?
    Pervarsion is a woman's neame!
Sae fare-t'e-weel. I'll sarve my king,
    An' niver, niver mair come heame.'

Now Jenny frets frae mworn to neet;
    The Sunday cap's nae langer nice;
She aye puts barley i' the broth,
    An' hates the varra neame o'rice.

Thus trifles vex, an' trifles please,
    An' trifles mek the sum o' life;
An' trifles mek a bonny lass
    A wretched or a happy wife.

                Susanna Blamire (1747–1794)

threep: argue

Peer Body

Several of Susanna Blamire's best dialect poems were written in collaboration with her friend Catherine Gilpin, sister of William Gilpin, author of Observations on Picturesque Beauty, *etc.*

Jenny, she's aw weet, peer body,
   Jenny's like to cry;
For she hes weet her petticwoats
   In gangin' thro' the rye.
               Peer body!

Gin she hed gane a mile about
   Or takken better care,
She hedn't mead sec durty wark,
   At dancing at the fair.
               Peer body!

For Jenny danc'd an' dript the fleer,
   The lads, they aw brast out,
An' Jenny cried, an' wish'd that she,
   Hed gane that mile about.
               Peer body!

'To seave a little durty mile,
   There's mony fuils like me;
An' mony mair to seave a pund,
   Is forc'd to mak it three.
               Peer body!

'I's nivver hear the last o' this,
   They'll tell it twenty ways;
An' some'll say I peed the fleer,
   An' water'd ower Strathpeys.
               Peer body!

brast out: burst out laughing

'An' some'll say I laid the dust,
    An' some I mead it mair;
But aw the lads'll laugh an'tell,
    She's gangin' to the fair,
                                Peer body!'

                        Susanna Blamire (1747–1794)
                        and Catherine Gilpin (1738–1811)

Reed Robin

Come into my cabin, reed Robin!
    Thrice welcome, blythe warbler, to me!
Now Skiddaw hes thrown his white cap on
    Agean I'll gi'e shelter to thee.
Just hop thy ways into my pantry,
    And feast on my peer humble fare;
I niver was fash'd wid a dainty,
    But mine, man or burd sal ay share.

Now four years are by-geane, reed Robin,
    Sin furst thou com singin' to me;
But, oh, how I's chang'd, little Robin,
    Sin furst I bade welcome to thee!
I then hed a bonny bit lassie,
    Away wid anudder she's geane;
My frien's was oft caw at my cabin,
    Now dowie I seegh aw my leane.

Oh, where is thy sweetheart, reed Robin?
    Gae bring her frae house-top or tree;
I'll bid her be true to sweet Robin,
    For fause was a lassie to me.
dowie: lonely

You'll share iv'ry crumb i' my cabin,
  We'll sing the cauld winter away;
I wunnet deceive ye, peer burdies!
  Let mortals use me as they may.

Robert Anderson

'It's Nobbut Me'

Ya winter neet, I mind it weel,
  Oor lads 'ed been at t'fell,
An', bein'tir't, went seun to bed,
  An' I sat be mesel.
I hard a jike on t'window pane,
  An' deftly went to see;
Bit when I ax't, 'Who's jiken theer?'
  Says t'chap, 'It's nobbut me.'

'Who's *me*?' says I, 'What want ye here?
  Oor fwok ur aw i'bed' –
'I dunnet want your fwok at aw,
  It's *thee* I want,' he sed.
'What cant'e want wi' me,' says I;
  'An' who, the deuce, can't be?
Just tell me who it is, an' than' –
  Says he, 'It's nobbut me.'

'I want a sweetheart, an'I thowt
  Thoo mebby wad an' aw;
I'd been a bit down t'deal to-neet,
  An' thowt' at I wad caw;
What, cant'e like me, dus t'e think?
  I think I wad like thee' –
'I dunnet know who 't is,' says I,
  Says he, 'It's nobbut me.'

jike: squeak

We pestit on a canny while,
  I thowt his voice I knet;
An' than I steall quite whisht away,
  An' oot at t'dooer I went.
I creapp, an' gat 'im be t'cwoat laps,
  'Twas dark, he cuddent see;
He startit roond, an' said, 'Who's that?'
  Says I, 'It's nobbut me.'

An' menny a time he com agean,
  An' menny a time I went,
An' sed, 'Who's that 'at's jiken theer?'
  When gaily weel I kent:
An' mainly what t'seamm answer com,
  Fra back o't'laylick tree;
He sed, 'I think thoo knows who't is:
  Thoo knows it's nobbut me.'

It's twenty year an'mair sen than,
  An' ups an' doons we've hed;
An' six fine barns hev blest us beath,
  Sen Jim an' me war wed.
An' menny a time I've known 'im steal,
  When I'd yan on me knee,
To make me start, an'than wad laugh –
  Ha! Ha! 'It's nobbut me.'

                                        John Richardson

Lal Dinah Grayson

Lal Dinah Grayson's fresh, fewsome, an' free,
Wid a lilt iv her step an' a glent iv her e'e;
She glowers ebbem at me whativer I say,

pestit: chatted, argued   *whisht:* silent   *ebbem:* straight

An' meastly mak's answer wid 'M'appen I may!'
  'M'appen I may,' she says, 'm'appen I may;
  Thou thinks I believe the', an' m'appen I may!'

Gay offen, when Dinah I manish to meet
O' Mundays, i't'market i' Cockermouth street,
I whisper, 'Thou's nicer nor owte here today,'
An' she cocks up her chin an'says. 'M'appen I may!
  M'appen I may, my lad, m'appen I may;
  There's nowte here to crack on, an' m'appen I may!'

She's smart oot o' dooars – she's tidy i't'hoose;
Snod as a mowdy-warp – sleek as a moose.
I' blue goon, i' black goon, i'green goon or grey,
I tell her she's reeght, an' git 'M'appen I may!'
  'M'appen I may,' she'll say, 'm'appen I may,
  Thou kens lal aboot it, but m'appen I may!'

There's nut mickle on her – we ken 'at gud stuff
Laps up i' lal bundles, an' she's lal aneuf;
There's nowte aboot Dinah were better away
But her comical ower-wurd 'M'appen I may.'
  'M'appen I may,' it's still, 'm'appen I may.'
  Whativer yan wants yan gits 'm'appen I may.'

An' it shaps to be smittal whoariver I gang,
I can't tell a stwory – I can't sing a sang –
I can't hod a crack, nay! – I can't read or pray
Widout bringin' in her dang't 'M'appen I may.'
  'M'appen I may,' it cums, 'm'appen I may;'
  Asteed of Amen, I say 'm'appen I may.'

But she met me ya neeght aside Pards'aw Lea yatt –
I tock her seaf heam, but I keep't her oot leat,
An' offen I said i' my oan canny way,

mowdy-warp: mole   *smittal:* infectious

The Lake District

'Will t'e like me a lal bit?' – 'Whey, – M'appen I may!
  M'appen I may, Harry – m'appen I may;
  Thou's rayder a hoaf-thick, but m'appen I may!'

I prist her to wed me – I said I was pooar,
But eddlin aneuf to keep hunger fray t'dooar.
She leuk't i' my feace, an' than, hoaf turn't away,
She hung doon her heid an' said 'M'appen I may!
  M'appen I may!' – (low doon) – 'm'appen I may,
I think thoo means fairly, an m'appen I may.'

We're hingin' i't bell reaps* – to t'parson I've toak't.
An' I gev him a hint as he maffelt an' jwoak't.
To mind when she sud say 'love, honour, OBEY,'
'At she doesn't slip through wid her 'M'appen I may.'
  M'appen I may, may be – m'appen I may,
  But we moont put up than wid a 'm'appen I may.'

Alexander Craig Gibson

Billy Watson' Lonning

O for Billy Watson' lonnin' of a lownd summer neeght!
When t'stars come few an' flaytely, efter weerin' oot day-leeght –
When t'black-kite blossom shews itsel' i' hoaf-seen gliffs o' grey,
An't honey-suckle's scentit mair nor iver 'tis i't'day.
An' nut a shadow, shap' or soond, or seeght, or sign 'at tells
'At owte 'at's wick comes santerin' theer but you, yer oan two sel's.
Ther' cannot be anudder spot so private an' so sweet,
As Billy Watson' lonnin' of a lownd summer neeght!

---

hoaf-thick: thick-head	*maffelt:* talked silly	*lownd:* calm
flaytely: timidly	*black-kite:* bramble	

* 'Hanging in the bells ropes', i.e. the period during which the banns are read.

T'Hempgarth Broo's a cheersome pleace when't whins bloom full
  o' flooar –
Green Hecklebank turns greener when it's watter'd wid a shooar –
There's bonnie neuks aboot Beckside, Stocks'hill, an' Greystone
  Green –
High Woker Broo gi'es sec a view as isn't offen seen –
It's glorious doon on t'Sandy-beds when t'sun's just gan to set –
An' t' Clay-Dubs isn't fast aslew when t'wedder isn't wet;
But nin was mead o' purpose theer a bonnie lass to meet
Like Billy Watson' lonnin' of a lownd summer neeght.

Yan likes to trail ow'r Sealand-fields an' watch for t'comin' 'tide,
Or slare whoar t'Green hes t'Ropery an' t'Shore of ayder side –
T'Weddriggs road's a lal-used road, an' reeght for coortin toke –
An' Lowca' lonnin's reeght for them 'at like a langsome woke –
Yan's reeght aneuf up t'Lime-road, or t'Waggon-way, or t'Ghyll,
An' reeght for ram'lin's Cunning-wood or Scatter-mascot hill.
Ther's many spots 'at's reeght aneuf, but nin o' ways so reeght
As Billy Watson' lonnin' of a lownd summer neeght.

Sec thowtes as thur com' thick lang sen to yan, a lonterin' lad',
Wid varra lal to brag on but a sperrit niver sad,
When he went strowlin' far an free aboot his sea'side heam,
An' stamp't a mark upon his heart of ivery frind-like neam; –
A mark 'at seems as time drees on to deepen mair an mair –
A mark 'at ola's breeghtens meast i't gloom o' comin' care;
But nowte upon his heart has left a mark 'at hods so breeght
As Billy Watson' lonnin' of a lownd summer neeght!

Oor young days may'd be wastet sair, but dar their mem'rys dear!
And what wad yan not part wid noo agean to hev them here?
Whativer trubles fash'd us than, though nayder leet nor few,
They niver fash'd us hoaf so lang as less an's fash us noo;
If want o' thowte brong bodderment, it pass't for want o'luck.
An' what cared we for Fortun's bats, hooiver feurce she struck?
It mud be t'time o' life' at mead oor happiness complete
I' Billy Watson' lonnin' of a lownd summer neeght!

Alexander Craig Gibson

aslew: amiss   *slare*: walk slow

The Lake District

A Sneck Posset

A sneck-posset is what a man gets when the door is shut in his face.

Niver agean, Eddy! Niver agean!
If I moo'n't hev a lad 'at 'ill coort me my lean,
At'ill hod by ya sweetheart, an' me be that yan,
    I mun bide as I is till I dee.
Thu's coddel't Keat Crosstet, Ann Atchin, Jane Blair,
'Becca Rudd, Mary Mo'son, Ruth Lytle, an' mair;
Thoo says it's o' fun, an' sec fun ma' be fair,
    But it doesn't seem jannic to me.

I favour't the', ey! abeun o't'lads aboot;
I thowte, like a feul, 'at thu'd sing-elt me oot
Frae t'udders, an' I've been reet sarra't, na doobt,
    To trust sec a taistrel as thee.
Reet-sarra't? Ey, mess! I was warn't gaily weel –
I was telt hoo thu'd feul't an' than left Greacy Peile;
An' what reet hed I to believe thoo wad deal
    Ayder fairer or fonter wid me?

Fwoke telt me thoo com of a slape, sneeky breed; –
'At a tungue sec as thine seldom hung iv a heid; –
'At twice i'three times when thoo said owte, thoo leed;
    But I fanciet that hardly cud be.
For 'Speatry, I kent, was a hard-spocken pleace,
An' I thowte 'at, may-hap, thu'd been wrang't aboot Greace; –
God help me! – I thowte I read t'truth i' they feace,
    When thoo swore thoo cared only for me.

We're silly, us lasses – We're maizlins, I know!
We're t'meast tean wi'them 'at oor frinds meast misco';
An' when we're tean in, we've to shear what we sow,
    An' to rue sec mistaks till we dee.

jannic: honest	*slape:* slippery
sarra't: served	*'Speatry:* Aspatria
taistrel: good for nothing	*maizlins:* simpletons

382

Canny Cummerlan' or Oor Mak O' Sang

But leet com' i'time, an' it o' com' at yance,
I so't fair aneuf, but, to give thee ya chance,
I went by mysel' to Jane Loncaster's dance,
    Just to see if thoo dud care for me.

Theear, hoaf oot o' seat, a bye corner I teuk,
An' thoo dudn't cu' nar; nut a smile nor a leuk
Dud te kest to poor me, as I dark't i'my neuk,
    An' wunder't I'd trustit i'thee.
Thoo stack till Bess Bruff like a cockelty bur;
An' she cutter't wi' thee just to greg Harry Scurr; –
When t' cushi'n com'in thoo teuk t'cushi'n tull hur,
    An' thoo glimed, when thoo kiss't her, at me.

But Harry an' Bess mead it up iv a crack;
An' noo, 'at thu's hed a begonk, thoo cu's back;
But if *thu's* fund oot *thine*, I've fund oot *my* mistak';
    An' I'll ho'd mysel' heart-heal an' free.
Sooa Neddy, gud lad, dro'thy steak, an' be ga'n;
Amang thy oald chances thu's m'appen finnd yan
Ma'be fain, though thu's snaip't her, to hev the' agean,
    But, Eddy! that yan isn't me.

Alexander Craig Gibson

A Furness Song

Cm Roger to me, as thou art my son,
An' tak the best counsel o' life;
Cum hidder, I say, wi' out farder delay,
An' I'se warn't t'e I'll git the' a wife – I will!
    Sooa I will, sooa I will,
An' I'se warn't t'e I'll git the' a wife – I will!

greg: tantalize   *begonk:* disappointment
glimed: looked sideways   *snaip't:* snubbed

The Lake District

Put on the best cleas 'at iver thou hes,
An' kiss ivery lass 'at thou meets;
Ther's sum 'ill leak shy an' tak it awry,
But udders 'ill co' the' a sweet – they will!
    Sooa they will, sooa they will,
But udders 'ill co' the' a sweet – they will!

The first bonny lass that Roger did meet
Was a farmer's fair dowter, her neam it was Kate;
She dudn't exchange wi' him hardly a word,
But she fetch'd him a slap i' the feace – she did!
    Sooa she did, sooa she did,
But she fetch'd him a slap i' the feace – she did!

Says Roger, if this be like laitin' a wife,
I'll nivver ga laitin' anudder;
But I'll leeve sing-el o't'days o' my life,
An' I'll away yam to my mudder – I will!
    Sooa I will, sooa I will,
An' I'll away yam to my mudder – I will!

James Pennington Morris (1830–1898)

Leuken' Back

Oald thowts cum rammelin' back ta me
Fra days 'at's lang gone bye;
Oald thowts 'at stir me heart an' bring
A dimness ta me eye.
Ah see agean t'green fields ov heame,
T'oald hoose on t'breest o't'fell,

laitin': seeking

An' Ah've a langin' ta return
Ah can't finnd words ta tell.

In mind Ah picture t'hawthorn bleum,
An' t'smell ov new mown hay
Cums up fra fields whor white gulls hawk
For moths at dusk o' day.
Ah see t'grey owl, a ghwost-like shade,
Flit by on soondless wing;
An' like a dream fra t'worchet dyke
Ah hear a white-throat sing.

Ah meet wid menny a weel-kent feace
'At greets me wid a smile,
Tho' weel Ah know be t'oald grey kurk
They've slept a gey lang while;
Bit in me heart ther memory's green
As t'grass in t'fields ov Spring,
An' will be while Ah've heart ta feel,
Wativer t'ears may bring.

When young we lang ta stray fra t'heaf,
Whoar we war bworn an' bred;
Nor waw ner dyke 'll hinder us,
Ner owt 'at's deun or sed.
Bit when we're nar oor journey's end
We leeve in dreams oor past,
An' just like t'grey gowks deuh in Spring,
We finnd t'oald heame at last.

E. R. Denwood (1882–1958)

worchet: orchard   *waw:* wall
ears: years   *gowks:* cuckoos

Aw Maks

It taks aw maks teh mak a wurrl.

T'ole whaker sat on t'rwoadside seat,
Solemn an deep in thowt,
Musen on t'ways o' man wid man
An t'changes time 'ed wrowt,
When up ther comes a stranger-chap,
Jus' newly come teh t'toon –
A ootener, t'wes plain teh see,
Takken a furst leuk roon.

'What swort o' foaks leeve here?' akst he,
An t'whaker maks reply:
'What swort, good friend, war t'foaks thoo left?' –
Sez t'stranger wid a sigh:
'Suspicious, narra, mean ez muck,
An meast unfair, Ah fear!' –
'Ah's sorry, friend,' t'ole whaker sez,
'T'seamm mak o'foaks leeve here.'

Months rowld alang until yah day
(It may soo' rayder queer),
Anudder stranger akst t'ole man:
'Wha' swort o'foaks leeve here?' –
'What kind war t'neighbours thoo'd afoor?'
T'ole whaker asks ageann –
'Finest in t'wurrl, a champion lot,
Good neighbours ivvery yan!' –
Beamed t'ole man's feass like t'risen sun,
Steul tull his eye a tear,
'Than, friend, thoo'll fin;' wes his reply:
'T'seamm mak o'foaks leeve here.'

ootener: off-comer

William Sanderson

Lent

Roddy Webb, as he was known to many of us, was the founder of the Cumberland Literary Group, and a man with a vision of a regional renaissance. Most of his work was in standard English, but a few dialect verses show that his early death may have robbed us of one of the few writers ready to use the dialect, not merely for Georgian or folk-style verse, but as a legitimate language for poetry of the present century. The rhyme, quoted at the beginning of the following poem, is well-known in West Cumberland, and celebrates the six Sundays from the beginning of Lent to Easter. The fourth Sunday in Lent, being Mothering, or, as it used to be called, Refreshment Sunday, is omitted from the list, since it is regarded as a short respite from the fast, when the Simnel Cakes were baked and the hired men and girls at the farms were allowed the day off to visit their mothers. Carling Sunday is a diminutive of 'Care Sunday', the old name for Passion Sunday; and 'carlin' pez' are small dried peas or beans which were eaten on that day.

'Tid, mid, misere,'
Coont t'weeks ov Lent awaay,
Bairns an' elders aw can saay,
'Carlin', Palm an' Easter daay.'

Lent brings aw t'glents ov t'spring,
Cleanin' up an' freshenin'.
As t'blackies dowly sing
Here t'bonny church bells ring.

Pasche eggs noo t'windows prank:
Nivver let t'laal bairns grank.
Yan or ten it matters nut
What t'udder fellers got.

Nowt but carlin' pez ya week,
Than fur palms we aw mun keek.
Canst mind Arlecdon's bit prayer
On this daay, their Filly Fair?

blackies dowly: blackbirds solitary   *keek:* squint, i.e. look out
grank: complain

Than t'Easter cleas fit in.
Gud thysel' wid what thoo's gitten,
New cwoat matched wid new hat, seen
Smart oot seyde an' smart widin!

'Carlin', Palm an' Easter daay.'
See hoo t'weeks hev passed awaay,
Com' wid better thowts an' heart,
Second spring-teyme noo maay start!

J. Roderick Webb (1920–1952)

The Four-Year-Old Boy

I's not very big yet,
But I think I could get
Where you'd want to be,
If you'd nobbut take me.

I's wanting to be with you,
And doing things as you do;
I know there's things I can play
If I stop by myself all day;

But ye see I's wanting to come,
I's not wanting to stop at home.
Ye needn't take hold of my hand,
I can manage grand.

But if things is terrible tall,
Like a rock or a wall,
Happen ye'd give me a pull.
And, if becks is full,

Happen ye'd give me a ride;
And up fellside,
If it's very rough and steep,
I'll give ye my hand to keep.

But, if ye'll nobbut take me,
I'll come where ye want to be,
And I truly think I could get
If I isn't very big yet.

Margaret Cropper

Black Pheasants

Betty Wilson's Cummerland Teals, first published separately in the West Cumberland Times, were at one time enormously popular, and copies of the paper-backed editions are still treasured in many West Cumberland homes. The author, Thomas Farrall, was a school-master of Aspatria, and, though his style is simple and his humour naïve, he managed to catch the local idiom extremely well. It will be noticed that there is not a high percentage of pure dialect vocabulary in his work, but it probably gives a better idea than anything else we have of the pronunciation and turn of speech of the ordinary people of West Cumberland just at the time when the dialect was beginning to decline.

Ov aw t'fwoaks o' Emmelton [Embleton], Widdup [Wythop], or Secmurder [Setmurthy], theear nivver was a fellah keener o' devarshun nor ooar Bob. A gud temper't swort ov a chap he was, to be shure; helpy amang t'nabours; 'onest as t'day's leet; an' a gud wurker when he hed a mind; bit somehow or udder t'mind was seldom theer when t'hay was i'dry cock, or t'cworn ruddy for hoosin'. He wad git up seun i't'mwornin', an' toak as if he wad duah aw ov a day, an' wad git his brekfast, an ga reet off till Widdup Mill, to t'Blue Bell, or t'Peel Wyke, an' mebbe drink a full week. Sumtimes he tel't us aw his rises ower ov a neet, an' sum ov them war queer eneuf, Ah duah ashure ye.

Well, menny a 'ear sen, Bob was drinkin' at t'Peel Wyke two or three days, just aboot mid-summer, when he could ill be spar't at heam, but what car't Bob for that. At that time t'cwoach-horses used to be chang't at Smiddy Green, an' Jobby Hodgin waitit on them – seah ye may kalkilate it wasn't yisterday.

Pooar Willy Harvey keep't t'Peel Wyke, an' him an' Bob was toakin' just as oald Deavy Jonson druv' up. Oot gits a fellah wid a dubble-barrel't gun, an' two greet ghem [game] bags strap't ower his shooders. He was varra polite, an' noddit, an' ran back an' forret, prancin' like a cat on a het gurdel.

Well, ooar Bob cudn't mak oot what he was efter, seah be way of introdukshun, Bob ses,

'Gaun ta shut, mister?'

'Yes,' sed he.

'What ur ye gaun ta shut at this time o't' 'ear?'

'O, fessents,' ses he.

'Fessents! at this season?' sed Bob. 'Wey, man, they're just breedin', an' if ye war to kill yan noo, ye wad be tean ta Cockermouth in a crack [moment].'

At this, t'fellah leukt rayder doon i't'mooth, leetit a segar, tuk a drink ov his yal, an', efter puffin' away for ten minnets, ses he,

'It's a bad job.'

Bob ses, 'What is?'

'Well,' he ses, in his oan mak o' toak, mind, 'Ah was stoppin' at t'Bush Hotel, at Carel [Carlisle], last neet, an' a lot o' fellahs an' me got on toakin' aboot fessents, an' Ah sed theear was hundreds aboot Widdup, an' they aks't hoo Ah knew; an' Ah sed Ah'd seen them. They rayder disputit me wurd. Seah at last, fra' less ta mair, Ah bet them fifty pund at Ah wad shut two duzzen afooar to-morrah neet. Noo, they wad likely know weel eneuf 'at it wasn't t'season; neah-boddy wad let me shut an' as ther wad be nin ta be gitten wid silver gun, that is, wid munney, they wad win ther wager.'

Well, t'fellah humm't an' he haw't, an' toak't mighty fine, for Bob cudn't tell hoaf o' what he sed, an' t'reason o' this was, 'at he com' fra' Lunnun. He caw't his-sel sum-at like a Cocker.

'Neah matter,' thow't Bob, 'whether thoo's a cocker, setter, or spaniel; bit Ah knows ya thing thoo is, an' that's a big feul.' Yit Bob didn't say seah; let Bob alean for that; his pokkets wer' empty, an' his pint full, at t'Cocker's expense. It wadn't answer ta 'frunt him, at least nut than. Seah they sat an' supp't an' crack't on till towards eight o'clock, t'fellah varra nar bet what ta duah, an' Bob hardly knowin' hoo ta help him, nor, Ah dar say, nut carin' a heap as lang as his pint was full.

At last t'Cocker says, 'If you'll help ta git meh a quantity o' fessents, Ah'll give ye five pund for yer labor.'

Well, five pund sartinly was a tempter for Bob, 'at hed sitten two or three days, owder on sumboddy's cwoat lap, or he'd been hingin' up, as t'sayin' is, aback o't'bar dooar. Than Bob begins to ask t'fellah if ivver he'd poach't enny, an' he sed he hedn't, nor he'd nivver shutten enny fessents bit yance, when he fand sum yung uns in t'nest in a tree, an' shot them throo t'branches.

'Fessents' nest in a tree?' ses Bob.

'Yes,' ses t'Cocker.

Bit t'truth just then flashed across Bob's mind 'at fellah didn't know a fessent when he saw yan, seah Bob consider't a bit, an' at last he ses,

'Well, Ah mun try ta help ye; we'll sit till barrin' up time, an' than we'll off when aw's whyet.' [quiet].

Than, efter revivin' t'deed yal 'at was i'ther stomaks wid a sup o' Mrs Harvey's rum, away they went sneakin' off at t'deed time o' neet, bent on plunder. Theer was neah boddy ta bodder them much i'them days, an' they nobbet met oald Ann Simpson till they gat till t'pleace whoar t'fessents war.

T'Cocker ses, 'They shurely sit nar t'hooses.'

'Oh, ay,' ses Bob, 'clwose till.'

Well, Bob gat furst up ya tree, an' than anudder, an' fand burds plenty. He twin't ther necks roond, an' threw them doon, an' t'Cocker pop't them intill t'bags.

'Clean full,' ses t'Cocker at last.

'Aw reet,' ses Bob.

Wi' that he com doon t'tree, an' away they sally't off ta t'Peel Wyke. T'Cocker went ta bed, an' Bob laid on t'swab aw neet; seun i't'mwornin' 't'Cocker gat up an' order't brekfast for two. Ham an' eggs an' a chop, an' Ah know nut what, was neah deef nut for Bob ta crack, seah efter he'd whyte astonish't t'Cocker be cleanin' up ivvery plate, they coontit t'burds ower, an' fand they hed two duzzen, an' ten ta beut.

'Stop,' ses Bob, 'we mun put a lock o'shot in them.'

Well, they hung them up be t'waw [wall] side, an' smatter'd away at them till they was gaily well riddel't.

Than t'Cocker drew oot five golden sover'ns an' gev them ta Bob, paid for him a gud dinner an' a bottle o' rum; an' just wi' that t'cwoach druv up. In gat t'Cocker wid his burds, 'an as t'horses mov't off, he wat't his hat, an' mead his'sel varra daft.

Whedder he wan his bet wid his Black Fessents nowder Bob nor me ivver hard tell; bit Ah think Carel fwoak wad know 'at they war nobbet *Crows*!

Thomas Farrall (1837–1894)
Betty Wilson's Cummerland Teals

Index of Authors

393

Index of Authors

Index of Authors

Index of Authors

(NB. William Hutchinson's *History of Cumberland*, in the form in which it was published, was the work of a number of authors whose contributions cannot always be identified with certainty. Such contributions, when included in this anthology, are therefore indexed under the name of Hutchinson.)